ON THE FUTURE OF HISTORY

ERNST BREISACH

ON THE FUTURE OF HISTORY

THE POSTMODERNIST CHALLENGE
AND ITS AFTERMATH

The University of Chicago Press
Chicago and London

ERNST BREISACH is Graduate and Research Professor of History Emeritus at Western Michigan University. Among his books are *Historiography: Ancient, Medieval, Modern,* 2nd edition (1993) and *American Progressive History: An Experiment in Modernization* (1993), both published by the University of Chicago Press.

THE UNIVERSITY OF CHICAGO PRESS, CHICAGO 60637
THE UNIVERSITY OF CHICAGO PRESS, LTD., LONDON
© 2003 by The University of Chicago
All rights reserved. Published 2003
Printed in the United States of America
12 11 10 09 08 07 06 05 04 03   1 2 3 4 5

ISBN: 0-226-07279-7 (cloth)
ISBN: 0-226-07280-0 (paper)

Library of Congress Cataloging-in-Publication Data

Breisach, Ernst.
    On the future of history : the postmodernist challenge and its
aftermath / Ernst Breisach.
        p.   cm.
    Includes bibliographical references and index.
    ISBN 0-226-07279-7 (cloth : alk. paper)—ISBN 0-226-07280-0 (pbk. :
alk. paper)
        1. Postmodernism—Social aspects. 2. Historiography. I. Title.

HM449.B74 2003
306—dc21   2003006765

CONTENTS

A PREFATORY AND INTRODUCTORY NOTE

Part 1 of this volume offers an ample introduction to the story of the postmodernist challenge to history. Therefore, this introductory note is limited to stating the reasons for writing this book and for the approach chosen. The vast literature on postmodernism may lead some to question whether another book on the topic could be useful. Such doubts vanish with the realization that there is a dearth of books that focus directly on the relationship between postmodernist and historical thought. That is especially true if, as this volume attempts to do, the postmodernist challenge is seen not as a theory of an extra-historical quality but is viewed as a historical phenomenon that has been conforming to the usual pattern comprising a rise to prominence, an exuberant flourishing, and—at present indications—a dampening down of revolutionary intents to partial modifications of historical thought and practice. The approach also recognizes postmodernism's reach to basic propositions about the human condition, thereby rescuing the postmodernist debate from its confinement to methodological issues in an abstract theoretical space. Exceptions to the confinement had already been taken by those who have held fast to the public role of history. Viewed in this wider perspective, the postmodernist challenge to history acquires a dramatic quality as its aspirations collide with long-standing Western traditions in historical thought and practice.

Writing this volume proved arduous. The vast literature on postmodernism offers sometimes difficult reading. An innovative vocabulary joined the wide interdisciplinary reach into philosophy, literary criticism and theory, anthropology, and cultural studies in taxing the persistence of the inquirer. In this context, I wish to express my sincere appreciation to the great number of scholars who have enriched my understanding of the subject matter through their work, discussions at conferences, workshops, and informal meetings, and through the exchange of ideas after my own lectures. As I modified and refined my views, my appreciation of the collegial character of historical thought and practice gained new strength.

PART I

A PRELIMINARY EXPLORATION OF THE POSTMODERNIST CHALLENGE

Two Turns of Centuries and Two Crises

The parallelism has been striking, perhaps also a bit deceptive. In the decades leading up to the twenty-first century, scholars engaged in a postmodernism discourse that abounded with warnings about a crisis of or challenge to modernity and its views on history. A look backward to the last turn of centuries revealed a debate among scholars also filled with warnings of a crisis in historiography. In either case, the call was for a drastic change.

In the late 1800s, Carl L. Becker and Henri Berr worried about the viability of history in light of what they saw as the more rapid modernization of the social sciences. They would be joined by Frederick Jackson Turner, James Harvey Robinson, and Karl Lamprecht in calling for and pioneering a New History.[1] Their ideas, joined with those of historians who followed the pioneers, would supply the primary matrix for twentieth-century historiography. While these innovators and their successors would set different specific directions in their works, they all wished to change the ways of "doing history" toward what they considered a modern historical understanding. The suggested remedies demanded that preferences be given to (in Turner's words) "deep, anonymous structures and forces" over "surface phenomena" (individuals and events), predictable and measurable patterns over the contingent, the general over the unique, the many over the individual, the masses over the elite, and the broad context of life over the emphasis on politics, diplomacy, and war (now seen as event history). To these features were usually added a strong empiricism and a more or less pronounced progressive view. During the twentieth century the New History—primarily in the form of social history—developed in many variants with strong national accents. Among them were the American Progressive history, the social science–oriented history, the history of the *Annales* group, Marxist history, and the German *Historische Sozialwissenschaft*.

Now, the terms crisis and challenge have once more become common coin. For the new reformers, the grand hopes that had accompanied the New History movement had dimmed. Disenchantments with the course of □ **3** twentieth-century events and the perception of an impasse in proceeding toward the modernist goal of full explanation and truth have provided a climate favorable to a radical criticism of modernity, including the manifestations of what had once been heralded as the New History. The postmodernists who dominated the theoretical discourses of the 1980s and 1990s called for the rejection of modernist ways of "doing history." Their preferences favored the contingent, discontinuous, marginalized, oppressed, unique, perspectival, and ineffable. Rejected were the modernist view of history as progress and the whole modernist complex of truth finding.

The key question suggested itself here: whether any of the variants of postmodernism would play the same role for twenty-first-century historiography that the New History did for its century. At this point, the parallelism between the two turn-of-century changes in historical understanding failed. Both changes did indeed aim at new ways of historical understanding. In the 1880s and 1890s, the projected change was to shape historical thought into its fully modern form, while in the 1980s and 1990s, postmodernists strove to undo the results of that modernization. Yet the postmodernists suggested changes in historical thought and praxis that would negate not only the modernist but much of the longstanding theoretical framework of "doing history." A change so formidable that talk abounded of the "end of history" or the "end of man." Both were indicative of postmodernists reaching for a theory with impact on history not only as a separate scholarly discipline but also as a key endeavor of human life.

The Puzzling Term "Postmodernism"

In light of the postmodernist endeavor's scope it is not surprising that assessing the postmodernist challenge has been hampered by a lack of agreement on what the term "postmodernism" meant. Some scholars have denied that the term referred to a cultural phenomenon with sufficient commonalities. Others found it not only useful but also justified. Gianni Vattimo thought that the ubiquity of the term has evoked the impression that "the idea of 'post-modernity' lies at the center of contemporary intellectual debate in the West."[2] Perhaps so, but that ubiquity has been matched by a corresponding vagueness regarding the term's meaning. The mixture of prominence and haziness even prompted a postmodernist scholar to remark that "in the last two decades the word postmodernism has shifted from awkward neologism to derelict cliché without ever attaining to the dignity of concept."[3]

Postmodernist scholars themselves have created obstacles to a ready understanding of their concerns and ideas. Frequent complaints have cited their use of much off-putting jargon. But more important has been a reluctance— often on principle—to formulate customary theories to which the term postmodernism might be attached. Even prominent postmodernists of the 1980s and 1990s have issued occasional calls for greater precision in postmodernist thought. They have raised objections to the "medley type" or "anything goes" postmodernism with its collages of postmodernist, Marxist, Freudian, and assorted other modernist concepts. Wolfgang Welsch saw too many post-modernists treating the term postmodernism as a "Passepartoutbegriff" (a catch-all concept with many meanings).[4] Umberto Eco spoke harshly of a "postmodern babble" and confessed that it was his "impression that it [the term postmodern] is applied these days to everything the speaker approves of."[5] Adversaries, such as the sociologist Ernest Gellner, were still harsher. "Postmodernism is a contemporary movement. It is strong and fashionable. Over and above it, it is not altogether clear what the devil it is. In fact, clarity is not conspicuous amongst its marked attributes."[6] Others, baffled if not disenchanted, have harbored the suspicion that postmodernism was little more than a brilliant word game, a short-lived fad, a product of a hyper-active intellectual fashion industry, or simply an extended aftermath of the 1960s counter-culture movement rather than a significant phenomenon.

Attempts to remedy the vagueness have encountered the problem that a postmodernism defined "precisely" would draw tight borders around post-modernism and give preference to one meaning of the term over others. For a large segment of postmodernists, that would violate their very injunction against exclusions. As a solution, some scholars have suggested minimally exclusive definitions, such as speaking of postmodernism as the period in which determinacy fades and indeterminacy prevails (Ihab Hassan).[7] Others saw postmodernism as a new, grand sensibility or climate of sensibility rather than a systematically structured theory. For Susan Sontag the new sensibility reversed centuries of attempts at rational mastery of the world that through the use of its canon created a secondary world. Now, "the heavy burden of 'context'" would be lifted as the new sensibility knew none of the old binary distinctions, including that between high and low cultures.[8] Gianni Vattimo justified his speaking of a postmodern age by citing a new and widespread sensibility, defined as "a widely shared sense that Western ways of seeing, knowing and representing have irreversibly altered in recent times."[9] The loose unity effected by such a shared sensibility would substitute for a tight and systematic theoretical base, which many postmodernists, for their own reasons, had not created and would never create.

Some scholars have found the confrontation with a sheer endless series of complexities, questions, and paradoxes "a massive but also exhilarating confusion that has given important new impulses to and opened new territo-ries for intellectual exploration."[10] More typically, however, the impression of being caught in a maze called forth voices of skepticism and doubt. One scholar saw the term postmodernism referring to "a hydra-headed decen-tered condition in which we are dragged along from pillar to post across a succession of reflecting surfaces, drawn by the call of the wild signifier."[11] He would rather abandon it for one with a clearer meaning. More realistic has been the statement of resignation that "although the term postmodernism has led to all kinds of misconceptions, it cannot be replaced, at the present time, with a better one."[12]

The term endured because it was useful and justified. In recent decades, ardent and intensive debates on postmodernism have been occurring, first, in the fields of architecture, literary criticism, and philosophy, then, in the arts, music, anthropology, religion, Islamic studies, and others. While they have been marked by a goodly measure of faddishness in style and content, the quantity and vigor of the ongoing debates and publications linked to postmodernism as well as the fundamental issues raised should caution against assuming toward postmodernism the attitude appropriate toward a mere fad: not to study and assess it but simply to wait for the end of its inevitably short stay in the limelight. Postmodernism has not been—as often proposed—a freakish phenomenon. Although postmodernists have presented their views as a sharp rupture with modernism, indeed, an ultimate one with many of Western culture's traditions, such a claim to utter singularity has represented more a statement of hope and intentions than one of reality. Postmodernism did fasten onto some long-standing trends in Western intellectual development.

The Hesitancy of Historians to Respond

Although postmodernists have predicted that life in postmodernity would render traditional historical understanding obsolete, responses by historians came hesitantly. That reluctance of historians to engage postmodernists in debate earned them criticisms for complacency. Keith Windschuttle found historians unaware of what happened to their discipline. Others found that historians, lacking theoretical finesse, "simply fail to register the intellectual history of their own time," and abandon their discipline to the general fate that made "disciplines tend toward sclerotic self-satisfaction."[13] Nancy Partner found the historians' "stiff-upper-lip doggedness . . . quite interesting and entirely commendable, although the collective motives and institutional forces that account for it are merely self-interested and self-perpetuating."[14] Some of that criticism was justified. Yet the roots of the historians' reticence reached deeper.

Historians, for plausible reasons, have rarely responded with alacrity to opportunities to engage in theoretical debates. First, they have felt confident about their own complex and sturdy body of epistemological principles and practices (often simply referred to as methodology)—the result of repeated adaptations to and absorptions of rhetorical practices and philosophical propositions over the centuries. Hence, the frequently cited hostility to theory should really be seen as a deliberate caution toward accepting theoretical challenges fully and too readily. Even the innovative scholar Lucien Febvre pronounced against too much attention to theory when he observed that "it is not a good thing for the historian to reflect too much upon history. All the time he does so his work is held up."[15] Febvre pointed here to the reluctance of historians to engage in "pure" theory detached from historical practice.

The second and weightier reason for the historians' reluctance was provided by the long-standing suspicions of those disciplines in which much of the postmodernist thought originated: literary criticism and philosophy. History has always been precariously lodged between the domain of philosophy with its universal abstractions of timeless quality distilled from the complex experience of life, on the one side, and the domain of literature with its imaginative reconstructions of life free of the obligation to reflect the past as it once had been actually lived, on the other side. While philosophical and literary elements have helped shape historical accounts, history has persisted as an autonomous and mediating venture located between the two endeavors. That despite the fact, that from time to time, history had seemed destined to be absorbed into one or the other of these two disciplines and to disappear as a distinctive mode of understanding human life.

The most recent phase in history's struggle for autonomous status came with attempts to rework historical understanding into a science. In that context, history's borders to philosophy and literature were redefined to establish history as a distinct academic discipline and profession. In America, memories of that struggle have remained particularly keen. Here it had taken on the shape of a fierce battle to purge philosophy and literature from history on behalf of the unfettered autonomy of the new historical discipline and profession.

However, autonomy never has meant total separation. Even in the late 1800s, the connection between philosophical concepts and historical theories, methodologies, and interpretations remained firm. The seemingly "natural" prevalence of empiricism, even positivism in the new profession, obscured that connection for a long time. The rise of a new critical historical theory in late-nineteenth-century Germany (Wilhelm Dilthey, Wilhelm Windelband, and Heinrich Rickert) and to a lesser degree in France (Alexandre Xenopol) highlighted anew the ties between the two disciplines. In the United States, part of the young historical profession experienced the impact of William James's pragmatism and John Dewey's instrumentalism, particularly in the case of American Progressive history (James H. Robinson, Charles A. Beard, and, for a few years, Carl L. Becker).

When historians have objected to philosophy they have primarily referred to the so-called philosophies of history, which explained historical events on a grand scale. Already in the early 1800s, Leopold von Ranke had drawn the dividing line when he had opposed Hegel's grand philosophical scheme of history on behalf of a history more closely tied to empirical research. In the late 1800s and early 1900s, the American scientific historians had fought against philosophies of history—most often "Fall of Rome" theories—that they saw as short-circuiting proper empirical inquiries via speculative approaches. This procedure seemed to threaten history's scientific standing, which secured history's proper modernity as well as the status of the new historical profession. In the United States, the effect of that struggle would be a particularly strict separation of history from philosophy—a separation more categorical than the one in the increasingly complex and intense German and French discussions about the proper approaches to historical truth finding.

The turn-of-the-century distrust of literature was even wider and deeper. Far from being a new phenomenon, it represented no less than the modern phase in history's long struggle against Aristotle's dictum of the superiority of poetics over history. Yet, for centuries, the Aristotelian dictum had not prevented history and rhetoric from a close although tension-filled symbiosis. That changed with the emergence of the ideal of a scientific history—first in the moderate form of the German *Geschichtswissenschaft,* which still owed much to philology, and, then, in the less accommodating form of the scientific history in the mold of the natural sciences.[16] Frederick Jackson Turner expressed this sense of triumph over literature when he assured his students that the historical discipline was now free of literature.

Memories of that recent phase of history's struggle for autonomy vis-à-vis philosophy and literature would prove a formidable obstacle to the postmodernist penetration of historiography. The historians' reticence to pay attention to postmodernist calls for the wholesale revision of the historical enterprise—issued by scholars with a philosophical and literary bent—was therefore not capricious or inertia-driven but rooted in a basic wariness. Historians saw no reason to participate in a redrawing of disciplinary borders under less than auspicious conditions. Nevertheless, in the long run, they could not ignore the need for an engagement with an intellectual movement characterized by such terms as postmodernity, postmodernism, and posthistory—every one of them with revolutionary implications for historical theory and praxis.

The Ambiguous Challenge: Postmodernity and Postmodernism

The stipulation of a postmodernity as a distinctly new age, produced either by an already existing or just emerging new set of social and cultural conditions, seemed to pose no threat to historians. First, the postmodernists' acknowledgment of two periods, modernity and its "post"-aftermath appeared to fit the traditional manner of thinking in chronological periods. Second, the issue of periodization brought postmodernists, nolens volens, onto the territory of historical inquiry, where they would encounter the discipline's rules of discourse.

However, such comfortable thoughts were soon dispelled. When the postmodernists stipulated postmodernity as an age unprecedented in all aspects, they deliberately broke the chronological mold. Furthermore, historians came to realize that the vision of history, appropriate for postmodernity, affected not only the issue of periodization (the grand order of history) but also history's whole infrastructure, that is, its epistemology with its large body of assumptions, rules of inquiry, and models of interpretation. The more radical the claims for the uniqueness of the postmodernist age became, the less postmodernist thoughts on history would be compatible with existing modes of historical inquiry and interpretation.

Postmodernists encountered their own vexing problems with the chronological implications of the term postmodernity. Many of them found it to be in conflict with their denials of an inherent historical order. Periods as chronological (diachronic) entities implied unwanted totalities. Other scholars have questioned claims to absolute uniqueness for postmodernity. Umberto Eco, for example, spoke of postmodernity as just the modern instance of the recurrent periods of mannerism throughout history.[17] Even the prominent proponent of postmodernism Jean-François Lyotard showed much vacillation when he dealt with periodization in history. While hostile to grand style history, he affirmed at times a distinct postmodern period. He saw the age as shaped by "the condition of knowledge [prevailing] in highly developed societies."[18] At other times, he doubted the strict separation of a postmodernity from modernity because "postmodernity is not a new age, but the rewriting of some of the features claimed by modernity."[19] Wolfgang Welsch even spoke of *unsere postmoderne Moderne* (our postmodern modernity), transforming postmodernity into the last, perhaps highest phase of modernity.[20] Despite these disagreements, the concept of a distinct postmodern period has remained intact, indeed even dominant in postmodernist thought. Enthusiastic proponents maintained that we do not "have a choice about this. For postmodernity is not an ideology or position we can choose to subscribe to or not, postmodernity is precisely our condition: it is our historical fate to be living now."[21] More often, scholars have made the same claim implicitly.

The second term, postmodernism, experienced its related problems. It has been widely used (and will be in this book) as connoting the concepts and theories postmodernists considered appropriate for the social and cultural conditions of postmodernity. Many scholars have been critical of so sweeping a claim. For them, the term postmodernism designated only one of many responses to the real or perceived crisis of modernity. That put postmodernism on the same level with such contemporary movements as feminism, environmentalism, and neo-Marxism.[22] Neo-Marxist theoreticians have been particularly intent to diminish wider postmodernist claims. Some of them have argued that postmodernity was "also, and perhaps more than anything else, a *state of mind*."[23] Therefore, postmodernism as a critical and oppositional movement was a reality, postmodernity was not. However, a proper inquiry into postmodernism must accept the larger claim made for it, namely that it referred to the culture of postmodernity. That view yielded a fuller and more accurate assessment of postmodernism.

The Unambiguous Challenge: Posthistory

The claim that postmodernity represented a unique and unprecedented period found its justification in the stipulation that postmodernity would be posthistoric. The vision of modernity's posthistoric aftermath has clearly and sharply separated postmodernists from modernity's other critics and opponents. Whether postmodernists explicitly used the English word posthistory or the French sounding, but actually German neologism *Posthistoire* or simply implied such a stage in their works, the reference has been to a period (if it could be called that at all) of infinite duration with an utterly new mode of human life.[24] The term posthistory expressed well what Andreas Huyssen, in a different connection, characterized as "the [specific] temporal imagination of postmodernism, the unshaken confidence of being at the edge of history."[25] The term posthistory and its associated phrases "end of man" and "end of history" stipulated that the segment of human life had ended for which history had claimed to offer explanation and understanding.

Some postmodernists have tried to soften that image and have argued that the term posthistory referred only to the end of history as now practiced by historians—"*the end of the peculiar ways in which modernity conceptualized the past; the ways it made sense of the upper and lower case forms* (emphasis in the original)."[26] But, while postmodernists have not conjured up apocalyptic visions of an end to it all, their intentions have gone well beyond technical revisions in historical inquiry. The majority of postmodernists have either stated clearly or implied strongly by the logic of their arguments that the turn to postmodernity would constitute not just a break *in* history (traditional ways of "doing history") but one *with* history (the historical dimension of life itself). Postmodernism may have had as its first aim to describe, explain, or bring about the end of modernity. However, its ideals and concepts spelled out the characteristic features and processes of postmodernity that made necessary radical changes in historical thought and practice. While the exact road to the "end of history" as well as the specific features of posthistory have been contested issues among postmodernists, the implicit or explicit presence of such expectations for the future has been the bond that gave a measure of coherence to the many varieties of postmodernism. Therefore, the stipulation of a posthistoric condition offers itself as the best criterion for what to include in this study of the phenomena termed postmodernism and postmodernity as they relate to historical thought.

■   2   **AN ADVERSARIAL IMAGE OF MODERNITY**

Chronological Vagueness

The prefix "post" in postmodernity (the period) and postmodernism (that period's thinking about and coping with life) has carried besides the temporal connotations of "after" and "beyond" in equal measure those of "anti" or "contra." That adversarial attitude extended well beyond the narrow confines of the epistemological debate to all aspects of the modern historical thought. As the postmodernists of the 1980s and 1990s have seen it, there must be a decisive, all-encompassing cultural revolution.

Considering the importance of the issue, the lack of postmodernist debates on the chronological and formative limits of modernity has been surprising. Only a few postmodernists, among them Michel Foucault and Jean Baudrillard, have tried to locate such chronological limits.[27] That lack has been veiled by the fortuitous agreement among most postmodernists that the Enlightenment must be seen perhaps not as the beginning point but as the ultimate defining moment for modernity and modernism. The long and intense historical controversy about the Enlightenment's exact nature and standing—a radical break and genuinely new creation or a phenomenon with remarkable continuity as a secularized version of the Christian tradition—was circumvented.[28] Also, the postmodernist inclination to view modernity as a calamitous era ruled out the moderate view of the Enlightenment as a complex phenomenon that bestowed on the human race remarkable benefits as well as severe problems. Such a view would have favored a "carry-over" into postmodernity of some seemingly beneficent ideas and concepts of modernity. None of postmodernity's versions favored that prospect.

Progress as Defining Feature

Not surprisingly, then, progress, depicted as the Enlightenment's quintessential view of history, dominated postmodernist discussions of history. And postmodernist critiques have never been far from equalizing the progressive interpretation of history with the endeavor of history in general. And in matters of progress, postmodernists chose the most uncompromising variant of progress as their antagonist: progress as the relentless and also merciless march of reason through time toward a totally new stage of human existence. Such an understanding of progress as reason's unfolding toward complete human emancipation had the greatest affinity with the concept of progress articulated by the Marquis de Condorcet.[29] Alternative, less exuberant views on progress were neglected by postmodernists, including those of François Quesnay and Turgot, with their combination of empiricism and an ideal natural order of things, those of Voltaire and David Hume with their hints of skepticism, even pessimism, and those of the scholars of the German and Scottish Enlightenments with their more complex sets of ideas and themes and the undogmatic simple amelioration view. Condorcet's scheme of history articulated best those features of progress that would be the main targets of postmodernist criticism. It stipulated that (1) the human race had a unitary development, (2) history was unilinear since its universal *telos* moved all developments toward the emancipation of the human race from ignorance, superstition, error, and the misery connected with them, (3) reason acted as *the* critic and destroyer of the old and the builder of the new order in all areas of life, (4) increasingly rational human beings acted as history's agents in building the knowledge needed for human control of the world, (5) the past was a by-product of little value produced by the continuous replacement of inferior by superior (more rational) ways of thought and life, (6) the past's surviving residues were important obstacles to the realization of the rational end stage, and (7) the end of history would see the triumph of the "empire of virtue" over the "empire of fate," in which that which "is" became identical with that which "ought to be" and fully realized reason would create happiness, freedom, and peace. At that point, with irrationality vanquished, the drama of progress would end. Human knowledge and control of life would reach at least near perfection. The prospect of such a triumphal ending transformed the progress view from just another interpretation of history into a message of immense appeal and persuasive power.

Surprisingly, the ultimate presence of a posthistoric age in the modernist progress theory has been largely ignored by progress's advocates and critics alike. In that final phase, whatever its exact features might be, progress and, with it, history would have run their course. Therefore, the crucial parallelism between modernity's end stage and postmodernity's envisioned posthistoric future was ignored. That unexpected and unwanted link stemmed from the irony of antagonistic relationships. The very process of arguing against modernity lodged elements of modernism in postmodernism. And while postmodernists differed in their perception of a posthistoric end stage—most would not even make such an end explicit—the logic of their argument has always included a version of it. The end of modernity could easily be construed as the end of history.

As for historians, they have usually shied away from dealing with or referring to such grand conceptualizations of history that touched on ontological matters. However, in practice, they have all along dealt with such fundamental questions when they have defined the "real" structures and forces of history or the human condition. In the case of the Enlightenment, there had been a peculiar ontological reduction that has been well known to historians as the process of secularization. It aimed to reduce to one the two levels of beings affirmed by the Christian view of history that had been dominant during the medieval and early modern periods. The one remaining level has been that of the experiential-empirical world. Yet as many postmodernists have pointed out relentlessly, the Enlightenment's antimetaphysical ardor had been restricted to the rejection of religious explanations of the world and history. Reason's presence (as the permanent anchor for all) had been condoned in order to give legitimacy to progress as well as to the authoritative truth derived from it. Indeed, the postmodernist quest has often been linked to the twentieth-century attempts to purge metaphysics (now referring to that which was not strictly contextual) completely from Western culture—a quest that made plausible the view of postmodernism as advocating a radically new view of life rather than as a call for technical adjustments in epistemology.

Postmodernism's Opportunity: Progress as a Triumphal Burden

From the mid-1700s, the conviction spread that all of life's phenomena were best studied in terms of their development, that is, historically. For over a century, Hegel's and Marx's grand interpretations of history further enhanced the historical perspective's preeminent position. History represented the story of human emancipation from all vicissitudes and injustice. In its empirical variety, history benefited from its claim to be a science, which made it fully modern. In this so-called Golden Age of history, historians became advisors to rulers, presidents of republics, and activists in political and nationalist movements. History became a transforming force in Western culture, enhancing the aspirations of nationalism, industrialism, colonialism, and capitalism.

But history's triumph came at a great risk. After the fateful days of August in 1914, events reaffirmed those limits to human accomplishments that in modernity had been declared to be mere temporary obstacles to progress. The promise of full rationality and control over human life that had seemed so close at hand never materialized. Instead, twentieth-century historians, particularly those with any kind of progressive tilt, were faced with events so horrible and on so large a scale that they could no longer be seen as temporary setbacks on progress's victorious march. The audacious promise of constant progress toward that distant ideal end stage would become an increasingly heavy burden. Proponents of progress among historians found themselves ill equipped to cope with the experience of such failure. In its uncompromising version, the progress view of history lacked what prior interpretations of history had provided: explanatory mechanisms that made it possible to account for massive failures of expectations—at least temporarily—without falsifying thereby the theory itself.

Before modernity, history had been a narrative that reflected the wide range of human greatness and fallibility. Ancient histories had demonstrated how individuals and collectives realized their ambitions only to encounter limits that they could not overcome but which eventually overcame them. The perfect stage without history's turbulence, usually termed the Golden Age, had existed in the far distant past but was only an inspirational memory with little impact on expectations for the future. The shadow of failure was cast permanently on the world and was acknowledged intermittently in the accounts of historians. Philosophers, not historians, were engaged in designing solutions for the closing of the gap between the perfect and the imperfect, between the permanent and the temporary.

Medieval historians would speak of the unattainability of perfection or even lasting duration due to human sinfulness. Failures of individuals and collectives had no decisive influence on the *progressus*, the world's movement toward the fulfillment of time. The latter derived its dynamic force and its ultimate destination from the sacred sphere, an ontological layer (a layer of being) that was permanently insulated from the instability of history. The ultimate overcoming of failure—and with it the perfect fulfillment of human destiny—also would occur outside of the world of human history. Medieval chroniclers could discern in history the divine will without having to carry the burden to prove or bring about universal human emancipation.

In contrast, modernity had made history take on the task of demonstrating the progressive fulfillment of the promises of the Enlightenment. With no escape clause, progress's plot line—the march to complete human emancipation—could be disturbed only temporarily. Even immense human suffering must only be seen as a spur and step to further beneficent development. Yet inevitably, failures and the resultant disenchantments proved sufficiently significant to diminish the persuasiveness of the progressive hopes. Postmodernists have seen themselves as agents of reckoning. They had no use for suggestions that the project of modernity must still be finished or its dangerously high hopes with their attendant high risks be simply modified. The postmodern moment in which postmodernists would claim the right to succession to the discredited modernity seemed to be at hand.

3 THE POSTMODERN MOMENT

Ascertaining the Moment

Scholars have used a ready method to locate the transition from modernity to postmodernity—the postmodern moment—and the decisive intrusion of consciously postmodernist thought into the world of modernity. They have traced early appearances of the term postmodernism.[30] Four such cases have been located for the period prior to 1946. In 1870, John Watkins Chapman called for the radicalization of modern painting beyond the program of impressionism.[31] But postmodernism referred here only to a more thoroughgoing modernism. Half a century later, the cultural critic Rudolf Pannwitz's postmodern human being was a product of the crisis of European culture, but one who hid rather than solved the crisis. "Toughened by sport, consciously nationalistic, militarily trained, and religiously fervent the *postmoderne Mensch* was a superficially hardened weakling" unfit to usher in a new cultural period.[32] Then, in 1934, in Federico de Onis Sanchez's *Antología de la Poesia Española e Hispanoamericana* (1905–14) *postmodernismo* became the intermediate phase between *modernismo* (1896–1905) and *ultramodernismo* (1914–32) with an accordingly limited function.[33] And in 1945, Joseph Hudnut used the term in a discussion of modern architecture. His post-modern house elevated sensibility and tradition to equal status with scientific-technological considerations of prevailing modernist orthodoxy.[34]

None of these uses of the term corresponded to present usages. At best they could be taken as intellectual heat lightning, faintly signaling stormy weather ahead for modernism. Actually, the views of some prominent critics of Western culture during the same period, who did not use the term postmodernism, came much closer to present concepts of a postmodernist age. Friedrich Wilhelm Nietzsche, Henry Adams, and Max Weber could be invoked as examples.

In 1939 and later in 1954, the historian Arnold Toynbee used the term to designate a historical period as postmodern—first referring to the time after 1914 and then for the age since 1875.[35] In either case it was meant to signal the end of Western global dominance due primarily to the internal weakening of Western culture by an excessive individualism. Yet the affinity of his usage of the term "postmodern" to that by the postmodernists was deceptive. Toynbee's end of modernity and modernism came in the framework of his cyclical philosophy of history. The postmodern age was Western culture's stage of the decadence that recurred in every high culture, once total relativism prevailed and ushered in anarchy in thought (excessive relativism) and life (social turmoil, revolutions, wars). At that point, all cultures slipped into the anonymity and obscurity of posthistory. Yet such a posthistory lacked the newness, uniqueness, and affirmative quality demanded by postmodernists.

In the 1950s, the term postmodern found more frequent use. It would be significant for the future of postmodernism that the perspectives on postmodernism by some social science–oriented scholars (C. Wright Mills, Bernard Rosenberg, and an early participant in the postindustrialism debate, Peter Drucker) already differed widely from those by scholars in the humanities—foreshadowing the eventual dual development of postmodernism. Also, at that point, the term no longer saw merely idiosyncratic use but referred to intellectual currents.

Decisive Twentieth-Century Disenchantments

The postmodern moment was at hand when the concepts of postmodernity and postmodernism emerged as serious challengers to those of modernity and modernism in the debates on Western culture's development. That occurred after two of modernity's key premises lost their aura of certainty for many.

According to the first premise a sufficiently complete authoritative knowledge (truth) could be obtained about the past by the use of properly modern methods and interpretations. Nietzsche once remarked that since Copernicus Western culture had been on a slide downward toward nihilism. He referred to the vanishing certainty that had been offered by the essences and ideas of the ancients, God and the divine providence of Christians, and, he might have added, the Reason of the Enlightenment thinkers. After 1945, the progressive view's persuasive power showed a serious erosion as the impression of an inescapable impasse in truth-finding had reached critical levels.

In tandem with the faded hope to find stability for knowledge went a second disenchantment. After the Enlightenment, the promise of an authoritative knowledge had carried the promise of control over nature and human destiny. The promise had gained wide acceptance among a general public attuned to the marvelous advances in science, technology, and medicine. The disenchantment, particularly in Europe, began after World War I and increased steadily as the twentieth century kept on producing a long series of events that supplied testimonies against the progressive hopes once vested in human control: the inability of modern knowledge to stop the deprivations of the Great Depression, the shocking role of science and technology in increasing the horrors of war, the horrendous price exacted by tyrannical ideologies in their attempts to create the envisioned "new human being," and the so-far unimaginable Holocaust and other genocides.[36] The stark contrast between the hopes placed in the civilizing process through the growth of rationality and the gruesome realities made a mockery of the once strong expectation that the so-called cultural lag would be remedied in time. The lag was attributed to the slower speed of the ethical progress of the human race in comparison to the scientific-technological advances. To that must be added the sense of disenfranchisement on the part of minorities and women as well as the sense of loss created by the steady diminution of Europe's dominant position in the world.

Postmodernism emerged as a response to the double shock administered by life. The specific postmodernist theories would differ in exactly how the perceived failure of progress was accounted for. Yet all of them found the situation climactic enough to foresee more than just another period of history in the long row of periods. The postmodernist sense of mission could be best stated by paraphrasing Lucien Febvre's remark that "history in the last resort meets the same need as tradition . . . [it] is a way of organizing the past so that it does not weigh too heavily on the shoulders of men."[37] While modernists had seen it as history's task to lift the heavy burden of tradition from people's shoulders, postmodernists wished to free people from the burden of history. Thus, postmodernists, regardless of differences amongst them, took it upon themselves to be the historical force destined to either predict or bring about an end to history as so far lived and thought about.

■ 4 AT THE CORE OF THE POSTMODERNIST CHALLENGE TO HISTORY

The Call for a Revolution in Historical Thought

At the beginning of this preliminary exploration of postmodernism and its impact on historical understanding as well as historiography, the question was raised whether postmodernism would shape twenty-first-century historiography to the degree the New History of the 1890s and early 1900s had done for twentieth-century historiography. By now, however, the postmodernist challenge has taken aim at more than a transition from modernity to just another historical period. The driving forces of moral indignation and political considerations made for a more ambitious endeavor: a fundamental change in the understanding of the human condition. Therefore, its reach also has transcended the wish for modifications in historical epistemology and methodology toward a revolution touching the very basis of present historical understanding, particularly its concept of the inevitable historicity of human life. Hence, history and historians were substantially affected when postmodernists set out to create a theory of history that would fit into the postmodernity from which the detrimental features of the historical period would be absent.

Both, modernists and postmodernists, expected an era with a novel human condition once their views of the world had become the organizing principles of life. Guidance in that life would no longer come from the recorded past. Human life in postmodernity would have a new structure and dynamic. Postmodernists did not choose in the simple reductionist way to replace reason as the all-important force with another specific aspect of human life. In the postmodernism debate, which has focused on methods and interpretive approaches of history, this choice has not figured significantly. A surprising fact since not only was the choice crucial for postmodernism's views on postmodernity, it also obscured an agreement between historians and postmodernists on the crucial importance of time as a dimension of the human condition and a key disagreement. In a decisive shift, postmodernists based their hope for a postmodernity, completely and irrevocably set apart from the past, on a radically different valuation of the two basic human experiences of time—change and continuity. In doing so, postmodernists touched the core of the historicity of human life and historical thought: the historical nexus.

Questioning the Historical Nexus between Past, Present, and Future

The historical nexus linked together the past (available through evidential traces and interpreted memories), the present (with its need for decisions and actions guided by a knowledge, much of it derived from the past, that spoke with many voices), and the future (as yet an expectation shaped by the images of the past and the new features of the present). Thinking in terms of the nexus made the historian's main quest—the description, understanding, or explanation of the past—into more than simply the effort to produce a static, isolated image of the past. Antiquarians have aimed at such static images. Historians have always dealt with dynamic segments. A history of France in 1750 involved remainders and memories of life in the preceding decades as well as the expectations for the future held before and in 1750.

The nexus, as the typical dynamic structure of life and historical inquiry, involved both temporal experiences: change and continuity. Change was recognized as incessant and inevitable, its effect being a strangeness between past and present. Unavoidable elements of continuity diminished the strangeness, providing a countervailing and stabilizing tendency. This affirmation by historians that the two temporal experiences were always interwoven in the human condition in complex ways has given history its special kinship to life but also made the historian's task enormously difficult.

Historians have affirmed the ever-present intricate interplay between change and continuity, allowing only for short periods of dominance in life by one or the other, as reflected in history's revolutionary and static periods respectively. They also recognized the tension caused by the simultaneous and contradictory presence in individuals and groups of the longings for continuity and urges for change. This tension, produced by the forever shifting interplay between the temporal experiences, has been so pervasive that it should be termed an existential tension. Properly so, as long as the term was understood only as a descriptive one and not as yet another pan-explanatory, single causal force for every historical change. The fitting image of that tension would depict it as the energizer and modifier of life—a life seen as an incredibly complex and ceaselessly reconfigured web of forces. Far from being an abstract or separate force, the existential tension, as a key manifestation of the time dimension, has been seamlessly interwoven into all human activities, such as the meeting of needs; the satisfying of forever multiplying wants for ease, comfort, and pleasure; the gratifying of ambitions for power, status, and recognition; as well as the assertion of a sense of order with justice; the appreciation of beauty; the coping with death; and the affirmation of a realm of the sacred. All of them were subject to the pulls and tugs of the often contradictory, sometimes complementary longings for change and continuity. For historians, the content of life and the dimension of time could not be separated in life or theory.

Historical practice has on the whole conformed to that understanding. Postmodernist critics have pointed to the eventual failures of all nexuses, be they constructed in the praxis of life or in historical inquiry. The history of historiography has indeed been a testimony to a long line of efforts at nexus building, each of them undertaken in specific historical contexts. Yet, while the flow of life has eventually changed all nexuses or made them obsolete, they and their results did not become just so many figures drawn in shifting sand. Human fallibility did not make all historical insights arbitrary or illusory and all action futile. From past successes and failures, historians have glimpsed some rather steady perimeters of the human experience as well as recurrent features in the human condition. These perimeters and recurrences made visible sturdy elements of continuity—a permanence, albeit on a human scale—in life's incessant change. In turn, these insights gained have been used as guidance for people's lives and as part of the matrix of order for the historians' inquiries. But postmodernists have preferred to see in the failed nexuses the justification for considering the present endeavor of history as, in the end, illusory. Their key argument for a unique postmodernity would rely on a sharply different assessment of change and continuity's roles in human life.

As an endeavor to grasp the complex reality of past life, history has constructed a formidable body of methods and interpretive approaches in order to facilitate the analysis and understanding of the past with a minimum of simplification. Among that which must not be simplified was the constant interweaving of change and continuity in life. That has contributed to the complexity of "doing history" and made its results not perfectly but sufficiently true. Nevertheless or perhaps because of it, the cumulative efforts by historians have produced accounts of past human life of great richness—the only repositories of insights into the overall human existential experience. But postmodernists considered this complexity typical for the historical period only. In postmodernity it had no place.

The effects of the existential tension on human life have been made even more complex by the uniquely human capacity to reflect on life, particularly the ability to distinguish between the "is" on one side and the "wished for" or the "ought to be" on the other. That capacity has enabled human beings to construct historical nexuses not only on behalf of maintaining the existing order (the present linked to the past) but also of trying to bring about a different, more desirable future. This ability to envision a better or more just order of the human world also opened the way for an immense extension of the human desire for the reduction of the existential tension. In metahistories— as in the grand progressive schemes—the wish for a merely more satisfying future yielded to that for a perfect future in which the existential tension and the historical nexus would become irrelevant.

The most surprising finding about postmodernist theories (including the variety that adamantly opposed metahistories) must be the fact that they were formed on the metahistorical level. The postmodernist challenge to history was a radical one (in the sense of the word radical as a derivative of the Latin word *radix* for the root), motivated by profound ethical and political disappointments with modernity and the wish to do better. Still, modernity shaped the postmodernist theories' interpretation of time. In their analyses of modernity, postmodernists saw the progressive view of history suggesting an early stage dominated by change (under rationality's increasingly firm guidance) and a final stage of perfection (of lasting continuity). Thus, the existential tension was remedied in the course of time. On their part, historians learned much from the progressive view but reaffirmed the constant intertwining of change and continuity. Postmodernists learned a different lesson from the progressive model. The avoidance of the evil features of the historical period required the re-evaluation of the role of time in the shaping of history. In one case continuity, in the other case change was declared ultimately dominant and beneficial, while the other aspect of time was assigned the negative role of having caused the calamities of history. Depending on the postmodernist theory affirmed, either change or continuity would lose its formative power in postmodernity. The postmodernist revision of history was to be no mere technical change in methods and approaches but a change in basic views concerning the world and the human condition.

Historical, geographical, and generational contexts would assist first one kind of postmodernism and then the other to prominence—with different implications for historical thought. But the existential tension was to be resolved in both cases. Historicity would have to be redefined since the traditional concept of the nexus was declared to be characteristic only for one period of human development—the historical period. Or, even more restricted, nexuses were no more than pragmatic, contextual constructions of Western culture for coping with life.

5 TWO VERSIONS OF THE POSTMODERNIST FUTURE

POSTMODERNITY AS THE ULTIMATE ERA OF STABILITY

The Long Reach Back

Formative thinking for an early version of postmodernism occurred well before the actual postmodernist moment, when two seminal thinkers elaborated its core ideas: Antoine Augustin Cournot, a scholar of the French Second Empire, and Alexandre Kojève, a Russian exile living in the Paris of the 1930s. Both men affirmed progress, but they stipulated that its end stage would be far from the expected dynamic society of fully rational and free people. The proponents of progress, including Condorcet, had failed to grasp the real outcome of the modern quest for absolute knowledge and its correlate, absolute control. Instead of the ideal union of reason and freedom, a life with a narrow-gauged routine would mark the static or quasi-static postmodernity. The historical nexus would be dominated by continuity as the future would become an extended present. The crisis that was thought to have befallen the progressive view was only a crisis of our wrong expectations of progress. History, progressive in its course, found its true ending in a stage of dominant continuity with minimal change.

The Creative Phase

In the two decades after 1945, the context of life gained a greater affinity for this version of postmodernist thought. Disillusioned proponents of a non-Marxist socialism such as Hendrik de Man and Bertrand (Baron) de Jouvenel (des Ursins), discerned what the American sociologist C. Wright Mills located as the central lesson at mid-century: the Enlightenment's stipulation of a necessary connection between reason, morality, freedom, and happiness had been proven wrong. Universal and beneficent reason had become in reality the guiding force toward a human life of narrow dimensions. These proponents of postmodernism had a keen appreciation of the subversive side of progress, which turned mass production and consumption, rational control, and mass media from blessings into forces steering all into a stable state. The anthropologist Arnold Gehlen foresaw a posthistory in terms of a biological pragmatism. In America, Roderick Seidenberg envisaged it as the triumphant but spirit-deadening period of the technological culture. All of these postmodernists either spoke of or implied a posthistoric period marked by the petrification or crystallization of society as the true end of historical development. Much later, in the 1990s, Francis Fukuyama evoked a vigorous debate with a version of his postmodernism that recaptured Kojève's ideas and Cournot's enthusiasm.

This postmodernism had its prominence in Europe, particularly France and Germany. Its basic mood was not attuned to the America of the immediate postwar period. And the attention of historians was not attracted because the features of this postmodernism pertinent to history were closely related to the prevailing social science–oriented historical practice. However, the expected postmodernity with its posthistoric nature formed the exception. History as a significant part of life and the role of historians would virtually disappear. Debates would occur at the publications of major works. But a greater urgency for debate would depend on the prospects of realizing the envisioned postmodernity.

The Term "Structural Postmodernism"

The naming of this early group of postmodernists was guided by their key retention of a knowable world of objectively given structures and forces. The term "structural postmodernists" seemed to be the most appropriate designation for them, because it indicated a historical reality that could be grasped in its inherent dynamic and order. However, the term "structural" must be clearly differentiated from the term "structuralist," which, as will be seen later, refers to a group of scholars whose affirmation of structures was of a specific kind.

POSTMODERNITY AS THE ENDLESS STAGE
OF TOTAL FLUX

The Emergence of a New Postmodernism

The 1960s favored the emergence of a second group of postmodernists that had its home base in the humanities—especially literary criticism, continental European philosophy, the arts, and architecture. Traces of this type of postmodernist thought, even the occasional use of the term post-modern, could be discerned from the late 1950s onward in the writings of Charles Olson.[38] Then, Irving Howe and Harry Levin spotted, still in a critical vein, elements of the new postmodernism: the loss of faith in a truth that represented reality, the breakdown of traditional large-scale ordering schemes in the literary and social world, and the dwindling of a systematic base for action. In contrast, Leslie Fiedler enthusiastically embraced the dismantling of fixities and of limits in American culture. A special aim was the destruction of the cultural hierarchy with its high ("elitist") and a low ("popular") culture, which for him bespoke an oppressive distinction. Other writers celebrated the toppling of the Western self from its pedestal. A drive gathered strength to darken the image of progress and, with it, the whole heritage of the Enlightenment. The rejection of traditional views of truth was most immediately directed at progressive versions of history. That rejection included the American progressive sense of history with its certainty about the universal emancipation of humankind from all social and economic afflictions as well as the Marxist philosophy of history and its end stage of ideal economic justice.

By the 1970s, a significant cultural transformation was underway. The presence of the term postmodernism in the titles of some prominent works by American and European scholars indicated the ascendancy of the term and the ideas it stood for: Ihab Hassan's *Dismemberment of Orpheus: Toward a Postmodern Literature* (New York, 1971), and Charles Jencks's *The Language of Post-Modern Architecture* (London, 1977) and Jean-François Lyotard's *The Postmodern Condition* (Paris, 1979; English, Minneapolis, 1984). French philosophers, among them Michel Foucault and Jacques Derrida, had already published works that left no doubt about the aspirations of the new postmodernism to be the dominant way of thinking about the world, life, and history. Roland Barthes's turn toward a poststructuralist perspective would have a decisive influence on the postmodernist transformation of historical narrativism. Hayden White's *Metahistory* (1973) played the key role in that transformation in the United States.

The Rejection of Metahistory and Authoritative Truth

These postmodernists did not see the crisis of modernity originating in an improper understanding of the working and aim of progress. Instead, they regarded the very assertion of one encompassing and universal history as a grand and dangerous illusion and cited as proof the hegemonies, dominations, and tyrannies of the twentieth century. All grand conceptualizations of history must be rejected. The proper course of action was *not* to construct yet another long-range historical nexus claiming universal validity and authoritative truth, which would produce new hegemonies, tyrannies, and oppressions. Historical nexuses beyond a minimal and temporary scope were artificial closures that introduced an illusory permanence (in historical theory, continuity) with subsequent oppressive attempts to enforce their validity.

These postmodernists also focused on the second perceived crisis of modernity—the intellectual malaise blamed on an epistemological impasse: modernity's failure to gain a certainty for knowledge untainted by subjectivity. But they did not do so because they were motivated by the drive to find new ways to gain authoritative knowledge. Such attempts were futile and dangerous. These postmodernists focused on the link between the authority of truth and power. The emphasis in truth-finding shifted from reason and empiricism to desires and drives, especially power. Debates on truth became couched in terms of opposition to oppression, hegemony, privilege, establishment, domination, legitimation, and enforced homogeneity. The solution to the problems posed by metahistory and claims to authoritative truth was the stipulation of the absolute dominance of change over continuity in postmodernity. "Closures" and nexus-building would be impossible. A total revision of the infrastructure of historical thought and practice was called for.

The key instrument for such revolutionary changes in history's epistemology was found in the participation in the so-called Linguistic Turn. In the linguistically constructed world, truth would have neither permanence nor stable foundations and hence no privileged authority. Language changed from being the neutral medium between consciousness and the outside reality to being itself the only accessible reality. Mostly overlooked in the stipulation of the Linguistic Turn as the ultimate basis for this postmodernism has been that the view of reality as a web of ceaselessly and aimlessly shifting linguistic relationships has as its fundamental premise a world of total flux. Henceforth, the only acceptable continuity was the continuity of change since it was an "empty" or formal nonoppressive continuity.

The Term "Poststructuralist Postmodernism"

For naming this group, the terms anti-structural or a-structural offered themselves. Yet as the analysis will show, elements of structure—albeit unwanted—were present even in the works of the most prominent postmodernist scholars. Therefore, the better denotation will be one that already has been widely accepted for this group: poststructuralist postmodernists. The term places these postmodernists into a definite cultural and temporal setting—the period after the flourishing of literary and anthropological structuralism. And, above all, it mirrored its basic perspective on the world and history.

■ 6 **THE PROJECT OF A POSTMODERNIST THEORY OF HISTORY**

The postmodernists' case against the progressive view of history was based on the discrepancy between visionary expectations and reality. Each of the modern philosophies of history—be it that of Condorcet, Hegel, Marx, or others—stipulated an end stage of history, established through the perfection of one or another aspect of the human condition. Their ethical and political motives made postmodernists reaffirm (surprisingly) the concept of a proper human condition. However, they have not envisaged a triumphant ending in which progress (change) ended in a state of full rationality (continuity). Instead, structural postmodernists foresaw a postmodernity in which a tightly limited routine life warranted the life of perfect continuity. Poststructuralist postmodernists would establish their postmodernity by persistently barring closures (establishments of illusory and damaging continuity) in a world defined as endless flux. Both postmodernist ventures foresaw the end of the historical period with all the evil that human beings could inflict on one another. That commonality of assumptions and purposes also justifies the use of the term postmodernism or, as it has been put, "homogenizing the conversation on postmodernism and its implications."[39] In both cases, the historicity of human life was put into question by redefining the world and the human condition.

For the present inquiry, the crucial question will be the one after the feasibility and shape of a postmodernist theory of the human condition that lacked the features of what now was called the historical period and of the old ways of inquiring into it. Could the postmodernist expectations of a new human condition be translated into a consistent and persuasive theory that knew not the messy fullness of temporality but only the pure dominance of change or continuity? In other words, could the historians' mediating approach between such binary elements as change and continuity, object and subject, construction and interpretation be replaced by a theory of history that stipulated a world with no need for such mediation?

This book explores, analyzes, and assesses these questions and issues. In each section, theories by prominent postmodernist scholars relevant to historical thought are presented. An assessment follows of the viability of these views for serving as the basis for a new historical thought. Space is also given to the often ardent debates between postmodernists and historians.

PART 2

POSTMODERNITY AS THE TRIUMPH OF
CONTINUITY: STRUCTURAL POSTMODERNISM

7 POSTMODERNISM'S EMERGENCE IN AN UNLIKELY SETTING

A search for postmodernist traces in Western historiography between 1850 and 1914 seemed to be an unpromising endeavor. In these years, modernity, both in theory and the praxis of life, radiated an unprecedented confidence that stifled doubts about progress. European societies expanded their economic base by industrialization within the framework of capitalism, spread their political power across the globe, and enhanced the comfort and health of many of their citizens. The United States fulfilled its "manifest destiny" in becoming a truly continental nation—one prosperous and powerful. The theoreticians of progress could paint the expectations for the future only in bright colors. In the contemporary historical nexus, the future could still be seen as free of the past's vicissitudes. Even most prominent critics of the Enlightenment's rationalist version of progress—such as the Marxists—pitted against it yet another version of a radiant future.

In intellectual endeavors, the certainty of truth came to be seen less in terms of traditional fixed essences (except for reason and progress) and more in those of development. Scholars who searched for order in the ever more rapidly changing world tried to discern above all history's driving forces and their direction. With the world itself in constant motion, history with its sense of dynamic replaced theology and philosophy as the key explanatory discipline. The historical approach prevailed in scholarly inquiry. Where formerly permanence had meant timelessness, now it was defined in historical terms as continuity in development. History, in turn, took on the obligation to demonstrate truth in terms of progress. So far an endeavor to understand life with its complex interweaving of destabilizing change and stabilizing continuity, history had become an all-explaining and secular redemptive venture—a burden that seemed light in the late 1800s.

In the second half of the nineteenth century, the progress theory of history experienced another reshaping, when progress-through-science scholars merged their views on progress with those of the eighteenth-century rationalists. The historical interpretations of such late-nineteenth-century scholars as John W. Draper and William E. H. Lecky spoke of an unstoppable "upward" development of the human race, sustained by scientific and □ **29** technological innovations. In the future, human control over nature and society would be fully realized and so too would be the freedom of individuals.

Yet some scholars sensed a fundamental contradiction in the progressive views of Hegelians, Marxists, and progress-through-science historians. In each case, the end stage of modernity stipulated the presence of both the triumphantly free and rational human being and the victorious quest after total control over the world of nature and society. The odd angle at which the two stood to each other went unnoticed. Structural postmodernists would build their case on the suspicion that progress worked in a manner and with objectives sharply different from the enthusiastic expectations prevailing at the time. The end of modernity would be a postmodernity in which continuity would prevail but secured in a manner modernists did not suspect. In this postmodernity, life and historical thought would take on a sharply different shape. Even before structural postmodernism reached its prominence as a major current in Western thought in post-1945 Europe, a few scholars grasped some of its major themes.

■   ## 8 AN EARLY REDEFINITION OF PROGRESS'S DESTINATION

Antoine Augustin Cournot

In light of the prevalent cultural euphoria, it should not surprise that the contrary pronouncements on the goal of progress by the mathematician-philosopher Antoine Augustin Cournot (1801–77) did not attract much attention.[1] Born only a few years after the death of Condorcet, Cournot related Condorcet's historical vision to a scientifically conceived cosmic ordering process. History mimicked the cosmos, which displayed the struggle between *hazard* (chance) and *reason* (order). The latter was destined to prevail in the end stage of total continuity.

Progress toward a Static Postmodernity

History reflected the cosmic ordering process in its three stages. In the first stage instincts and the environment cooperated in shaping the initial, not-yet-fully developed human beings into a natural social whole.[2] In contrast to the scholars of contemporary evolutionary anthropology, Cournot did not envisage that originary period as "primitive." Yet, in the context of the cosmos of chance, the natural harmony and unity proved temporary. Gradually, the process of social differentiation produced many different "branches of the human family" and spread relentlessly into all aspects of life. Once more, in contrast to the dominant evolutionary anthropology, Cournot maintained that not all people would develop further. Some would never participate in the next, the historical stage.

The second stage was one of increasing differentiations in all aspects of life resulting in a period of instability—that of history. At first glance, this period offered no improvement as it resulted from the disintegration of the harmonious whole. Instability prevailed, sustained by conflicts. Cournot portrayed the age as the "time of warfare and conquests, of the founding and destruction of empires, the rise and fall of dynasties, of castes, of governments, aristocratic or popular . . . [when] superior human beings of all kinds, conquerors, legislators, missionaries, artists, learned men, philosophers, exercised the most influence on their age."[3] All through this age, the energy of life was dissipated in a disorderly manner.

Into that disorder entered the progress of rationality. With it, views on history would change from fascination with events (producing a history of diffuse facts) to dedication to the rational and uniform (yielding a history of generalization, even laws). In line with such a trend toward greater rationality and stability of insights, Cournot offered a novel suggestion that would become the key tenet of structural postmodernism. Progress was bringing about an order diametrically opposed to that foreseen by the progress theoreticians in the vein of Condorcet. Progress the great accelerator of change turned out to be the ultimate force in the "preparation of delay."[4] Here, delay meant the slowing down and eventual end of progress caused by its own successes. Instead of moving toward the realm of freedom and all it implied for the human life, the history of the human race moved toward a new stability with unexpected features. Just as the cosmos proceeded from the dominance of chance to that of the Logos, so human history proceeded to its own orderly state of affairs—one of a rigid routine. "We leave the historical phase where the caprices of fate and the acts of personal and moral vigor have such influence, and enter into that where, in the main, the general and the masses enter into calculations; where one could calculate the precise results of a regulated mechanism." The violent swings of history were flattened out progressively as the "elements of civilization" gained the upper hand over the "elements of nature," the essential over the incidental, the general over the individual.[5] The masses, with their increasing influence and prominence, played a significant role in that process since they favored such stability.

That third stage brought what later would be called the posthistoric postmodernity. The historical forces, which had caused all the instability, lost their capacity to bring about noteworthy change. Reason, the force that tended to favor the general and predictable over the contingent, had wrought the proper order. Now it showed that progress had all along been a *progress vers la fixité*.[6] The world and its analysis reflected the same process—the advance from uncertainty to certainty, the subjugation of the particular to the general, and the transformation of history into *etiologie* (a broad study of life). But rather than an empire of virtue, the emancipation from chance brought not the freedom *of* choice but only the freedom *from* choice. The harmony of the cosmos, ordered and stable, was reflected in the society arranged *quasi geometrique.*

History, once dominated by the stories of dramatic events and great persons, became the story of the life of the masses in which predictable and routine elements prevailed over the contingent. Necessity of a primarily economic and physical sort triumphed over the unpredictability of events. History was "reduced to an official gazette, that serves to announce the regulations, statistical statements, the accession of chiefs of state and the naming of functionaries, and consequently ceases to be history in the sense in which the word is usually given."[7] Society now accented uniformity and functions. Cournot did not perceive such a future as an apocalyptic end of history or a slow and painful sliding into decay. He preferred another image for the future society—that of the beehive. Its life was rigidly organized, busy, productive, and uneventful.

In the new context where the dominance of continuity had resolved the existential tension between the desire for change and the longing for continuity in human life, the ambitions and strivings of human beings had lost their former intensity. After all, the gap between that which was and that which ought or was desired to be would have been nearly closed. As the properly ordered society reduced the existential tension to a degree insufficient for causing disturbances, history ended.

Sounding the Key Themes of Structural Postmodernism

Nearly a century before the structural postmodernists achieved prominence, Cournot suggested many of their themes. Above all, unimpressed by contemporary enthusiasms, he showed what he thought were the proper conclusions derived from the presuppositions and suppositions of the progressive view of history.

First, Cournot had grasped that progress's aim of a perfect or near-perfect ultimate stage entailed an almost total stability of the human world. Ironically, the end stage would be opposite in character to the change that brought it about. The exact nature of the dynamic force fueling progress's drive toward the end did not matter. In Cournot's case, the inescapable kinship between the cosmic trend to perfect order and progress's logic of perfection prescribed the end.

Second, the resultant state of utter fixity and stability fit formerly ardent hopes and aspirations into a human life within tight perimeters. Rather than the expected life of pure happiness in freedom, people would experience one of contentment within an unexciting and endless routine. For Cournot, it all amounted to a grand liberation, although the routine of the rationally organized life would stifle all hope, aspiration, enthusiasm, creativity, and moral struggle—features that together with freedom had lost their function in the new beehive society.

Third, the human condition at the end of history resembled that at the very beginning. Only the shaping force of the animal-like existence differed: nature in the one and reason in the other case. The existential tension had proven not to be an inherent feature of the human condition after all, but only a feature characteristic of the historical period. Continuity ruled supreme with minimal exceptions. Cournot did not consider the price too high for ending the historical period with its turbulence.

Cournot understood the ironic twist in modernization that would lead the course of history away from Condorcet's vision for a future in which fully emancipated, rational human beings would live with their freedom unimpaired in a new world of perfection and harmony. Progress was destined to achieve a pyrrhic victory. Its triumph brought the annihilation of dynamic reason. By its work and struggle reason had purchased no more than the return of human beings to a quasi-natural state of harmony. While prospects of such an ending would not have appealed to Cournot's contemporaries, imbued with different hopes, they would appear plausible to the structural postmodernists impressed by their twentieth-century disenchantments.

■   9 VIEWS WITH POSTMODERNIST AFFINITIES

A time of exuberant optimism about progress provided no incentives to pay attention to Cournot and his prediction of an ironic end of progress. Still, the period from Cournot to the 1920s experienced two other powerful critical assessments of progress in the vein of Cournot. However, Henry Adams and Max Weber no longer shared Cournot's cheerful outlook on progress's newly understood logic. Because their critiques made them—to paraphrase a Henry Adams dictum—incapable of drinking when the cup of triumph was offered, they have often been labeled simply cultural pessimists. But in the context of structural postmodernism, Adams and Weber were significant indicators for shifting attitudes on progress with affinity to postmodernist thought.

Henry Adams: Progress toward Cultural Entropy

Scholars have held a New England patrician's regret about the passing of the old order or simply a skeptical personality responsible for Adams's radical doubts about the widely asserted smooth fit between democracy, liberalism, science, progress, and industrialization. They have overlooked Adams's life-long quest to find the force that shaped the world and history into a unity. "The attempt to bridge the chasm between multiplicity and unity is the oldest problem of philosophy, religion, and science, but the flimsiest bridge of all is the human concept, unless somewhere, within or beyond it, an energy not individual is hidden; and in that case the old question instantly reappears: What is that energy?"[8] Adams perceived that force as cosmic energy, subject to natural laws. This led him to his conclusions about the path of history that bear a discernible affinity to those of structural postmodernists.

There was, once more, an overall triadic development from stability to an unstable state and on to an end in a new lasting stability. First came an age of unity that was maintained by instinctual promptings and, then, by religion. After 1660, the second, modern age produced new differentiations in a society transformed initially by mechanical forces and its concepts, then by electricity. Third and finally appeared the hazily defined ethereal state. While this superficially looked like the story of the ascendancy of the human race, the brilliance of progress held true only with regard to physical improvements. The actual development of human history followed that of the natural world in which Adams saw the working not of the law of the conservation of energy but of the second law of thermodynamics. The flow of time brought the dissipation of energy, which tended toward the state of entropy.

In history, the social energy that shaped temporary forms of unity also caused their decline when its initial strength dissipated. Historians often have spoken about exhausted states, empires, and societies, but have embedded such talk usually into cyclical theories of decadence. Adams, much in the manner of structural postmodernists, referred to one universal history with its development and end. As in Cournot's view, the much-vaunted idea of progress would be the major force that drove history to its ironic end in permanent stability. The acceleration of innovations and change witnessed not just to a greater human control over the world but also to the accelerating dissipation of social energy. The function of the modern period was thus ultimately a destructive one. Adams's vision of the end of history stood in stark contrast to both Condorcet's joyous expectations and Cournot's soothing cosmic harmony. In it prevailed the stillness and coldness of the absolute end of all in a permanent equilibrium.

Max Weber: Modernity's Iron Cage as Postmodernity's Model

One feature of Weber's thought brought him into proximity with the later poststructuralist postmodernism: his insistence that historians, like other scholars, in their quest to know could construct only ideal types (*Idealtypen*)—constructed concepts that temporarily ordered phenomena but did not represent or mirror reality. They certainly did not allow for their use as building pieces for grand historical schemes. But the ideal types would still retain too much of the venture toward finding the truth about reality for the antireferentialist preferences of the later poststructuralist postmodernists.

Weber linked up more closely with the structural postmodernists when he redefined the dynamics and aim of history. For what other scholars called progress, Weber substituted a more specific concept: the *Rationalisierungsprozess* (the process that made human life increasingly rational).[9] So far, only modern Western culture had achieved a thoroughly rational culture that was shaped and marked by science, technology, entrepreneurs, industrial capitalism, work ethics, and a rationally based system of laws. Like the structural postmodernists, Weber became fascinated by the ever more visible irony in that *Rationalisierungsprozess*, manifest as the radical divergence between its expected and actual results.

History was the record of the human adventure with its three types of social order and their different claims to legitimacy. They followed each other in a roughly chronological sequence: the charismatic, centering in one outstanding person; the traditional, relying on the sacredness of tradition and authority of those called to office by it; and the rational, endowing those with authority whom the legally constituted order designated. The charismatic and the traditional affirmations of truth and ethics had inspired grand emotions and sacrifices. In contrast, the rational order has been marked by the complete routinization of life that has resulted in the ultimate erosion and eventual destruction of the traditional world, including religion. Condorcet had delighted in reason's destruction of traditional thoughts and customs since they represented obstacles to rationality's mastery of the natural and social worlds. Weber, rather than seeing a future empire of virtue, happiness, and peace rising from the ongoing *Rationalisierungsprozess* discerned an *entzauberte Welt*—a disenchanted world without awe, mystery, and the tension between the given condition and the one aspired to. From it had vanished all depth of experience or simply the appreciation of contingency. Ironically, even reason's own claims, hopes, and prestige were eroded by modern doubt. Reason was checkmating reason.

In the advanced modern age, the dominant masses shaped life and society into a routine produced by purely material interests.

Bureaucratization prevailed among the new but by now already encrusted institutions—necessary stabilizers in a world cast off from its traditional moorings. Its routinization and quantification of life's problems suited it ideally for regulating modern life. "In co-operation with the deadening machine, it [bureaucracy] is already at work to produce the iron cage [*Gehäuse;* best rendered as iron cage] for the new servility of the future, in which the human being, like the fellahs of Old Egypt, lacking all will and power, will have to live obediently."[10]

The new society that had rid itself of tradition at the price of life in an "iron cage," left no room for true freedom, a meaningful life, and responsible action. Values with transcendent foundations, once considered trusted guides, now were reduced to disposable instruments for living. In the most advanced forms of modernism, the last remnants of a society of restraints and willingly deferred expectations disappeared, now seen as the outdated heritage of Calvinist asceticism for the glory of God. Thus, the ultimate society would have arrived with its flat routine, devoid of great expectations but safeguarded by bureaucrats. "In the American 'benevolent feudalism,' in the German so-called *Wohlfahrtseinrichtungen* (social service institutions), in the Russian factory system—all of them have ready the *Gehäuse* [iron cage] for the new servility."[11]

The gap between the "is" and the "wished for" or "ought to be," that spur to action for human beings throughout history, had been abolished and, with it, had vanished the truly multidimensional human life. The burden modernism had placed on history—that of demonstrating the relentless march toward perfection—had been lifted at a heavy price: a disenchanting ending to the grand hopes evoked by progress. Weber's assessment was less than sanguine when he described the late modern human beings as "specialists without spirit, sensualists without heart; this nullity imagines it has attained a level of civilization never before attained."[12] And while human beings never had real access to the meaning of history, they now lost even the illusion of such knowledge.

Weber himself did not accept stoically life within the merely given or the abandonment of the autonomous individual. In protest against the tyranny of routine and mediocrity, he called for the daily assertion of a vocation and awareness of responsibility. Later on, some poststructuralist postmodernists would call in a similar spirit for a life of perennial opposition. For their own and quite different reasons, both would find in their new world views no room for actions guided by any meaning and truth inherent in the world.

Traces of Postmodernist Thought in Historiographical Developments

At first glance, the historiography between the 1880s and 1914 appeared to be safely removed from fundamental doubts about modernity. The lives of historians were firmly embedded in stable national contexts. In such conditions, historians wrote historical accounts with a firmly held national focus and were largely unreceptive to doubts about the beneficent course of history. Historicism with its aim to understand the diversity of past cultural configurations flourished. But, itself often still with a nationalist bent, it lacked yet the hard edge to overcome the generally accepted teleological and unitary view of history.

Yet some of the structural postmodernist themes were present. The stipulated easy coexistence of human freedom and total human control of world and society in modernity's end stage appeared as a topic of discussion in various forms. First was the debate on the relationship between the values of democratic life and those of science. Doubts about a smooth fit between them were strong enough that the first article in the first issue of the *American Historical Review* reassured American historians on that point.[13] Earlier, in 1888, the British analyst of American culture, James Bryce, had discerned a discrepancy between American democracy and the emerging and soon dominant scientific history, which he judged to be elitist. For him the social implications of a scientific history and of democracy were in conflict with each other. Six years later, Henry Adams, in his presidential address to the American Historical Association, had criticized the generally optimistic tenor of the American historical discourse, particularly the naively harmonious linkage between a democratic society and the scientific history. Most American historians found his message disconcerting as it came at a point when, as they saw it, history was just winning its place among the sciences presumably without endangering its civic role.

Second, predictions appeared of an end of history that ran counter to those of human progress. Witness of that were Brooks Adams's *The Law of Civilization and Decay* (1895) and the popular "Fall of Rome" literature that were patterned after the age-old cyclical model of interpretation. In all of them could be found cultural end stages marked by features of a posthistoric postmodernity.

Third, the decades on either side of 1900 also experienced the call for a New History by Frederick Jackson Turner, Henri Berr, and Karl Lamprecht. Its most important themes were pronounced by Woodrow Wilson in his talk to the historical conference at the World Exposition in St. Louis (1904) and by James Harvey Robinson in his well-known *The New History* (1912): a turning away from isolated facts, politics, elites of power, and distinct events and toward generalizations, inclusion of all aspects of culture, the masses, and "the grand silent forces."[14] As historians set out on the path to make the New History a reality, they elevated the status of the "people" but diminished radically the importance of the individual. The extinction of that now diminished role would be a defining feature in both types of postmodernism.

Then, the guns of August 1914 ushered in a new climate of historical thought in Western civilization, one more conducive to asserting alternatives to the progressive view of history, to questioning the possibility of a certain and authoritative truth, and to pronouncing the powerlessness of the individual.

■   ## 10   THE FIRST TWENTIETH-CENTURY POSTMODERNIST: ALEXANDRE KOJÈVE

His Work and Its Context

Alexandre Vladimirovitch Kojevnikov (1902–68) or Kojève, as he was called as a French resident, was not fated to be quite as obscure a figure as Cournot had been. Cournot's work had foreshadowed uncannily the postmodernist transcription of Condorcet's triumphantly modernist message into the sober terms of subsequent centuries. Kojève reshaped the Hegelian version of the progress theory (or more accurately, elements of it) in the spirit of structural postmodernism for a generation still shocked by World War I and facing virulent ideological conflicts. For that role, his life prepared him exceedingly well.

His personal voyage as an exile from the Soviet Union (branded a class enemy, who nevertheless still professed Communist sympathies) led him first to Berlin and then, through the intervention of Alexandre Koyré, to Paris. At that time his intellectual framework had become quite varied: Marxist but lacking the constraints of orthodoxy; sympathetic toward eschatology through his study of Vladimir Soloviev (later by his acquaintance in Paris with Nicolai Berdyaev) without accepting the Christian faith; Hegelian without the assertion of the Absolute Spirit; vitalist in Nietzschean terms; and existentialist in the early Heideggerian mode. Tellingly absent in all of that was Condorcet's contention of an essentially rational human being, an affirmation of the world of reason, and a history patterned accordingly.

Kojève's work was created in the politically and intellectually turbulent Europe that had seen a sharp decline in the persuasive force of the progress view. The word crisis began to be affixed to the connotations of progress and its vision of Western culture's future. With the actual present as well as the expectations for the future lacking sufficient promise, intellectuals were receptive to views of the past that no longer suggested a story of a steady human ascendancy to a greater rationality.

Toward a Postmodernist Hegel

As substitute for his friend Koyré, the thirty-one-year-old Kojève delivered lectures on Hegel in a seminar at the Ecole des Hautes Études (1933–39).[15]

The intellectual climate of France was never the same afterwards, as Kojève's ideas influenced a group of illustrious scholars.[16]

Hegelianism in the German idealist vein had difficulties in making inroads in a country where variations of Auguste Comte's positivism and Henri Bergson's vitalism dominated intellectual life. The gradual ascendancy of Marxism provided some incentive for the study of Hegel whose invasion of France was also assisted by Jean Hyppolite and Jean Wahl. Kojève strengthened the influence of Hegel when he tailored Hegel to the preferences of twentieth-century intellectuals. He brought forth not "the most authoritative" but a highly idiosyncratic, free-style Hegel interpretation, which transformed Hegel's philosophy into anthropology.[17] History as the Hegelian self-realization process of the Spirit (really a *Selbsterkenntnisprozess*) yielded to a process of human self-realization. But both developments ended up in the same manner: in a condition of utter stability.

The Human Condition Redefined

Once more, the unitary march of history toward its end stage occurred in three stages. However, Kojève, as would most other postmodernists, focused his attention on the second—the historical stage and its aftermath.

In accord with his anthropological Hegelianism, Kojève found one source of history's dynamics in the human condition itself. His concept of that condition owed much to Heidegger's stipulation of the crucial human confrontation with nothingness, manifest as death. René Descartes's and Condorcet's emphasis on reason and consciousness, dominant in Western culture, was replaced by that on the existential, anxiety-filled encounter with the fullness of life. Heidegger would speak of human beings as strangers to the world—as "being thrown into the world." That immersion into life happened in the constant awareness of the future, which held the certain annihilation by death. This unique process of identity formation was to keep the human being equidistant from being considered a thing with a predetermined identity and from merely being a vessel of potential rationality.

But Kojève wished to write history in the Hegelian vein. The (early) Heideggerian view of human historicity derived from the individual's total immersion in life—one solitary in nature—did not produce human history. Only if the human being was by necessity a member of an effective collective with a distinctive dynamics could there be a historical stage.

The Crucial Conflict

Kojève found the driving force for the historical process by modifying the Hegelian interpretation of history in the Heideggerian mode. It would be radically world immanent, still move everything into a unitary direction, engage in conflict, and originate in a new conception of how the identity of human beings was shaped. Kojève rejected an inherent, stable, and clearly defined identity for human beings—be it the creature of divine making, Marx's alienated being or *homo oeconomicus,* the rational creature of the Enlightenment, or the freedom-seeking being of liberalism. He accepted the Heideggerian negative definition of the human being as not being-in-itself possessing a permanently fixed nature or essence but shaping itself in a life led in central awareness of death and the threat of nothingness. Trying to escape nothingness and being unable to gain a truly stable identity, human beings strove to establish as firm an identity as possible. Hegel had spoken of two typical reactions: to acquire for themselves strong identities (to be masters) or to permit others to define their identities (to be slaves).[18]

In their choices of identities, human beings were not motivated by reason but by desire. Kojève—following Hegel—saw desire as an experience that by necessity involved others, in this case, the desire to be recognized by others. The intent to satisfy that desire made human beings historical beings. Ironically, the desire to be recognized by others achieved its key status not by its usefulness but by its relative uselessness for coping with life. To Kojève, the very lack of a natural function made it a truly human desire. Kojève made it the force shaping the identities of two types of historical agents—the masters and the slaves. They differed from each other by their reactions to the threat of death. Those would become masters who in their struggle for full recognition by others were willing to face death (seen here as a purely natural event). All others (by far the majority of the human race) would be slaves, who preferred self-preservation to the risk of death that accompanied the struggle for full recognition by others. They paid the price by their lower status.

Kojève historicized this master-slave struggle when he made it the core of the story of history. Kojève, then, took a further step in historicizing the conflict when he identified the contending types, master and slave, with two social institutions: the master with the hierarchical state and the slave with the egalitarian family.[19] He also transformed what could have been a confrontation ad infinitum between two static types of human beings into a history that drove toward a defined end. The posthistoric postmodernity would free human beings from the burden of history. Earlier conflict theories of history had known only temporary settlements, mere mitigations that left intact the permanent opposition between masters and slaves.

The End in Posthistory

Condorcet, Hegel, and Marx had conditioned modern scholars and the public to thinking in terms of an end of history in a static stage (admittedly one more sanguine in nature than Kojève's would be). For Kojève, their concepts were outdated. As he saw it, the decisive move toward the end of history would come with the stilling of the desire for recognition in the state of absolute equality. That, by necessity, brought the triumph of the slaves because equality befitted them. The institution of the family had always given the slaves recognition as human beings without regard for recognition by others. In contrast, the state was based on the hierarchical principle and was the domain of the masters. The telos of history transformed the state after the pattern of the family under the impact of the rise of the slaves. Kojève based his prediction on the observation that the slaves, with work as their lot, transformed the world and thereby created the substance and process of history. The world they created gave them a claim to absolute equality. At that point history itself would come to its end since the dynamic force behind all struggles, the desire for recognition, would become dysfunctional. With the equality of master and slave accomplished, the existential tension (energized by desire) between the "ought or expected to be" (the motive for change) and the "is" (the tendency toward continuity) would also have been closed. Thereafter, there would be no reason for negating existing conditions for their perceived incomplete or unjust order. The grand dynamic of history would fade away in a permanently static state. In the absence of the force that had created opposites, the posthistoric reality would not be riven by tensions nor would contingencies of a serious sort disturb the new routine of life.

The postmodern era of universal and absolute knowledge would begin. At one time only Hegel—the wise man—had understood all of history, "because on the one hand, he *lives* in Napoleon's time, and, on the other, is the *only* one to *understand* him (emphases in the original)."[20] Now all people would. The search for truth could end. No fundamental changes would occur, particularly not the bloody wars and revolutions of history. The life of contemplation and routine would know no end. What thinkers from Condorcet to Marx and beyond had longed for, the rule of freedom over necessity and the end of human alienation, would be realized on Kojève's terms.

Kojève's Ambiguity on Human Life in Posthistory

In the political entity that would emerge after the end of history—in Kojève's formulation the "universal and homogeneous state"—all citizens would be equal, undivided by race, class, or any other separating feature. As for history, it would be reduced to exhibiting the now irrelevant past in museums for the curious idle. Inquiries into the future would also become irrelevant since the future would be no more than the extended present. The subject of the traditional and the modern ages, the human being as the agent of history, would fade away too. This meant that the anthropological development ended not with the gloriously rational human being, but with living bodies in human form, but lacking true human creativity.

Kojève wavered in assessing the quality of life after the end of history. At first, he defined the final stage in pleasing terms. While the quest for truth and with it philosophy as well as the horrors of revolutions and wars would disappear, "all the rest can be preserved indefinitely; art, love, play, etc., etc.; in short everything that 'makes man *happy*' (emphasis in original)."[21] At that point, Kojève was sure that the "the disappearance of Man at the end of History, therefore is not a cosmic catastrophe: the natural World remains what it has been from all eternity.... Man remains alive as an animal in *harmony* with Nature or given Being (emphasis in the original)."[22]

Yet in a note to the second edition, he betrayed doubts about such a cheerful assessment of the purely biological human condition. "Hence it would have to be admitted that after the end of History, men would construct their edifices and works of art as birds build their nests and spiders spin their webs, would perform concerts after the fashion of frogs and cicadas, would play like young animals, and would indulge in love like adult beasts. But one cannot say that all this 'makes Man *happy*' (emphasis in the original)." He granted only that "the post-historical animals of the species *Homo sapiens* ... will be *content* as a result of their artistic, erotic and playful behavior inasmuch as, by definition, they will be contented with it (emphasis in the original)."[23] Even worse, "'the *definitive annihilation* of Man *properly so-called*' means the definitive disappearance of human Discourse (*Logos*) in the strict sense (emphases in the original)." The new human being would react to the spoken signals only with conditioned reflexes, making for discourses that resembled the "'language' of bees."[24] It did not matter, since in the posthistoric world there would be not only no "search for discursive Wisdom but also that Wisdom itself. For in these post-historic animals, there would no longer be any [discursive] *understanding* of the World and of self (emphasis in the original)."[25]

A Postscript

The issue of when exactly the end of history would occur and who would be the instrument for bringing it about, remained open. At one time, just as for Hegel, the pivotal figure was Napoleon, who universalized modernism in the image of the French Revolution. At the time of his lectures on Hegel, Kojève stressed Stalin as the new decisive figure and, later, rejected that view.[26] Then, countries rather than persons became the fulfillment agents. In 1948, the United States appeared as the state approaching the stage of equality—a pioneer for the global conditions of the future. Later, however, he saw the "return of animality" by far furthest progressed in the United States, with its boredom of the eternal present.[27] In 1959, Kojève found himself enamored by traditional elements of Japanese culture: tea ceremony, *No* theater, aesthetic suicide, and some elements of the Samurai life—all of them useless rituals, preservers of an aristocratic life in a consumer society. The dull routine of the end stage would be alleviated by the useless but inspiring remainders of the past.

Kojève himself ended up as an official for planning in the French Ministry of Economic Affairs; a position much in line with his conviction that the event-history was over and the future of the human race depended now on the institutions serving stability and their administration. Then, years after Kojève's death in 1968, his ideas inspired Francis Fukuyama's *The Last Man and the End of History* (1992).

■   I I   **THE FLOURISHING OF STRUCTURAL POSTMODERNISM (1945–65)**

THE SETTING

In the two decades after World War II, Europe lived on two experiential levels. The rebuilding process provided much support for the progressive view. As conditions improved, life became gradually easier and yielded more hope. After all, the Great Depression had not returned; innovations and inventions fostered convenience and comfort; the harnessing of nuclear power still promised a wholly beneficent and unprecedented control over nature; mass production of consumer goods eased the lives of many; health care became more effective; a democratization of power and, to some degree, affluence defused social tensions; and the welfare state offered unprecedented security. And those advocating a social revolution could take hope from French and Italian Marxists with their still intact expectations for an ideal future.

But memories of the just experienced human catastrophes were still vivid. The human suffering in its modern form, epitomized by the Holocaust, had proved to be nearly incomprehensible. Ideologies, be they the defunct fascism or the still seemingly vigorous Communism, had become irremediably tainted. These memories shaped the creative work of a group of European scholars, a few of them former ideological activists, whose disenchantment proved to be especially keen. The result would be a postmodernism that retained the emphasis on the logic of progress that prescribed a posthistoric ending, now painted in much darker colors. That static posthistoric postmodernity had no resemblance to the formerly expected states of happiness and perfection. The turbulence of the historic period would end with the triumph of stability (the continuity of the same). Human ambitions and activities would no longer be stimulated by constantly alternating desires for change or continuity. The "ought to be" and the "is" would be nearly the same and the existential tension defused.

For Americans, their efforts and sacrifices of the war had brought some compensation. The superior power, status, and affluence of the United States led many to conclude that progress had indeed shown to be an accurate interpretation of the world's development. That also seemed to confirm the American view of history as progressive universal emancipation in a *novus ordo seculorum*. Historiographically that view had its expression in the consensus school with its affirmation of a basic unity, stemming from centuries of collective experience and a stable set of shared ideas and habits. The emergence of doubts about progress in America would come in the late 1960s, a time in which the prominence of structural postmodernism's prominence was fading quickly. Hence, that postmodernism remained a predominantly European affair. Nevertheless, it was an important cultural current that shaped the historical thought of many contemporaries but also witnessed to postmodernism as a phenomenon that was not isolated to the postmodernist variety prominent in the decades to either side of the recent turn of centuries.

AN IDEOLOGICAL PATH TO POSTMODERNITY: HENDRIK DE MAN AND BERTRAND DE JOUVENEL

Two representatives of the disillusioned political Left, Hendrik de Man and Bertrand (Baron) de Jouvenel (des Ursins), produced postmodernist reflections on their age in political exile.[28] In their works featured prominently a profound disappointment with those elements of modernity that formerly had been sources of hope—the masses, the industrial economy geared to mass production, and the welfare state. These elements turned progress away from its once expected goal.

While de Man and Jouvenel expected modernization to produce a posthistoric state of inertia, they like other postmodernists rejected any linkage of their diagnoses to the similar end stages found in decadence theories. In Hendrik de Man's *Vermassung und Kulturverfall* (1951), the cyclical historical theories of Oswald Spengler and Toynbee were seen as improper generalizations from temporary national moods: Spengler from the German bitterness about the defeat in 1918 and Toynbee from the nostalgia for a vanishing empire.

Hendrik de Man

A disillusioned de Man cautioned historians not to prophesy in terms of grand theories of history but to rely in their projections for the future on the analysis of large-scale forces beyond human control. From such a critical analysis, de Man concluded that these forces worked to create not Condorcet's empire of virtue but a postmodernity he called posthistory. The key to understanding the unexpected developments was the ironic twist of history that made the very forces in which modern hopes were invested—individualism, mechanization, and democracy—stifle gradually all change and innovation. The major victim of progress would be progress itself.

The masses, the intended beneficiaries of progress, were not willing, but only unwitting agents of the development toward the static posthistoric state.[29] They yielded to the power of the machine that proletarized production, and they were coopted by a pleasure-rich but in the end destructive commodity system. Thus, the triumph of the masses came to have a perfect fit with the entropic posthistory. In the latter, *Kultur* (here art, literature, and philosophy, all in the sense of high culture as civilizing agent) was deprived of its dynamic principle: the search for truth and beauty where results were judged according to accepted standards of achievement. In the posthistoric postmodernity, all aspects of *Kultur* became mere tools for the psychological mastery of life.

As progress proceeded, the agents of change weakened. The emerging society favored a life in which continuity marked by sameness prevailed. In turn, the ideal of uniformity, the hallmark of mass production, produced an art and architecture devoid of any connections with regions, communities, or any other existential unit. Artists and writers turned into experimenters in self-expression who were incapable of creating a style that represented more than a short-lived fashion. Art and literature became mere technical enterprises.

History ended when the highest human achievements, the machine and the mechanization of production, turned against their creator. They deprived human beings of their unique human qualities, limited their consumption to standardized articles, destroyed the sense of workmanship, and leveled all differences past life had created. Modernism's lofty ideals and its actual results stood in stark contrast to each other. Postmodernity did not turn the modern version of utopia into reality but yielded a life of existential boredom triggered by a feeling of emptiness. Worse, human ingenuity had shaped a situation without escape. Even the communication revolution, hailed by so many for its liberating influence, contributed to the static state. The overabundance of stimuli resulted in an ennui that brought about the need for even stronger stimuli to gain attention in the cacophonous world. That overstimulation and the attending ever-shorter attention span deadened in the masses all reflection and fostered pure superficiality. The masses, once the hoped-for agents and intended beneficiaries of the emancipatory rationalization process, instead experienced a primitivization and new infantilism. Unfit to be agents of change they became perfect inhabitants of the posthistoric static order. History itself would end as present and future would be forever the same.

Bertrand de Jouvenel

Jouvenel focused his critical attention on the emerging new absolutism: the liberal and democratic welfare state that rendered all past agents of historical change impotent. In that state, a human creation born of the progressive hope for a truly humanitarian society with absolute freedom and human dignity, state authorities would in the end control every aspect of life, whether it be health, wealth, comfort, expressions of thought, art, education, welfare, and security. In this "social protectorate," as Jouvenel called the new society, life would be a "sweet slavery" marked by the enforced endless repetition of the same routine. A quiet tyranny of laws, regulations, and rules enforced the entropy of absolute belonging. "We are the witnesses of a fundamental transformation of society, of a crowning expansion of Power. The revolutions and *coups d'etat* which are a feature of our epoch are but insignificant episodes heralding the coming of the 'social protectorate.' A beneficent authority will watch over every man from the cradle to the grave, repairing the disasters that befall him, even when they are of his own making, controlling his personal development and orientating him towards the most appropriate use of his faculties." Such a posthistory puts into doubt the central premise of the progress theory and the core belief of modernism that the greatest desire of human beings was their freedom. "Where the idea comes from that men hold despotism in detestation, I do not know. My own view is that they delight in it."[30] Jouvenel suggested that the desire was for a despotism gently and seductively applied. History's true thrust aimed at that stage.

AN ANTHROPOLOGICAL PATH TO POSTMODERNITY: ARNOLD GEHLEN

Recourse to Anthropology

In the intellectually turbulent but fertile Weimar Republic, the young Arnold Gehlen linked his scholarship not to history but to an anthropology with a strong philosophical and historical bent. Anthropology had by then acquired a firm status as an intended replacement for the traditional philosophical, theological, and historical interpretations of the human condition.[31]

    When Gehlen chose a biological approach to anthropology he distanced himself equally from all remainders of German idealism and the heritage of the Enlightenment. In the 1930s and early 1940s, that choice facilitated a modicum of collaboration with fascism, which was never well founded. Gehlen's human being was shaped in a dynamic interchange with the environment and not by stable racial characteristics. His inevitable disillusionment with the Nazi regime led Gehlen to a social psychological approach that offered a greater latitude for theorizing than his former narrowly biological interpretation. The American social psychologist George Herbert Mead's influence was one trigger and admiration for a pragmatic empiricism the other. How then did Gehlen arrive at his concept of a postmodernity as posthistory?

Human Development from Instinctual to Institutional Control

The human being of the historical period was for Gehlen not the rational subject of the Enlightenment. Instead, he defined the human being in the vein of Friedrich Wilhelm Nietzsche as the *noch nicht festgestellte Tier* (the, in its nature, not yet stabilized animal). The logic of that view, buttressed by his preference for a radical pragmatism and an increasingly influential existentialism, made Gehlen see human beings as gaining their identities through their actions. No metaphysical elements needed to be considered in his sociobiological world because scholars "can ignore theories of a dualistic kind."[32] The proper categories of analysis were utility and action.

In line with other postmodernist schemes, the first phase of history was a long period of stability (the *paleolithicum*) in which human beings had a rather strong instinctual equipment that nevertheless was still insufficient for the tasks of human life. That insufficiency produced much insecurity. Human beings, always craving stability, began to interpret the world, thereby creating mental instruments for coping with life. The resultant elements of order became pragmatically effective when they were objectified in rationally constructed institutions that stabilized the human condition.

The second phase of human history, peaking in modernity, was marked by systematic interpretations of life—the ideologies—that built even more powerful institutions. On the one hand, ideologies were sources of upheavals internally and externally, since "to bend reality so that it comes close to the purity of the ideal, is always a bloody affair."[33] On the other hand, the ever more powerful and tighter net of institutions calmed the human life as it relieved human beings, by now instinctually weak and without firm identity, to an increasing degree of the necessity to make decisions and to take risks. The masses were seen as noninnovative and risk-averse and, hence, effective supporters of that new order.[34] Increasingly, the growth of institutions compensated for the fading strength of instincts and, finally, for the loss of belief in a fixed human nature. Rather than being stabilized from the "inside," the human being became the externally *festgestellte* being (that is, one with an identity imposed from outside).

From the gradual drift toward the ultimate state there was no escape. All elements of tradition would be gradually destroyed in the interest of the smoothly functioning social whole. A "tidal wave of superficiality" would sweep away all elements, such as ideals, values, and even truth, that once had been considered absolutes. The ambitions and aspirations they sponsored had accounted for the turbulence of history.

The arts, purged of all aspirations beyond functional ones, were made unproductive for the collective when all attention shifted to the self. Philosophy, deprived of the search for ultimates, would not transcend a simple hedonism. Philosophies extolling self-insight and self-control lacked all pertinence in the thoroughly planned social environment that prevented all situations requiring more than routine decisions. Equally redundant had become quests after the meaning of things or the arguments over ethics. And the sciences generated endlessly new insights without true development. All of these now redundant intellectual ventures had been produced in the historical period by an excess in human energy (*Antriebsüberschuss*). They had always lacked a proper pragmatic goal. Now, the human life no longer knew the tension between the imperfect present and the envisioned better if not perfect future, between the given and the ought to be or simply hoped for, and between shifting longings for change and continuity. All of that now revealed to have been no more than temporary adjustment problems.

Postmodernity and the End of History

In the third phase, the development had reached a stage in which the human condition had adjusted totally to the new reality. At that point, history ended in posthistory. The unexpected had happened. The exceptional dynamic of modernism had led to the utter stability of the fully developed technological society. In it, the power of the institutions had become unbreakable— ironically by the actions of those who had wished for a totally different order. The welfare state represented that perfection of the institutionalized order. In it, the dominance of institutions succeeded in inculcating a system of useful habits (*Habituationssysteme*) in all members of society. With it, utter predictability and sameness marked the human life. Left without functions, ideologies would fade from the scene and no new ones could find support.

While the individual seemed to be valued, its purely functional existence made such individualism a mere facade. As a mere being of habits, the individual lacked true existential weight. The institutions that totally sheltered human beings also alienated them from all that formerly was thought to be truly human but in posthistory had become nonfunctional. And, in the absence of the conscious, reflective, and creative individual, the agent of change in history had met its end. When Gehlen spoke of posthistory (Gehlen called it *das Post-histoire*) he characterized that final state of constructed stability as crystallization or petrification.[35] With other structural postmodernists, Gehlen shared the dilemma that he had charted an inevitable progress toward a stable posthistory that he as a person did not welcome.

A SCIENTIFIC-TECHNOLOGICAL PATH TO POSTMODERNITY: RODERICK SEIDENBERG

Seidenberg's *Posthistoric Man* (1950) was published in a period of nearly undisturbed American faith in progress toward a rational world, vouchsafed by science and technology. If noticed at all, the book was criticized as the work of a dilettantish futurologist. Undaunted, Seidenberg developed its thesis further in his *Anatomy of the Future.*[36] The works seemed isolated pieces since nobody noticed their parallels to other structural postmodernist writings. An important sign for his link to the structural postmodernism showed already in the triadic structure of his historical interpretation: a stable stage founded on natural features; its gradual disintegration in the subsequent unstable historical age; and the re-establishment of a stable order of ultimate duration in postmodernity.

Humanity's Journey to a Posthistoric Postmodernity

The first stage of human development was an instinctually founded and stabilized one. Yet in the end, human instincts, favoring stability, proved insufficient for the enduring mastery of life. Their dominance yielded to the destabilizing power of intelligence (the force of change).

Instability marked the second stage that provided the subject matter of history. Its key development was the struggle of the steadily weakening instincts against the ever more powerful intelligence. Instinctually rooted stabilizing values and concepts were replaced by constructs with a rationalist basis. The modern society emerged, based on agreements, codes of law, and conscious control. Connected with the increase in intelligence was the self-acceleration of rational organization. But in a structural postmodernist mode, Seidenberg asserted that the true goal of progress and the specific accomplishment of the stage called history was the permanent stabilization of the human world through intelligence. For millennia, no force had been strong enough to establish stability on its terms. But the telos inherent in human development and, thus, in progress was the re-establishment of a stage of wholeness, stability, and harmony. Seidenberg found that now "mankind is passing through a nodal point in its development."[37] The trend was irreversible because intelligence brought "the progressive transformation and domination of every aspect of human existence under the principle of organization."[38] Its end point came with the third, the postmodern age.

The Posthistoric Human Condition

Already in the 1940s, Carl L. Becker had discerned the ironic self-stabilizing tendency of progress. "In such a stabilized and scientifically adjusted society [brought on by progress] the idea of progress would no doubt become irrelevant as progress itself no doubt becomes imperceptible or nonexistent."[39] Seidenberg agreed. Human beings would achieve stability by exchanging for it their capacity to create and innovate. The price had to be paid when the constant acceleration of change would eventually "be nearing a climax in a state of virtually ceaseless change."[40] What was left afterwards was a decline of the ratio of historical change, "presaging an increasingly stabilized condition in human affairs as man adapted himself with ever greater precision to his furthest boundaries, as to some mathematical limit toward which he would move with ever more mincing steps."[41]

In the postmodern age, an ironclad determinism—humanly made—would rule. The very natural laws, discovered and constructed by human beings rather than prescribed by nature itself, now governed human actions. "And in the degree they become crystallized and final—because of some irreducible statement of their relationship, or because man no longer has the power of further penetration into unknown regions—they will inevitably come to function as fixed perimeters of the future."[42] There would still be "incongruous outbursts against the ever more encompassing of rational intelligence" but they amounted to no more than mere rear guard actions.[43]

Science had made the ultimate period real by devising the machine. At one point, Western culture, having become supercharged with the trend toward organization by intelligence, had "crystallized" with the introduction of the machine. Just as crystallization concluded a natural process so did the machine end the one of organization by intelligence. At that moment, the modern age also ceased because it had achieved its task—the ultimate detachment from instincts and its world.

Posthistoric People and Society

The last stage would be inhabited by posthistoric people who fit the new condition of utter fixity and stability. They would realize that human freedom, so cherished in the past, had constituted no more than a feature of the human condition in the age of instability, caused by the "discordance under the impact of opposing forces."[44] In the posthistoric stage with the tightest organization intelligence could produce, freedom had no place because it had no function. Human beings, the would-be masters, had to accommodate themselves completely to the creation of their own intelligence. They had exchanged a human existence that knew choice, decision-making, searching for sense and meaning, and struggling for inner autonomy, with all the risks and instability adhering to them for one of utter stability, permanence, and security. The new society had an icy grandeur, but in its nature it recalled Cournot's image of the beehive, although it was really the construct of intelligence and not a biological phenomenon. "We are thus forced to concede that man may, indeed, that man will, under the compulsion of his deepest trends, move ever closer to that condition of high socialization found pre-eminently among the insects."[45] The drama of the second period in human development, extensively described and puzzled over by traditional historians, ended in a "blind and aimless state of fixity." Such a "triumph of intelligence seems like a bitter and ironic anticlimax."[46]

The long-desired vanishing of the cultural "lag" had occurred in an unexpected manner. The discrepancy between the fast speed of progress in scientific, technological, and economic endeavors and the slower one of ethical and social change had been resolved by the disappearance of the inner-directed and problem-conscious individual whose problem the lag was in the first place. Or in terms of this account, the envisioned posthistoric stage lacked the existential tension produced by the simultaneous presence of longings for change and continuity that had given such intensity to human aspirations, hopes, ethical struggles, religious strivings, and visions of an end stage.

Historians would become annalists of the routine changes in a routinized society. The past they had at one time portrayed was only the now-irrelevant account of a vanished historical period. From its story of a vain movement from problem to problem without proper solutions nothing could be learned for life in the posthistoric stage with its entirely different human condition.

■ 12 THE FADING OF STRUCTURAL POSTMODERNISM AND A TRIUMPHAL EXCEPTION: FRANCIS FUKUYAMA

The Recovery of Progress's Positive Image

The accelerating globalization in the post-1945 world raised entirely new questions about progress. On the one hand, particularly, globalization supplied a new opposition to favorable views of progress. On the other hand, the spread of the capitalist market economy into all corners of the world and its competition with Communist regimes as well as democratic socialist countries brought a variety of defenses of progress. The strongest support for progress views of history came from the so-called modernization theories.

These saw progress fueled primarily by economic forces that were guided and enhanced by technological innovations and capitalist ordering principles. They implied a promise of a universal human condition free of the most burdensome cares, problems, and sufferings of the past. In the 1960s, these theories found their most effective version in development theory. According to it, world history demonstrated the repetition of a development that began in early modern Europe with capitalism's assault on traditional economic practices and cultural traditions, seen as hampering development, and reached its goal in the stage of mature mass production.[47] On their part, futurists or futurologists expected electronic and communications technologies to usher in a new age. Its characteristics came close to Condorcet's vision. Finally, a fervent debate about postindustrialism brought a different perspective to the debate on the shape of the future (Daniel Bell, Amitai Etzioni, Alain Touraine). With the collapse of Communism in the late 1980s, the debate about a new world order acquired new intensity. At that moment, a work representative of structural postmodernism gained much attention.

Structural Postmodernism Returns in a Triumphal Mode

At a time when scholarly attention had become fixated on poststructuralist postmodernism, one of structural postmodernism's best-known works, Francis Fukuyama's *The End of History and the Last Man* (1992) appeared. Seemingly well out of season, it startled most observers, few of whom understood its connections to earlier thinkers like Immanuel Kant, Hegel, and especially Kojève. The impression prevailed of facing a somewhat freakish apparition.

Fukuyama's *The End of History and the Last Man* returned structural postmodernism to a position of note by exhibiting an attitude of optimism if not of triumph. Decades of disenchantment and skepticism about an inherent meaning in history were rejected by Fukuyama's affirmative answer to the question "whether, at the end of the twentieth century, it makes sense for us once more to speak of a coherent and directional History of mankind that will eventually lead the greater part of humanity" to a stable status.[48] That unitary development originated in the dynamic nature of the human condition, which tended toward the completion of history in a world of liberal democracies. When looking for the dynamic principle leading history to that end, Fukuyama rejected modernism's choices of dominating forces, such as Marx's ways and means of production, Sigmund Freud's sexual impulses, and Charles Darwin's environmental adaptations.

He located the decisive force in "that part of man which feels the need to place *value* on things—himself in the first instance, but on the people, actions, or things around him as well. It is the part of the personality which is the fundamental source of the emotions of pride, anger, and shame, and is not reducible to desire, on the one hand, or reason on the other. The desire for recognition is the most specifically political part of the human personality because it is what drives men to want to assert themselves over other men, and thereby into Kant's condition of 'asocial sociability' (emphasis in the original)."[49] The drive to have one's worth recognized by others (presently often defined merely as the search for self esteem), first accented by Plato as *thymos* (spiritedness), was for Fukuyama the ultimate force and hence the proper explanatory concept.

Hegel and Kojève had used that desire and the varying degrees of its presence in individuals to account for the turbulence of history. In Fukuyama's terms that turmoil resulted from the collision of the aspirations of those driven by *megalothymia* (the ambition to be recognized as superior) with the claim to equality by those not willing to risk much for recognition (*isothymia*). As for the universal order of history it has shown the progress from irrational to rational forms of coping with the discrepancy in the desire for recognition. The goal of history has been the proper accommodation of both versions of the desire for recognition.

So far, traditional societies had tended to maintain schemes of *megalothymia* and the modern social theories and practice had fostered *isothymia*. In short, the social ordering systems had favored either masters or slaves. Unable to solve the basic complexities connected with satisfying *thymos,* they all foundered, be they traditional monarchies or governing systems sponsored by modern ideologies of Marxism, fascism, and nationalism. Put into Fukuyama's terminology, it could be said that the Left has favored solutions in favor of *isothymia* and the Right has opposed them.

In the aftermath of the French and American Revolutions, liberal democracy has represented the final and universal institutional framework for the proper channeling of the desire for recognition. Liberal democracy succeeded in doing so because it created a society that permitted freedom and inequality to coexist in a dynamic system of checks and balances. Therefore, it would "constitute the 'end point of mankind's ideological evolution' and the 'final form of human government', and as such constituted the 'end of history.'"[50]

The posthistoric stage would still permit, within stringent limits, an oscillation between the poles of equality and excessive self-assertion—a kind of safety valve dynamics that allowed for a history of small dimensions. It "would not mean that the natural cycle of birth, life, death would end, that important events would no longer happen, or that newspapers reporting them would cease to be published. It meant, rather, that there would be no further progress in the development of underlying principles and institutions, because all of the really big questions had been settled."[51]

Fukuyama admitted that the quality of life after the end of history could cause some doubt. "It is reasonable to wonder whether all people will believe that the kinds of struggles and sacrifices possible in a self-satisfied and prosperous liberal democracy are sufficient to call forth what is highest in man." After all, "Hegel—as opposed to his interpreter, Kojève—understood that the need to feel pride in one's humanness would not necessarily be satisfied by the 'peace and prosperity' of the end of history."[52] But the fate of the posthistoric concept hinged on people deciding to be content with this resolution of the existential tension in a relatively stable postmodernity with institutional limits to the desire for recognition. Fukuyama was convinced that liberal democracy would provide the proper balance between what once were history's disruptive forces and would be able to maintain indefinitely the triumph of continuity.

A Cool Reception

Fukuyama's work met mostly negative reactions. Empirical scholars rejected it as metahistory, especially the stipulation of an end to history. "Wild speculation" was a typical characterization. Few reviewers recognized its links to structural postmodernism. The thesis that liberal democracy was the penultimate solution to the human situation was challenged especially by those who denied that the collapse of the Soviet Union equaled the demise of Marxism.[53] And the book fit ill into the ongoing debate focused on a postmodernism that affirmed the dominance of change and the historians' rejection of metahistories.

■   13 **INSIGHTS AND PROBLEMS**

Only in a limited sense did structural postmodernists grant the presence of a crisis of representation. Theirs was not a call for a complete remodeling of the infrastructure of historical knowledge via the linguistic turn. They simply recalled the well-known lesson that all human actions have intended and unintended consequences to explain and resolve the much debated crisis of progress and modernity. The highlighting of the unexpected or ignored tendencies of progress would make visible the "true" aim of progressive developments and yield the proper indications for the future's shape. Progress would be vindicated, albeit in a manner not expected.

That gap between the realities created by progress and the expectations from progress was one between reality and illusions. The latter centered on the final emancipation of humanity, resulting in freedom, equality, virtue, and happiness. The reality of progress knew the change from reason as liberator to reason as instrument of control that created technology, bureaucratic organization, mass production, and communication—all of them creating sameness.

When they stated their view, structural postmodernists presupposed that the reality outside of human beings had its own dynamic and structure that could be known using proper procedures. Results showed an increasing stabilization of the human realm. Progress was increasingly spinning out of human control and led to a human condition human beings had not aspired to. But it was not against their deepest desire either because, as postmodernists saw it, progress revealed the true human desire after security (not freedom). The society best suited for fulfilling that desire was the static postmodernity. In it, the aspirations of human beings were tamed in the interest of avoiding the vicissitudes of the historical period. That perfection came in gray and dull colors, except for Cournot's and Fukuyama's visions. The human experiences in the years between 1930 and 1960 elicited little triumphalism.

In retrospect, structural postmodernism invited three observations and reflections. First, in contrast to the postmodernism that would follow, its expectations and predictions were rather easy to verify. Western culture did manifest some of the trends to stabilization. These postmodernists could be credited with having located and understood a so far neglected dimension of progress. Despite its usual association with dominant change, progress did foster powerful elements of stabilization.

Second, the ambiguity besetting the reach of the structural postmodernist model would point to a problem in all postmodernist thought. If the claim to validity were global, human development in all cultures would eventually come to a halt. The predicted static postmodernity would point to a new human condition. If not, a much older model for nexus building could claim validity: the cyclical one. With Western culture alone entering entropy, the posthistoric postmodernity could be diagnosed as a not so unusual period of decadence. The structural postmodernist theory would turn out to have been a version of the cyclical nexus construction and not a new universal view of history.

Third, historians would play a minuscule role in the static postmodernity. Nexus building would lose its quality of being a venture in the society of rigid routines. The past held no interest except as a negative, outdated example of the human condition. Historians could tell the story of the instability of human life in the historical period and how it ended by progress's own negation of modernity's illusory hopes. The present (once a stage in the unstoppable progress toward a future of stability) was becoming ever more identical to the future. Historians could act only as annalists of routine changes and natural events.

Despite such dire prospects, historians remained unconcerned about structural postmodernism. First, while structural postmodernists theorized about history, they were considered, at best, only philosophers of history. These postmodernists also only challenged the contemporary perspective on progress's working, consequences, and ultimate aim. For that task no revolution in historical epistemology was needed. The postmodernists found that much of the prevailing historical methodology sufficed if applied unaffected by visionary hopes. The infrastructure of history was safe. But such epistemological restraint estranged structural postmodernist works from the theoretical discussions of the 1960s and 1970s, with their intellectual forum located in the humanities. In them, language began to attain a dominant position. Being attuned to and even shaping that new intellectual climate, poststructuralist postmodernism would pose a much more immediate challenge to the existing discipline of history—one that aimed straight at the philosophical presuppositions and the epistemological base of history. Therefore, the attention of historians was soon absorbed by that different challenge to their discipline.

Yet the disappointment with reason's actual transformation of the world did reverberate in thinking about postmodernity. The view that reason had changed from sponsor and guide for human progress toward full human emancipation of some sort to a mere instrument of control of the natural and human world stimulated various reactions: the protests against a commodified and strictly administered world by the scholars of the Frankfurt School or Critical Theory, the emphasis on the historical importance of the private world of individuals by Michel de Certeau, and the highlighting of the consumer society by Mike Featherstone.

PART 3

POSTMODERNITY AS THE AGE OF DOMINANT CHANGE: POSTSTRUCTURALIST POSTMODERNISM

▪ |4 A PRELUDE TO POSTSTRUCTURALIST POSTMODERNISM

NAME, MOTIVE, AND TASK

The Name

Structural postmodernists had foreseen a resolution of the crisis of modernity in a static postmodernity. Historiography, although untouched in its epistemological infrastructure, would have to tailor its accounts to fit into the now limited postmodernist framework of human experience. Since the late 1960s, poststructuralist postmodernists have argued the case of a quite different postmodernity. In its simplest meaning the term poststructuralism referred to the chronological fact that this postmodernism appeared after structuralism had waned. Claude Lévi-Strauss's anthropological version had lost its prominence and Roland Barthes had stopped working strictly in the mode of structuralist linguistics and literature.

As in the case of structural postmodernism, the term poststructuralist postmodernism was not chosen because a uniform group of scholars set out to revise our thinking about modernity and progress in accord with a well-formulated, unified program. All of them, however, shared in a profound disenchantment with the main tenets of modernity: that full rationality would provide complete knowledge and that one of its important results would be the beneficial and complete control over human destiny. The starkly different reality led poststructuralist postmodernists to design theories that denied the autonomy of reason as well as the desirability of control.

In pursuit of that goal poststructuralist postmodernist thought emerged from the works of a few seminal thinkers who proceeded quite independently from one another. But while some of them even rejected the postmodernist designation, all of them shared a sufficient range of important tenets. Most important among them was the intent to redefine the world as devoid of intrinsic meaning and fixity. The wished-for total break with the human condition of the historical period would then be possible. A new view of historicity would bar the ideal of recapturing the actual past (the truth of it), the connection of this past to the present and the expectations for the future (the historical nexus) and the traditional uses of history (the pragmatic □ **59** aspect of history). The world of dominant change would prevent the rise of dangerous illusions. In doing so, this group of "idiosyncratic and difficult thinkers . . . have challenged the primacy and security of meaning, of history, of narrative, and of the idea of 'man' which is constructed by these practices."[1]

Motive and Program

The special attention given to truth and truth finding has fostered the tendency to treat the postmodernist challenge as a purely methodological one. Yet, the poststructuralist postmodernists were not primarily motivated by a desire to rescue historiography from a perceived epistemological crisis. At the core of their concerns were the shadowy sides of the twentieth century, especially the human catastrophes and the construction of a view of the human world that—if implemented—would make their recurrence impossible. Central to these attempts to bring about such a world would be an injunction against the most detrimental of modernity's features: the claim to a truth of universality and permanence that bestowed authority on its holders.

The most immediate targets of the reconstruction were the concepts of the Enlightenment, especially progress. Here and in other cases, the solution was not sought in the devising of new and better versions of authoritative truth but in abolishing even the quest for such a truth. The latter did not fit into the desired nonhegemonical world. The abolition would also delegitimize progress, which as truth in motion necessarily sponsored hegemony, oppression and marginalization, and all other schemes of history promising universality and permanence. Such claims were termed "metaphysical" (a term now used for claims to any duration across contexts) and had to be purged. The poststructuralist postmodernist world would need to be one in total flux. Therefore, while the immediate postmodernist critique was directed at the Enlightenment and progress, the logic of the endeavor would affect all of traditional historical understanding.

The Task

The construction of a theory adequate for a world of total flux would prove to be a dizzyingly difficult task. The redefinition of truth would set the perimeters within which two other issues in the postmodernist revision of historical understanding had to be resolved. In matters of order and meaning in history and the uses of history, postmodernist scholars had to acknowledge the same demand for nonauthoritative findings. They had to dispense with the notion of an inherent order in favor of one of pure and full contingency and construction. As for the use of historical accounts that offered guidance to human action, standards had to be found that carried persuasive force without claiming authority of a binding kind.

In light of the radicalism of the endeavor, critics and advocates alike have often seen the poststructuralist postmodernist venture as a sudden invention. A closer look, however, revealed it as a historical phenomenon with strong roots in the past. An attempt had been made by the ancient Heracliteans to give change exclusive dominance over human life. More immediately, there have been two decisive developments that made the stipulation of a world of flux easier: the upgrading of language to the main constituent of thought (the linguistic turn) and the redefinition of the connection between thought and life (the philosophical or hermeneutical turn). Both turns pointed scholarly inquiry away from entities with stable identities and objective forces and structures. Historical inquiry would have to change accordingly. The two main poststructuralist postmodernist schools of thought—the poststructuralist narrativists and the French poststructuralist postmodernists—have taken these turns in different ways and to different degrees.

TWO DECISIVE INTELLECTUAL TURNS: LINGUISTIC AND PHILOSOPHICAL

The Linguistic Turn: The Term

In its most general meaning, the term refers to a series of twentieth-century developments that pushed language and also literature into the center of attention in the humanities.[2] Many Western intellectuals saw in this elevation of language the ultimate emancipation from error and illusion and their historically demonstrable terrible consequences. For others, the term told of a flight into language—a way to resolve a widely perceived impasse in truth finding.[3]

In regard to history, the turn has referred to an entirely novel tie between language, literature, and history. These endeavors have had for many centuries close albeit rather tense associations. Examples for a rhetoric-related if not rhetoric-dominated history stretched from ancient historians to the *trattatisti* of the fifteenth and sixteenth centuries to the so-called literary historians of the nineteenth century. At times, advocates of the linguistic turn themselves have pointed to that long-standing relationship in order to make their own turn appear less threatening. Yet the recent turn toward language and literature had a vastly more ambitious goal than the one to which traditional rhetorical history had aspired: to undo the direct link that had been thought to exist between consciousness and an extralinguistic reality. For poststructuralist postmodernists the absence of that link was deemed necessary for the realization of their ideal of a totally fluid world. An intellectual revolution would eventually elevate language to the status of effective reality.

The door for the emergence of such a world was opened early in the twentieth century by the work of Ferdinand de Saussure in Geneva and of Roman Jakobson and the Opajaz group in Moscow.[4] Later, their views would be referred to as linguistic structuralism.

The Genevan Connection

Saussure radically altered the relationship of language to knowledge. Traditionally, language had been seen as the form or medium that reflected reality through concepts produced by consciousness. Language derived from the giving of names to the perceptions of reality. Thus the reality of objects and persons preceded language or, in other words, that which was experienced (the natural or given) preceded the conventional (the agreed upon). Order and meaning inhered in nonlinguistic reality, could be detected by consciousness, and then was depicted in language. Thus, in the eighteenth century, Johann Gottfried Herder and, later, the romantics could see language as the expression of the soul of a people. Soul was understood as the collective consciousness continuously shaped and reshaped by collective experiences. While, later on, the scientific historians differed sharply from Herder's and the romantics' views on the nature of the world and history, they, too, maintained the dominance of consciousness over language. The latter offered itself as the neutral communication medium to the searchers after facts and the subsequent connections of facts to historical accounts.

For Saussure, language had neither the essential relationship to the objects that traditional language theories had assumed (language as a mirror) nor was it the neutral medium scientifically inclined scholars had thought it to be (language as instrument). Also rejected was the mediating position that one part of the meaning of the word was due to relationships to other words and another part to the linkage to reality.[5] Such views were still too much in the tradition of the proponents of a natural or perfect language in which words and objects had their proper congruence.[6] Neither did the nominalist view find support in which the origin of language resided in the human invention of names for objects without an inherent link between objects (still real) and words.

Now, the relationship between word and object (the referent external to language) yielded to that between signs (words) and other signs. Language was a self-contained, ever-shifting system of signs. No word stood on its own. The sign (word) in turn was a combination of the verbal signal or the signifier (*signifiant*) and the verbal meaning (the concept or idea) or the signified (*signifie*). No sign had any meaning apart from its relationships to other signs. Nevertheless, Saussure's linguistic world remained rather stable in its signifier-signified relationships. Also, Saussure's scholarly ambitions did not reach beyond linguistics. The implications of his theory of language's absent link to reality (the nonlinguistic referent) were not taken up until much later.

In order to realize the world without inherent stability of any kind and with an order supplied by purely formal configurations, the poststructuralist postmodernists would strip away the last vestiges of a reality into which, according to Saussure, language was still embedded. They saw in Saussure's theory—once stripped of all stable elements—the instrument for resolving the perceived epistemological impasse in Western thought. His approach seemed to banish the key problem besetting any philosophy produced by the reliance on the individual's consciousness—the burden of subjectivity in truth finding. Now, truth and meaning were removed from the influence of the individual and its circumstances. They were constructs accomplished by the linguistic system, which remained a totality. From it, the referent (the object of reality) could be absent but not the signified (the concept). After the linguistic turn, the world of signs would have an uncertain connection with the world of the extralinguistic "reality," if any at all.

The Russian Connection

In 1916, a group of scholars in the so-called Opajaz group, with Roman Jakobson as its most prominent member, began to make its contributions to the linguistic turn in Western thought.[7] For these linguists, language consisted of combinations of phoneme (phonological elements), which had no inherent meaning but produced meaning by the differentiations they created. As in Saussure's theory, all meaning was relational, that is, not inherent in the phoneme or their combinations—words—but in the relations of words to one another. That made the realm of language to a high degree autonomous. But that groups' interest also included literature, where they scrutinized the functions of the author, authorial intentions, language, and the means and forms of communications.

The Moscow linguists emphasized the autonomy of the literary work—the text—from all extraliterary connections. Standing by itself, a text was best analyzed in terms of its linguistic techniques of production. The dramatic quality of a literary work came from the re-forming and re-shaping of its language. As for the production of meaning, these linguists stressed the importance of the reader. The analysis of a text must not focus on the author's intent (mind and psyche), because the text represented a polysemic sign (being diverse in meaning). With all readings being equally valid, there could be no more authentic meaning of the text, whether set by the author or anybody else. Since the conceptual world had been "decentered" (lacking the authoritative individual), there also could be no more authoritative literary or historical criticism. The importance of these developments for poststructuralist postmodernism would be decisive. Its proponents expected the linguistic turn to take them to a metaphysics-free world. Being without stable features, the world could be one of unimpeded construction. The linguistic turn held the promise of being able to conclude the purge of metaphysics, a term now referring to anything lasting across many if not all contexts.

The Philosophical Turn: The Term

This turn represented the second significant development in the shaping of a cultural environment favorable to the emergence of poststructuralist postmodernism. In reference to history, the phrase "philosophical turn" referred to a renewed interest in the philosophical aspects of historical debates in Germany and France. Its manifestation came in historical theory's rise to greater prominence in the late 1800s. The spur for that rise was the struggle against positivism's attempts to gain and maintain the dominant position for its rigorously empiricist ways of "doing history."

An increasing number of intellectuals had concluded that the modernist promise of an authoritative truth based exclusively on reason and science was unredeemable. Indeed, the radical rationalism, with its Cartesian ego that stood independently and sovereignly above all else, had already brought about a situation in which modernity had eroded not only the buttresses of traditional truth but also those of its own. A new certainty would have to be found in an entirely different view of the human experience. Nietzsche struck the cord in his "On the Use and the Disadvantages of History for Life" that reverberated in much of the subsequent criticism of modernity.[8] He complained about Western culture's loss of immediate and direct contact with life and blamed it on the strict separation of subject from object, the aim of objectivity, and the reliance on supposedly objective facts. From now on, all of these must not be considered necessary conditions for truth but rather barriers to a full understanding of life, past and present. Scholars must condemn modern Western thought as barren and, in historical matters, antiquarian. The historical approach, once valued as supplying the proper perspective on past life and reliable knowledge about it, must again inspire action and innovation in the present. Historical truth found its validation only in the praxis of life and not in the correspondence of statements to past life.

Ill Wind for Rationalism in the World of Spontaneity and Discontinuity

Philosophies, such as Henri Bergson's vitalism, which saw human thought as energized by direct links with life, came to be favored. The driving force was no longer rationality pushing toward its ever fuller realization, but, in a sign of things to come, drives and desires. Discontinuities, ruptures, and contingent connections, and not reason's clear path marked life's course. The *élan vitale* remained as the only element of continuity. As a result, life now was largely inaccessible to reason. Understanding human life from the "inside," rather than by the use of causal explanation, led to knowledge. Intuition and the grasping of the whole rather than the atomistic fitting together of small empirical facts to large-scale constructs was required. The observers, historians among them, were never separated from life but submerged into the flux of life. As participants, they had no way to gain a detached observer status. Truth was affirmation of life in the midst of life.

Vitalism bequeathed much to the New History and its twentieth-century versions as well as to poststructuralist postmodernism. But the process of transfer to the two endeavors was uneven. In each case some messages were accepted, others rejected. The poststructuralist postmodernists would un-reservedly affirm the vitalist world in constant and total flux, energized by desires and drives, and dotted by ruptures, contingencies, and discontinu-ities. Yet they could not accept the prominence of such totalities as life as a whole and the other remaining elements of permanence such as the variously defined ultimate life forces.

The diverse reactions of the New Historians to the life philosophies would foreshadow their relationship to poststructuralist postmodernism. The pioneer of the *Annales* group, Henri Beer, bowed to the ideal of see-ing life as a totality when he called for a synthetic history in the face of the incipient fragmentation of historical knowledge. But the vitalist neglect of continuity and praise of contingency did not appeal to most New Histo-rians. They had rejected the very history that provided the most room for contingency—military, political, and diplomatic history—and had labeled it a "surface-of-life" concern only. Into its place stepped a history shaped by "deep" and presumed to be primary driving forces such as Karl Lam-precht's collective psyche (*seelisches Diapason*), Marx's economic, Fernand Braudel's geographic, and Freud's sexual forces. They were forces of per-manence, varying only in their specific manifestations and open to at least sufficient explanation by empirical methods. Thus, beginning with the 1960s, the variants of the New History (especially social histories) would by virtue of their cognitive structure oppose poststructuralist postmodernism.

An especially significant difference in the reception of vitalist concepts showed up in the case of the immersion of the historian into the flux of life. Postmodernists and other critics of modernism would see in that the final step in the deliverance from the dominance by the individual consciousness and its, in their views, dangerous ideal of *the* truth. While most historians continued to work in the empirical manner, attempts were made to cope with the problem by making allowance for the historian's immersion in life. How-ever, the possibility of a sufficient degree of the historian's detachment from the context of life was preserved. Wilhelm Dilthey replaced positivist fact-finding with the analysis of the *Erlebnis* (an inner- directed understanding of specific configurations of life). Yet he persisted in searching for general categories of historical thought and critique that would provide an intelligible stabilizing order for the flux of life. Benedetto Croce, who ventured further toward a more fully contingent world, tried to show the inevitability of the historian's immersion in life and the invigorating quality it had on history. As they have throughout the centuries, historians would adjust to the new challenges coming from philosophy as far as they could without endangering the key principle of the correspondence of knowledge to reality. In contrast, the poststructuralist postmodernists would accept the most uncompromising version of the vitalist view of life as in constant flux for their theories on knowledge and truth that lacked all permanent elements. That held the promise of the longed-for world free of all traces of metaphysics.

THE CONTEXT OF POSTSTRUCTURALIST POSTMODERNISM'S RISE

Paris: A Suitable Location

In a major irony, poststructuralist postmodernists came to prominence by mounting a fierce attack on the Enlightenment in the city that once had been the Enlightenment's symbolic capital. In the Paris of the 1960s, the final act opened in a long intellectual drama with reason as the tragic hero. The original plot, provided by the Enlightenment-sponsored modernism, saw reason growing ever stronger, guiding human beings to greater heights of knowledge, even to the control of their world and, with it, toward a happy, peaceful, and virtuous existence. Now, the disillusionment with modernity and modernism did its work. The experience of a partially self-induced erosion of the hope for an impeccably rational and authoritative truth, the experiences of the shadowy side of modernity starkly visible in the twentieth-century catastrophes, and a social order perceived as "old" and unjust led to a sense of failure among many intellectuals and artists. They set out to reinterpret progressive reason into a hero who was full of good intentions but beset by destructive and fatal flaws.

The Paris of the 1960s and 1970s offered a perfect stage, when seeing intellectual history as drama. Postwar France searched for a new national identity in a setting marked by memories of defeat that often overshadowed those of victory, problems of physical rebuilding, a turbulent end to centuries-old French imperial ambitions, a groping for European unification, and a dangerous cold war. Caught up in a clash between old institutions and an innovative spirit, France became for a few decades filled with an intense intellectual ferment. The challenge to progress posed by the broad cultural upheavals of the 1960s turned into a broad attack on what was seen as modernity's core belief: a supreme and autonomous reason and the progress sponsored by it.

The Ebbing of Three Intellectual High Tides

By the end of the 1960s, three grand interpretations of the human world and its history that had dominated the French intellectual scene after 1945 were rapidly losing their persuasive force: Marxism, existentialism, and anthropological structuralism. Some of their concepts would yield material for new poststructuralist constructs, but most of them became objects for "deconstruction." To poststructuralists, Marxism represented the age of ideologies that had devoured millions of people, existentialism was the apogee of the mistaken exultation of the individual as most important agent in life, and structuralism demonstrated the rigidities even of systems with only a residual permanent (metaphysical) element at its core.

Marxism

In post-1945 France, many of the prominent intellectuals (including later postmodernists) had at least brief associations with the Communist Party. Yet a slow erosion sapped Marxist strength as the realities of the Soviet Union (its Gulag and imperialism) and the doctrinaire Marxism of the French Communist Party diminished Marxism's formerly persuasive force. Attempts to combine the new analyses of culture with Marxism (such as those by Sartre and Louis Althusser) brought forth sophisticated theories that, apart from their opaqueness, provided little guidance for action aiming at revolution or reform.

Then came the Communist failure to support the uprising in May and June of 1968—the famous Days of May, in which the New Left acted out its concepts of a revolution. Besides the calls for reform of the university system, its members defined the goals of their movement in terms of newly emerging ideas and ideals that carried poststructuralist marks. They were: a hostility to systems (intellectually, any organized set of concepts about society and, practically, any centralized state power that organized the economy or other sections of life); an emphasis on communication and consensus; the "manning of the barricades" without a clear guide for action; and a suspicion of power. In a sense, the great protests of 1968 initiated the stance of permanent opposition to whatever constituted the status quo and to plans for a new ideal age.

These attitudes were shaped into a loosely woven program by a group of intellectuals who were deeply disappointed by the events of 1968: the New Philosophers (André Glucksmann, Bernard-Henri Lévy, Guy Lardreau, Christian Jambet, and Maurice Clavel). Once more, important themes were sounded that reverberated later in postmodernist thought on history. These intellectuals condemned the "masters"—Plato, Marx, Stalin, and Mao—whose grand schemes for history and talk of absolute truth had evoked illusory hopes. Revolutions on behalf of the perfect society had merely produced the new tyrannies of ideologies or late capitalism's age of comforts and gadgets. In 1968, the masses acted out the revenge on the age of ideologies with its false promises. From now on, no grand schemes for the meaning of history must find believers. And the Third World, once thought to be different, disappointed by merely wanting to match the capitalist West. With power being equated with tyranny the proper role of the intellectual was the permanent opposition to systems of thought and their actual or attempted realizations in history. It all amounted to a rejection of hopes placed in political action on behalf of permanent ideals.

Existentialism

By the late 1960s, Jean Paul Sartre's existentialism, too, had run its course as an influential philosophy of life. It had tried to break the impasse in which the modern search for truth had found itself, when the once rational and objectively judging individual had vanished as a presupposition of philosophies. Existentialism had been a variant of philosophical phenomenology that had a strong hold on French intellectuals, beginning in the 1930s. Phenomenology had tried to ban the subjectivity that had plagued philosophy since the Cartesian elevation of the self and reason by employing a type of thinking about the world that would be insulated from psychological and external influences (Edmund Husserl). Sartre had joined Martin Heidegger's deviation from that objective on behalf of a direct and total connection between life and thought. Sartre used Heidegger's concept of *Dasein* as the basic definition of the human condition. *Dasein* referred to a human life marked by the experience of "being thrown" into a strange world that produced a fundamental anxiety. In this world of meaningless flux human beings tried to escape into a being like that of the things around them—the objects that lacked reflection (Sartre's "being-in-itself"). Yet the human being as an undefined being (a being "for itself") must not simply accept its identity from the human analog of things, the anonymous masses. Identities were shaped by reflective actions. These actions were never to be those prescribed by rules, customs, or other conventions. They were authentic actions, carrying the marks of genuine personal creations, and constituted strictly temporary but authentic personal identities—moments of meaning. However, after these moments had passed, the results of these decisions and actions joined immediately the objectionable world of inauthenticity, that world of the "in itself," which also included the writings of historians after the moments of creativity. Sartre's disdain for fixed identities and a structured meaningful world would fit into the poststructuralist image of the world in flux. But for poststructuralist postmodernists even the ever-so-short-lived true (authentic) human identity created by the individual in the moment of decision and action would still constitute an illegitimate attempt at stability and self-reference.

Anthropological Structuralism

Finally, as postmodernists would see it, even the anthropological counterpart to linguistic structuralism failed to solve the impasse in truth finding. On Claude Lévi-Strauss's structuralism still fell the shadows of metaphysics.

As a method for understanding the elements of order in cultural units and the commonalities between them, Lévi-Strauss's structuralism stipulated the priority of the whole over its elements and rejected the empirical approach of viewing the whole as an assembly of distinct self-identical parts (atomistically). This approach understated the shaping power of the relationships among the cultural elements. In a parallel to Saussure's system of language, Lévi-Strauss made these relationships create the specific configurations of the human world. But these relationships, in turn, were grounded in a stable realm of "deep" and purely formal codes and rules to which the ordering structures of a specific society were responses. These "deep" codes and rules were part of the human mental apparatus. Their historical manifestations (among them, linguistic orders, exchange and kinship relationships, and power relationships) were arbitrary and served to create and maintain temporary social order. In the new structuralist reality, identity was the unstable result of relationships within a system that changed constantly and had no overall direction. The world was in constant flux, but the "deep" codes yielded stability, which Lévi-Strauss still preferred to flux.[9] This emphasis on the timeless "deep" codes and rules gave anthropological structuralism a strong a-temporal, a-causal, and a-historical tendency.

For poststructuralist postmodernists the "foundational" character of the codes and rules was as much of a problem as the fact that it was an intolerable residue of stability—a remainder of permanence or, for them, metaphysics. Poststructuralism would derive its name from the program to purge this bulwark of stability. But Lévi-Strauss and the postmodernists did agree on the ethical objection to Western culture and its authoritative truth. For both of them, Western culture had been the source of all global ills. In the centuries of Western domination, the oppression of other cultures had been rooted in the claims to absolute truth for the progressive model. Poststructuralist postmodernists would widen this objection into a call for an end to the Western historical approach to understanding or explaining the world.

The French Poststructuralist Moment

The gestation of French poststructuralist postmodernism occurred in this period of fading intellectual currents. Two decades of enthusiasm for engagement on behalf of truth, certainty, and justice ended in distrust of such an engagement, now seen as the source of all that was wrong with the world. Shunning it, Roland Barthes and others took the linguistic turn and channeled their energies into the affirmation of the new semiological world view. The world would be seen as one of signs and texts properly studied by the science of signs (semiotics). All systematic inquiry was to be linguistic, recognizing the anonymous working of language as the sole ordering force. The new and exciting promise was one of a world of complete flux that lacked closures, fixed entities, and all permanence. Such a world signaled the final freedom from metaphysics and the vicissitudes caused by metaphysics—the bastion of the stable, essential, and permanent. The works of Michel Foucault and Jacques Derrida created the outlines of poststructuralist views of the world that were linked to both the linguistic and philosophic turns.

The American Echo

In the America of the 1960s and early 1970s, a weariness of modernity and the stirrings of vast social and political transformations augmented an increasing antirationalist, antiempiricist and antitraditional discontent in the humanities. Increasingly antagonistic studies of rational structures and explanations as well as of the rational and objective inquirer furthered a radical criticism of traditional theories of truth. The marks left on historical accounts by their contexts were no longer ascribed to inevitable failings in attempts at objectivity, but to deliberate acts of the historian's will on behalf of specific interest groups. Just as with other writings, historical accounts came to be viewed primarily as the expressions of power relations. Historical inquiry no longer shunned political advocacy. As in other countries, the American resistance to traditional ways of truth finding found a ready home in the humanities where strictly empirical inquiry never had held the prominent place as it had in the social sciences.

In American academe, neither Marxism nor existentialism had ever exerted an influence comparable to that in France. Therefore, the poststructuralist moment occurred less dramatically, specifically at Yale University and Johns Hopkins University. One could trace it back to a conference in 1966 at the latter university. In its proceedings, signs of a developing crisis in structural thinking became apparent in literary criticism, soon to be replaced by or renamed literary theory. By the early 1970s, Paul de Man, a member of the original Yale group of literary scholars, had fallen in line with one of the participants in the 1966 conference, Jacques Derrida. De Man began to erase the dividing line between fictional and historical accounts on the basis of his denial of objective links between the past and the accounts about it. The acceptance of elements of the new literary theory by other disciplines contributed to the spread of poststructuralist postmodernism in the United States. That expansion was energized, particularly in history, by the growing influence of French poststructuralist postmodernists.

Prospects

By the late 1960s, the outline had become visible of a most ambitious endeavor: to find an utterly new approach to knowing and living. Scholars engaged in the endeavor were confident that they had found the answers to the dilemmas of modern thought and, therefore, could lift the burden of progress off the shoulders of history. History would no longer need to demonstrate and actively cooperate in bringing about progress's fulfillment. Postmodernity would bring a human condition freed from the travails of the past by virtue of the dominance of change. In the absence of all elements of permanence or even long durations, now considered dangerous, life and its course would no longer be marked by the complexities of intertwining change and continuity. The existential tension would be defused by constant efforts at clearing impedances to change. To that end, the structural postmodernist expectation of modernity's end in a state of ultimate continuity must yield to one of endless change. Poststructuralist postmodernists set out to develop a new way of knowing, writing, and using history in a world of pure flux. The challenge to historians insisting on dealing with the fullness of life, including an undiminished dimension of time, was fundamental.

In the field of history, poststructuralist postmodernism has been championed by two groups of scholars: one clustered its works around the issue of the narrative, and the other focused more on wider issues in the theory of history. But both affirmed a world in ceaseless flux that had no inherent meaning or order. Historians could not rely, in comprehending and analyzing the past, on consciousness turning perceptions into concepts (conforming to the world) and expressing findings through the passive language. That perspective on the world was full of temptations of illusionary constants and the claims made for them. After the linguistic turn, language as definer of reality as well as of meaning offered to all scholars a world with infinite possibilities for construction unhindered by the stable features of objective entities. Although the shifting of accents made for important differences in approaches, the common denominators were strong enough for subsuming the two groups under the rubric of poststructuralist postmodernism.

■　　　15　**NARRATIVIST HISTORY IN THE POSTSTRUCTURALIST MODE**

THE PREPARATORY ROLE OF EARLY NARRATIVISM

For one group of scholars, poststructuralist postmodernism's influence on history came in the context of a long-standing debate: the one about the role of the narrative in history. The key issue in the debate was the historians' insistence on a strict separation of historical from fictional accounts (in modern terms, of historiography from literature). Aristotle's dictum that poetics was superior to history because it treated general rather than specific human situations has reverberated throughout the centuries. Historians would protest that the dictum was at least half wrong.

In the nineteenth century, the so-called literary historians considered language to be the neutral medium in which findings about the past were symbolically expressed. Via style, language was granted a limited active role in constructing historical accounts. For example, historians would debate which style of writing was appropriate for a democratic society's history. Earlier, historians had discussed that issue as the problem of the effectiveness of language to persuade. The *trattatisti* of the 1500s and 1600s pondered it when they argued over the relative value of the *historia nuda* (the unadorned narrative) versus that of history "adorned" for greater persuasiveness. These scholars, however, had no doubts about the goal to make historical accounts correspond to reality, only about the degree of their persuasiveness.

In the 1950s and 1960s, the debate about historiography acquired a stronger theoretical, especially epistemological component. A strong impetus for this component came from the narrativists of that period, who aspired to have the narrativist approach equal or even surpass in status the then prevailing versions of a scientific approach to history. The most radical of these prevailing versions were the cliometricians (advocates for quantifying evidence and interpretation), system theoreticians, and the neo-positivists. Carl Hempel and his advocacy of the Covering Law theory of history (1942) came to be the focal point of narrativist criticism. Its aim would be to show the limits of scientific history and to demonstrate the futility of claims to a total history when actually many aspects of life were neglected. The so-called analytical philosophers helped the narrativist cause by putting into critical focus the cognitive processes at work in the writing and telling of history (Morton White, Arthur Danto). William Walsh, Patrick Gardiner, and William B. Gallie strove to establish the plausibility of the narrative as a sufficient explanation of past phenomena. Linking statements using "then" served just as well as those stressing "because." Thomas Haskell put the early narrativist program succinctly: "narration is an especially supple form of causal reasoning."[10]

In the 1970s, when the most recent narrativists dealt with the issue of the telling and writing of history their work had a close affinity if not clear linkage to poststructuralist postmodernist thought. Among those who focused their scrutiny on the narrative and its complexity were Hayden White, F. A. Ankersmit, and Hans Kellner. The key ethical and political concerns of postmodernism remained in the background, although White's works showed their steady presence. As the 1980s progressed, poststructuralist narrativists could take advantage of this increasing recognition of the narrative as a legitimate way of historical thought. However, the range of their ambitions transcended such an achievement by far. The quest had become a narrative theory with its own presuppositions and methods and applicable to all historical accounts (now defined as narratives).

ROLAND BARTHES'S CHALLENGE

A change in one scholar's approach to matters—Barthes's break with structuralism—presaged profound changes for narrativist history. In 1967 Barthes published what would become a most influential essay, "Discourse on History." In it, he set out the themes that should guide the decisive changes in historiography.

While all of rhetoric had tried "the formal description of units longer than the sentence," he thought the moment propitious to create an entirely new "linguistic discourse." In it, the question was asked whether the time-honored distinction between the two types of discourses—fictional and historical—could or even should be maintained. Barthes did not think so. "Is there in fact any specific difference between factual and imaginary narrative, any specific feature by which we may distinguish on the one hand the mode appropriate to the relation of historical events—a matter traditionally subject, in our culture, to the prescriptions of historical 'science,' to be judged only by the criteria of conformity to 'what really happened' and by the principles of 'rational' exposition—and on the other hand the mode appropriate to the epic, novel or drama?"[11] Barthes's key counter-argument focused on the traditionally close link between reality and account or, in his terms, between referent and discourse, which made it possible to discern order and meaning of history from the study of the past as actually lived. Accounts could claim to be the providers of authentic and true statements. But "historical discourse does not follow reality, it only signifies it; it asserts at every moment: *this happened,* but the meaning conveyed is only that somebody makes that assertion (emphasis in the original)."[12] Historians had illegitimately abbreviated the signifier (word)-signified (concept)-referent (reality) triad into the wrong dyad: signifier-referent. The proper dyad was to be signifier-signified. In any case, traditional history had not produced the true image of reality but only a "reality effect" or the "referential illusion."[13] In the new narrativism "reality is nothing but a meaning, and so can be changed to meet the needs of history, when history demands the subversion of the foundations of civilization 'as we know it.'" He proclaimed that "the paradox comes full circle: narrative structure was evolved in the crucible of fiction (via myth and the first epics), yet it has become at once the sign and the proof of reality."[14] Interestingly, Barthes claimed for his view the position of being the conclusion of important developments—an admission of an otherwise frowned on objective developmental order.

Barthes's essay foreshadowed the profound changes poststructuralist narrativists would ask historians to make in the infrastructure of historical accounts. The transition from early narrativism to poststructuralist narrativism was indicated in Louis Mink's work. There, narrativism proceeded from being a cognitive instrument for reaching a determinate narrative to the narrative in which figurative (literary) elements were dominant. Mink's life was cut short before he reached a clear stance. The decisive turn to a narrativism as an important segment in the poststructuralist postmodernist context came with Hayden White's *Metahistory* (1973). In the wake of this pioneering work, a series of scholars elaborated theories of history that were based on the proposition that the modernist paradigm has lost all persuasiveness and that the narrative, free of the correspondence ideal of truth, would be the appropriate solution. Taking the linguistic turn, they redefined the relationship between the historical account and the actual past in a manner that made reality (understood as objective entity) either minimally or not at all accessible to any inquirer.

NARRATIVISM, POSTSTRUCTURALIST POSTMODERNISM, AND THE HISTORICAL WAYS OF INQUIRY: WHITE, ANKERSMIT, KELLNER

David Harlan spoke of the return of literature to the field of history and proclaimed that it "has plunged historical studies into an extended epistemological crisis."[15] The term "crisis" really referred to the resistance by historians to abandoning what they had seen as their endeavor's mediating position between disciplines that search either for the world of pure permanence or of pure contingency. White offered the alternative to that by defining a historical account as "a verbal structure in the form of a narrative prose discourse that purports to be a model, or icon of past structures and processes in the interest of explaining what they were by representing them."[16]

Truth and Evidence in the New Narrativist Perspective

Empiricists spoke of evidence as elements of the past that could be converted into facts by the use of critical methods and rules. With language still the neutral medium, this direct link of consciousness to past reality had given facts the key position in historical inquiry. Their accumulation would yield a greater approximation to the truth by revealing the structures and forces at work.

In the linguistic world of poststructuralist narrativism, the actual past was not effectual. The cumulated (now, "so-called") facts represented a chaos that received its order and meaning in the course of the construction of the narrative. They had no continuity of their own and did not add up to a story since life did not conform to the story format—it had no beginning, purposeful development, and clear ending. Thus, the body of evidence no longer represented visible traces of the past from which, by the use of inference (in a quasi-forensic procedure), could be reconstructed historical accounts mirroring the actual past. Also, evidence, because it was mediated linguistically and rhetorically to historians, could not supply the factual base in the empirical sense. Neither could the traditional methods of gathering facts since they themselves were constructs shaped in accord with the grand metaphor of empiricism. The pieces of evidence were discursive products that reached the inquirers linguistically prefigured. In the construction of historical accounts, the stories told by the people in the past met the story-making process in the present. Resonating in the two sets of stories—those of the past and the present—were the respective motivations for the emplotments.

Thus, Barthes and Hayden White spoke of facts as having a linguistic existence only.[17] Facts had no special claims to authority because they, too, were rhetorical creation. The important traditional division of evidence into primary and secondary kinds vanished, and was now revealed as an artificial division among rhetorical constructs. White pointed to the debate among scholars since the Enlightenment about the proper designation of findings as "real" where "one man's 'reality' was another one's 'utopia.'"[18] Ankersmit put it succinctly when he relied on the "narrative substances" of the linguistic world, which he saw as "substantial" only in the sense of being stabilizing verbal categories (such as Renaissance, Reformation). They did not subsume actual events, structures, or other phenomena but referred only to textual elements meant to shape or reshape a text.[19]

Poststructuralists considered it impossible to ascertain a transcendent signified—the past "out there" that yielded the evidence. As for the actual past, "this referential past is epistemologically a useless notion—something like Wittgenstein's wheel in the machine that is turned but does not drive anything else . . . narrative substances do not refer to the past, nor is such reference required from the point of historical debate."[20] That went far beyond the admission by historians of an inescapable degree of uncertainty about past reality, since not all facts were known and facts contained elements that could not be sifted rigorously. Only occasionally historians would spin their doubts close to postmodernist proportions. In 1910, the American historian Carl L. Becker had already suggested that facts were primarily constructs.[21] Then, after 1926, he formulated a theory of facts that moved historical accounts of the past into the area of myths—until he faced up to the real threat of fascism and abandoned so complete a denial of an authoritative truth.

Now such radical rejection of certainty became the rule. Narrativism's main thrust was not to tell the story as it once happened ("straight," that is transparent to past actuality) but to tell it in the sense of constructing it ("crooked," that is open to other narratives; Hans Kellner's terms). This thrust limited referentiality to intra- or intertextual scope. Reality became that which texts shared. At times, Ankersmit has spoken of "representationalism" as a manner of "doing history" that transcended epistemological and hermeneutical approaches. Such representationalism recognized that neither language nor the historian were transparent to reality, which meant that "we do not look at the past *through* the historian's language, but *from* the vantage point suggested by it (emphasis in original)."[22]

Postmodernism's ethical and political motive, manifest in the rejection of any certainty derived from a claimed correspondence of the historical account to reality, reappeared as the link between rhetoric and ethics. Poststructuralist narrativists accepted the corollary of their redefinition of evidence and facts—the absence of an authoritative truth in history. The appropriate way of "doing history" was clear. "Historians do not 'find' the truths of past events; they create events from a seamless flow, and invent meanings that produce patterns within that flow."[23] They cannot get the story "straight" only "crooked." The authority of sources is an effect created rhetorically only. That which has been called objective truth was unreachable and any contention that one had reached it dangerous. Hence the reality of logic must yield to that of rhetoric. The same held true for the subject matter of history. Telling had now become the proper way of explanation.

In a crucial change these narrativists had detached the narrative from any stable anchoring place and set it afloat in their world of flux. That detachment would deprive any narrative, particularly that of progress, of its privileged position. In a nutshell, postmodernists wished to replace the old maxim "search for unity (truth) in diversity" with the new one of "acknowledge diversity of truths as only good unity." The price was history's loss of its quest to narrate with sufficient authority the past in its specific actual uniqueness.

The New View of Order and Meaning

Where would order and meaning come from in the fluid world that could be warranted by the linguistically dominated historical inquiry and accounts? Speaking in terms of time, order and meaning had been seen as affirmations of continuity, that is, structures effective in many if not all contexts. That fit poorly into a world of flux from which the "real" and its inherent unity was banned. There, elements of continuity were constructed and were testimony to the actual discontinuity of the world. With poststructuralists having dug an unbridgeable epistemological moat between account and past extralinguistic reality, the source of order and meaning had to be relocated. Once more, signification would replace representation. Rhetorical invention would provide the answer.

Poststructuralist narrativists attributed the establishment of order in narratives to a creative act by the narrator. Historians must create meanings from meaningless debris. Without help from meanings inherent in reality, the ordering elements would need to be rhetorical in nature. Meaning resulted from the historian's activity, most often from the application of guiding metaphors (Ankersmit). Historical knowledge never was more than historical interpretation (now inscription or reinscription)—it was an aesthetic and moral enterprise, which did not transgress the boundaries of rhetoric. As an endeavor of aesthetics, history's "content is a derivative of style."[24] Style was chosen first and it determined what could be thought and expressed.

White spoke of "the poetic act which precedes the formal analysis of the field." The act was "precognitive and precritical." Thus, "the historian both creates his object of analysis and predetermines the modality of the conceptual strategies he will use to explain it."[25] The act imposed meaning on a past whose remainders offered no objective meaning to historians. Yet for White the poetic act was not chaotic, as it had limits in the presence of "deep" verbal structures. These limitations originated not in any inherent order and meaning of the subject matter (as reflection of reality) but in the limited number of possible rhetorical ordering strategies. White used the four main figures of speech, the tropes (metaphor, metonymy, synecdoche, and irony), as the "deep" structures or keys to the prefiguration of the narrative. Each of them, when chosen as the governing trope (master trope) for a historical account, established that account's rhetorical tonality. Yet irony held a special place as it inherited dominance after the narrative potential of the other three had been exhausted. Irony kept the process of giving meaning open. Such openness had a smooth fit to the world of constant flux. The present could shape the meaning of past phenomena at liberty.

Supplemental choices for shaping the historical account were supplied by strategies and categories. The first of the three strategies, emplotment, shaped the narrative into either romance, tragedy, comedy, or satire. Once more the choice from among them was that of the historian, independent of any "objective" context. The second strategy, the formal argument, concerned the relationships established between parts. It led to an order that was either formist (between discrete elements such as persons, events, or other limited entities), organicist (the relation to the whole), mechanistic (part to part relations), or contextualist (a web of relationships not unlike colligation). Third, the strategy of ideology, in which historians took a position on life in the present or, more exactly, on the discourse concerning change. For the latter, White offered the formal categories of anarchism (change without limits and stable order as aim), radicalism (sudden and radical changes), conservative (only necessary change), and liberal (orderly and restraint change).

Objectivity as Illusion

The epistemological chain reaction triggered by the severance of the referential link between the "past out there" and the historical account also reached the concept of objectivity.

Barthes set the tone when he declared that not the representation of reality but only the "reality effect" was the result of the historian's efforts. Historical narratives differ not at all from fictive narratives. Historians who claimed to do more and cited objectivity as legitimation for it were poseurs. Part of the objectivity "ritual" was the disguise of the historian as a "nonperson" and the prescription of an anonymous writing style that avoided references to the author. An elaborate technical apparatus (footnotes and citations as scaffolding) helped hide the author's role in the deception. "History seems to write itself." All was intended to create the "referential illusion, where the historian tries to give the impression that the referent is speaking for itself."[26] To that, poststructuralist narrativists added their special objection to the attribution of universal validity to scholarly objectivity. The latter concept was a purely Western cultural feature. The figure of the objective scholar hid the passions that motivated the Faustian searcher for the truth.

The denial of objectivity found additional support in the postmodernists' submersion of authors into their texts. This submersion, making authors nonpersons, was justified as it destroyed the illusion that human beings could escape language as their primary environment. The historian's authorial intentions (as cognitive acts) became insignificant compared to the text, which was the terminal point in the striving for "access" to "the historically real, the past real."[27] The text was the referent that had no exit to the nonlinguistic "real." The latter's meaning and order were constructs by readers and authors alike. In that sense, the historian was always a nonperson but not in the sense of the traditional attempt at the faux anonymity of objectivity. The immersion of the historian into the world, which historians had so ardently sought to neutralize in their quest for objectivity, had become not only acceptable but also proper in the linguistic reality.

Collapsing the Distinction between Research and Writing

The new perspective on facts also collapsed the long-standing distinction between research and writing. Research as the finding and critical scrutiny of remaining traces of past reality, and writing as the interpretive weaving together of these elements through themes and arguments had been seen as different but linked activities. Although the latter theoretically followed the conclusion of the former, practicing historians have experienced the activities as intertwined. Poststructuralists denied not only the "first the research and then the writing" sequence but also any difference that mattered between these activities. Or, putting it into their terminology, research did not produce the referential elements that the writing process configured into the historical text. Figuration, in the sense of free literary interpretation, must be the primary process. After all, "telling" was "explaining." For these narrativists, the true purpose of the elaborate research and documentation apparatus was not to yield the elements for the construction of the true image of past reality but only to conjure up the "reality effect" or the "referential illusion." True accounts did not result from interpretive renderings of verified statements. There could only be multiple true accounts produced as linguistic creations. Thus, in his early work, White could speak of the historical text as fictional. In his later writings, he preferred the term literary. In either case, the "past" did not instruct historians. They created the "past."

The Historical Account and the Realm of Fiction

The poststructuralist narrativist reshaping of history's infrastructure made historical accounts that were in accord with the stipulation of a linguistic world in perennial flux possible. Language had left behind the role of being the mere giver of form to factual accounts for that of the creator of the reality described in historical accounts. Historians could no longer appeal to a reality that was exempt from language's dominance. As these narrativists saw it, the Cartesian celebration of a dominant consciousness that cognitively mastered reality had ended. Consciousness's products (such as ideas and concepts) were now linguistic creations. Language no longer conveyed meanings; it created and changed them. Not even the core endeavor of modernity, science, enjoyed any autonomy; it too must be seen as being inside language—just another way to narrate the world now deprived of its privileged position.

The story of historiography was reduced to the story of the changing use of rhetorical ordering elements. In White's case they were the tropes, strategies, and categories and in Ankersmit's case the guiding metaphors. As fictive or literary configurations, all narratives have relayed views of the past rather than the past itself. For Ankersmit, even the dimension of historical time was a construct of a specific context. "Historical time is a relatively recent and highly artificial invention of Western civilization. It is a cultural, not a philosophical notion. Hence, founding narrativism on the concept of time is building on quicksand."[28] Present followed upon present in an endless a-temporal sequence. Or as Ankersmit put it, we can presume that "autumn has come to Western historiography."[29] Ankersmit compared its works to the leaves that dropped from a tree whose trunk had been essences and foundations. With the latter having been shown to be illusions, there would never be another tree. Left to us in the story of historiography were masses of dropped leaves heaped in no particular order. Historians would from now on endlessly combine and recombine dropped leaves (texts) into ever new configurations. No longer could historical accounts claim special insights into life or the history of historiography trace any real developments in the understanding of history.

MOTIVES, VISIONS, AND PROBLEMS

White's insistence that all historical accounts were ideological at their core refocused attention on the ethical and political motive for the poststructural-ist postmodernist endeavor—the proper ordering of society. This insistence raised the question about the ideological basis for White's own work, which on the surface seemed to be nonideological. Although White occasionally has affirmed his Marxist stance, White's world view stipulated a completely fluid and as such meaningless world. Tropes imposed order and meaning on that world. They replaced the historical nexus with its combination of evi-dence from the past and interpretations. Tropes, selected by an antecedent poetic choice, offered a rhetorical continuity that remained open for ever new rhetorical choices. Thus they seemed to conform to poststructuralist narrativism's ban on closures. But the tropes defied the ban since they were clearly universal and permanent.

As for social practice, by now every nexus between past, present, and expectations for the future had been revealed as a rhetorical construct put onto a purely contingent world not only to a few cognoscenti, who could use the knowledge to dominate, but to all of the people. The possibility was offered for lifting the burden of history forever from the people, a burden imposed ultimately by pretensions to a truth *found* rather than *constructed*.[30] With that, the way was open for the reconstruction of society in terms of re-lentless change. While White protested that he was in no way a revolutionary, he did wish to empower human beings by telling them about their ability to reconstruct their lives in the fluid world. Hence the use of "linguistic" or "existential" humanism for White's views was quite appropriate.[31]

White's views on history supplied the key point of a new political program: the avoidance of oppressive authoritarian truth claims. Such closures on the basis of philosophical (metaphysical) elements, which promised permanence and stability, had been the tragic flaws of all ideologies. After the rhetorical turn in history, the past, with its remainders and reminders of futile closures, could and must no longer oppress the people in the present. Compared to nexuses, a tropological order harbored none of the restraints on the choices and temporary character of all phenomena proper for the new view of the world. White spoke of the wide-open, fully contingent, even chaotic world as "sublime." The adjective sublime indicated freedom, choice, and possibility for creativity. And the affirmation of that "sublimity" against essentialist notions must from now on guide historians. The rhetorical structures, although limiting, were not seen as interfering. The denial of sublimity by utopias, modern ideologies, and historiographies in the scientific mode had been the reason for the spectacular and decisive failures of previous nexuses.

Ankersmit emphasized the element of play but with less activist intent. In the linguistic world without exits "history . . . is no longer the reconstruction of what has happened to us in the various phases of our lives, but a continuous playing with the memory of this."[32] The history of historiography dissolved into a mosaic of timeless presents that displayed no patterns. Without referentiality, the history of historiography became a "*connoisseurship* of historical writing (emphasis in the original)."[33] Historians must not try to reconstruct the life of the past from supposedly objective remainders but need to constantly reflect on the processes that built historical accounts. All of that would make difficult any affirmation of the utility of history beyond giving aesthetic pleasure.

At the core of the narrativism in the poststructuralist and also postmodernist mode stood the stipulation of nonreferentiality—the assertion that the actual past (the period of the existential experience that could no longer be changed by decisions and actions) was veiled by linguistic and literary constructs from the gaze of historians. Hence historical narratives did not constitute a cognitively true but a completely rhetorically configured image of past reality. However, adherence to a strict nonreferentiality proved most difficult even in narrativist theory, perhaps even impossible. Testimony for it has been the presence of certainties that clearly transcended linguistic boundaries. Barthes had already stipulated one foundational element of objective and universal certainty: the narrative as form of comprehension was a given, just like life itself. On his part, White has always hedged somewhat on affirming a starkly linguistic or literary world. Extralinguistic or literary elements have intruded implicitly and explicitly into his narrativist ordering process.

The world to be ordered was "known" to be chaotic and in relentless flux. But that assertion presupposed a true knowledge of the world prior to its linguistic shaping. Accepted without question was also the ubiquitous and objective presence of the human desire for order in a (naturally) chaotic world. Even absolute standards did reappear when the view of the world of flux was considered more accurate and hence superior to previous views. That raised the question after the legitimizing argument for a judgment of "right" and "wrong" in reference to truth in a narrativism adhering to poststructuralist postmodernist suppositions. All these issues resurfaced in the long debate on the exact ontological status of the array of tropes, strategies, and ideological categories that did the ordering work for White. They were not constructed or historically developed. They were just there—ahistorically and irreducibly so. Yet they also were important for giving a dynamic structure to White's work. Analyzing E. P. Thompson's work on the rise of the English working class in White's manner, tropological stages could be traced, reaching from the awareness of similarity in status (metaphoric class consciousness) to the accumulation of experiences (metonymic class consciousness) to seeing themselves as parts of a whole (synecdochal class consciousness) to the ironic splintering of the triumphant working class. This dissolving of seemingly solid constructs by irony kept the tropological process open. Critics among historians could point to a double basis for what resembled a new metahistory: the long familiar cyclical pattern, moving from inception to success and the decline in importance, as well as to another reductionism—this time one to literary configurations or just language.

The profound stability of the ordering and thus meaning-giving tropes and other elements—another kind of foundation—stood in stark contrast to the desirable and "naturally" chaotic world of inherently meaningless flux (another a priori). Even the important poetic act itself, defined by White as a precognitive phenomenon, implicitly escaped the confines of the purely linguistic or literary and became "real." Finally, was the world truly so chaotic and meaningless that every formal ordering category could be arbitrarily applied to every past context? In the absence of any resistance from a nonlinguistic reality, could every account be shaped into a comedy or a satire, even such catastrophic events as the Holocaust? If not, what created the "resistance"? And what accounted for the shifts from one to the other mastertrope?

Just as poststructuralist postmodernism, narrativism equated the ethically and politically "good" with openness, fluidity, and undecidability (even chaos). Ironically that assertion found no persuasive or logical affirmative base in its own theory. In the inherently meaningless and chaotic world, all ordering systems were purely formal and represented in the end futile attempts at closure. They became simply exempla for the application of the ordering scheme. Yet poststructuralist narrativism's authoritative stipulations for an ordering system could find no foundation in that narrativism's theoretical framework. Therefore, the legitimation used most often relied on the favorable contrast between the past with its objectionable order and ordering systems, as well as its illusory self-understanding, and a future shaped by the proper societal order based on a "true" understanding of development.

As for history, White had foreseen and welcomed the end to history's claim to occupy "an epistemologically neutral middle ground that supposedly exists between art and science."[34] That required a choice between endeavors that focused on the creative/imaginative and contingent/unique (favoring change) and those that relied on the systematic/inductive and general/regular (favoring elements of continuity). Poststructuralist narrativists championed the former when they gave change unconditional dominance in the temporality of human existence. In matters of "doing history," such exclusive advocacy challenged the claim of history to the middle ground. The mediating position called for recognizing both approaches to life and, with it, the full dimension of time. If historians wished to grasp the reality of past life as it once had been actually lived, they needed to recognize the roles of both continuity and change. When poststructuralist postmodernists affirmed a world dominated by change with its infinite possibilities and variabilities, they replaced the historians' attempts to mediate—however imperfect their results have been—with the creative/imaginative acts of authors constrained only by literary and linguistic forms. The demands of the full existential reality at a specific time and place—including its materiality—found only a generalized recognition. This has proven to be most problematic for a consistent new theory of history writing. Most historians have seen in it an attempt to merge literature with history. Hence they have been reluctant to abandon their theoretically less "clean" but still fruitful mediating position—between consciousness, language, and objective reality, including change and continuity.

COMING TO TERMS WITH THE NEW NARRATIVISM: THE RECENT SCHOLARLY DEBATE

Narrativism and Intellectual History

White had put narrativism in the postmodern mode on the historical agenda. Some historians would agree with Nancy Partner that his impact on historians has been negligible. However, that assessment has to be qualified. The impact on the different fields of history has varied. In social history it has indeed been small, because the influence of the social sciences has remained by far stronger than that of literature. But on the other side of the historiographical spectrum, intellectual history with its proximity to literature, art, and philosophy left the door ajar for the influx of poststructuralist postmodernist thought. That history has all along dealt with the world of the immaterial, such as ideas, concepts, and meanings, always conscious of the element of construction in it. Its often-splendid isolation from the material world ended in the era of social history's dominance, when ideas and meanings became expressions of and subsidiaries to material forces. By the 1960s, intellectual history, with its subject matter unclear and its autonomy endangered if not lost, seemed even to intellectual historians to be in decline (William Bouwsma), a malaise (Robert Darnton), or a state of total collapse (Michael Ermarth).

Modern intellectual history had its roots in the Enlightenment's emphasis on reason's central position. In reason's world, ideas (such as freedom and equality) could be envisioned as powerful and autonomous forces, deserving their own history. Intellectual history as the history of ideas (a form of contextualized philosophy) was the product of that world. Poststructuralist postmodernists never tired to point out that such a history preserved the two-level universe: the higher realm of stable ideational forces and structures (such as essences and ideas) and the lower one of materiality, time and contingency. In the nineteenth century, the relationship between the two levels was variously interpreted. The higher level triumphed in Hegel's philosophy of history, which described the self-realization of the world spirit. Marx reversed the relationship making nonmaterial phenomena mere expressions of material relationships (class and class struggles). The New History of the twentieth century affirmed that view in a more moderate manner: thought and artistic creativity were molded but not determined by the social context (such as Peter Gay's social history of ideas).

In the new world of poststructuralist postmodernism, the debates over the right relationship between the ontological levels—now considered "metaphysical"—lost their rationale. The opposition between the autonomy of ideas and that of the material was resolved when White transformed the issue into a rhetorical one. When he affirmed the "sublime"—for him chaotic—nature of the world, which was tamed by meanings that were rhetorical constructs, the old term and endeavor "intellectual history" became redundant. In a sense, all of traditional history shared in that judgment.

But the nonreferentiality problem—the disjuncture between word and world—has remained the crucial issue for narrativism. In matters of theory, it appeared in White's work as the problem of ordering a chaotic (for him sublime) world and in that of Ankersmit in the problem the evaluation of narrative structures. Its persistence introduced opaqueness into poststructuralist narrativism's assertion of unconditional and ceaseless change. In practice, the problem diminished the persuasive power of the new narrativist truth finding. The difficulties showed in many of the contributions to Ankersmit's and Hans Kellner's *A New Philosophy of History*.[35] White himself continued to struggle with the issue when he strove to clarify the ontological status of his linguistic, even foundational ordering elements (particularly the tropes) in the chaotic world. In the end, his answer remained a formal structuralism in a poststructurally defined world that did not solve the ordering (referentiality) problem, but only reshaped it into the question after the nature of the formal categories.

Ways of Coping with the Problem of Referentiality

The narrativist version of the referentiality problem has been posed as the issue of the proper relationship between historical and literary accounts. In many ways, the discussions among historians have resembled the debates in rhetorical historiography engaged in by ancient historians and the *trattatisti* of the Renaissance. In them, too, had been present the struggles to draw the line of division. But these scholars never wavered in their certainty about the need to find if not the *verum* (the true) so at least its closest approximation, the *verax*. In contrast, ardent narrativists have argued for the then absent view that historical accounts were simply a special kind of fiction.

There have been attempts to reconcile seemingly irreconcilable positions. These attempts have ranged from the tolerance for fluctuating borders between history and literature to the joyful erasure of them to leaving the line of division between historical and fictional accounts artfully hazy. Nancy Partner revived the old rhetorical standard of persuasiveness, as it related to history writing in a mass society with means of mass communication.[36] She suggested a careful mixture of fictive and historical elements. Such "historical" accounts would appeal to a broad audience in the postmodern age. Partner put history still squarely in the area of fiction, but gave history a special position in fiction by virtue of rules, codes, and limits placed on what could be said. History was regulated fiction. The regulating elements, defined as "enduring linguistic elements," evoked the impression of reality and permanence. But being still at home in the general area of fiction, historiography could borrow the literary devices that gave drama and color to the otherwise long gray line of facts. Western historians could act out once more the "reality principle" so dear to their discipline. Thus, as Partner saw it, a sufficient degree of stability had been restored to history apparently without resorting to claims of referentiality. Such "historical" accounts, it was hoped, would appeal to a broad audience in the postmodern age. Partner deplored that the world of mass media had grasped and applied the principle of history as reality-fiction much more readily than the world of academe. Sometimes Simon Schama's *Dead Certainties* has been cited as another attempt to merge literature with history, although in scope and spirit the fit to poststructuralist narrativism was far from perfect.

Historians have not accepted the idea of such cohabitation between history and literature. They have remained skeptical of these attempts since they saw a sharp line of separation as necessary. Poststructuralist postmodernists objected, since such a line stipulating a categorical difference between the historical and the fictive reaffirmed referentiality and the necessary continuity to a world in which change now dominated unobstructed by objective obstacles.

Some scholars have tried to demonstrate the value for history of a narrativist approach without radical nonreferentiality. Paul Ricoeur stressed the link between the temporal character of human life and the narrative. Life as the existential experience (the actual experience of deciding and acting) was a narrative experience. The existential experience of temporality (prefigured time) was converted through the human narratological ability into narrative accounts (refigured time). Thus, the transformation did not represent a production of meaning in a meaningless world. Historical narrative accounts were refigurations that dealt with the existential experience at a specific time and place, involving specific persons. Fictive narratives did not. Therefore, while both accounts were narratives, historical ones had a truth obligation that differed from that of fictive narratives. They were in this sense referential. On the other hand, Ricoeur maintained that there was no avoiding the narrative, because it had its roots in the core of human temporal experience. But while all constructs were rhetorical/narrative in nature, they were in the end linked to the intelligible existential experience. Thus, history could "affirm the structural identity of historiography."[37]

Paul Veyne defined historical inquiry as the comprehension of plots and theories as plot summaries. Yet in the manner of the ancient historians, he looked for stable moral and political insights in the study of these plots. David Carr and Frederick Olafson also rejected the sharp discontinuity between the narrative (as ordered) and the world (as not ordered). Such an unbridgeable gap equalized fictive and historical accounts and transformed the narrative into a purely formal ordering mechanism. Instead, the "narrative is not merely a possibly successful way of describing events; its structure inheres in the events themselves."[38] Carr, too, pointed to the collective life as a locus of continuity. The narratives *from* the past (first order narrative) and those *of* the past created in the present (such as those by historians) differed, negating a simple correspondence. But the links between the prefigured past and the refigured past in the present also yielded sufficient continuity that contradicted the discontinuity view of poststructuralist narrativists.

A willingness to go well beyond a reluctant or veiled acceptance of referential knowledge marked Roger Chartier's work. He, who greeted with enthusiasm the elevation of language beyond the level of mere instrumentality, rejected "the dangerous reduction of the social world to a purely discursive construction and to pure language games."[39] Chartier's history could retain its mediating position, specifically in the "relations between the products of discourse and social practices."[40] Or put differently, history was able to reside "on the edge of a cliff" (Michel de Certeau) or on the edge of the void.[41] Historians needed not to suffer destructive vertigo in maneuvering their way between discourse and life. They must not "see historical discourse as merely a free play of theoretical figures and as one mode of fictional invention among others." Against the "dissolution of the status of history as a specific knowledge (a stance often taken by postmodernists), one must insist forcefully that history is commanded by an intention and a principle of truth, that the past, which history has taken as its object, is a reality external to discourse, and that knowledge of it can be verified." With it, the temporal aspect of stability and continuity returned with a positive connotation. And history can demonstrate "that the discrete knowledge it produces is inscribed within the order of a confirmable, verifiable knowledge."[42]

Dialogue without Closure or the Historian as Quasi-Participant

A systematic version of narrativism that carried the mark of French philosophical postmodernism's preference for the dominance of change originated from Dominick LaCapra. In his attempt to wake history from its "dogmatic slumber" and dreams of a positivist final knowledge of the past, LaCapra's main argument has been directed against what he called the documentary model of knowledge. In it, texts were mines for facts (elements of the past referent), which could be extracted.[43] Then the interpretive process shaped the body of facts into the historical account, often simplified by singling out one element of the total context to explain the past (reductionism). LaCapra's main objections were to the slighting of the complexity of the text in favor of abstract reductionist approaches and the connected refusal on the part of historians to be self-reflexive. His remedy was the textualization of the context and, with it, the abolition of the binary juxtaposition of that which was internal and external to the text. In place of the "objectivist" inquiry, the dialogue or conversation between historical text and historian has to be chosen. With both text and context now being signifying practices, historical inquiry became an interactive process. In it, historians would always be self-reflexive, that is, critically reflective on their inquiries, which would remain without closures. As text and inquirer influenced each other, new aspects were discovered (LaCapra's "working through"). The dialogical way of inquiry would replace the monological one. Truth resided in the ongoing "conversation" with its multiple ways of seeing and describing as well as the mutual shaping of observer and observed. A consequence was the choice of seeing historiography as an aesthetic endeavor or—as in the case of Holocaust studies—an attempt at reliving past experiences of others in a quasi-authentic way without conclusive ending.

A Crucial Debate: How to Write Properly about the Holocaust?

Grave doubts have been voiced whether historians could at all produce adequate accounts of the Holocaust using traditional methods. However, recourse to a purely linguistic referentiality experienced its own special challenges. All narrativist participants in the debate affirmed the Holocaust's catastrophic character but they wrestled with the rationale for and manner of the desired condemnation. In this assessment of the Holocaust a disturbing aspect of poststructuralist postmodernism became visible. Despite its relentless rejection of oppression and hegemony, postmodernist narrativists seemed unable to condemn, on its own terms, the Holocaust or even affirm that it occurred. The insistence on the rejection of all authoritative truth claims left both the assertion of the fact of the Holocaust and any judgment on it without proper legitimation. In the face of so severe a contradiction between the essentially ethical motivation of postmodernist narrativism and the internal barriers to its practical manifestation, a search for adjustments began.

Narrativist postmodernists, such as White and Kellner, searched for the "middle voice" on the matter. That meant to concede enough of the nonconstructed and nonlinguistic reality of facts to deprive the so-called revisionist historians of the ability to deny the Holocaust without a general concession to referentiality. The recourse to "intransitive writing" was to ban empiricism (as presumptuous), objectivity (as morally dubious), and formalism (as objectionably distant). However, the approach chosen broke down the wall of nonreferentiality to a noteworthy degree. The suspicion, voiced by critics, seemed to be confirmed that it was impossible to design and maintain a historiography as a rigorously poststructuralist narrativism that could serve the practice of life well.

What then was the impact of poststructuralist postmodernist narrativism on historical practice? A considerable number of works have shed light on the importance language and rhetoric has had in the construction of historical accounts. This recognition has been the most important contribution of narrativism to historical inquiry. For some time to come, narrative and language will not be regarded as silent and passive partners in the creation of historical works. But as a theory of history meant to replace traditional history with its full recognition of the dimension of time and of elements that in human terms are stable and can be grasped cognitively, poststructuralist narrativism has not yet commended itself to historians.

■   16 IN THE EYE OF THE STORM: THE POSTSTRUCTURALIST POSTMODERNIST CONCEPT OF TRUTH

THE TARGET OF REJECTION

The Call for Disarming "Truth"

In the controversy over the constitution and recovery of the past, postmodernist narrativists had dealt with the issue of truth when they followed the linguistic turn to the borders of literature and beyond. All order in historical accounts resulted from the imaginative use of the forms of literature and language. The French poststructuralist postmodernists chose a similar course but added philosophical considerations to the literary ones. The world was one of discourses and texts but its dynamic involved more than the forms of literature and language. For historians this meant that they would have to revise thoroughly the ways of "doing history." Not with the aim of remedying epistemological failings but to destroy the link between truth and authority that legitimated the exercise of power on behalf of truth. As the poststructuralist postmodernists never tired to point out, the insistence on the truth of progress had been directly linked to the human catastrophes of the twentieth century.

Epistemologically, the venture to abolish the direct cognitive connection between historical accounts and past reality through evidence took the form of a general campaign against the so-called correspondence theory of truth, which in various versions had shaped the writing of history since the ancient period. Its central assumption stipulated that historical accounts could be truly representational. The objective structures and events of the past (together with their order and meaning) could be represented with sufficient accuracy in historical accounts. Their words and sentences accurately reflected the world as the historian "listened" to the past through its remainders.

Poststructuralist postmodernists rejected this view of historical truth. Their critique focused on the merely auxiliary role granted to language and the stipulation of a direct (conceptual) link between consciousness and past life. While the poststructuralists did not deny the existence of the actual world—past and present—they maintained that reference could never be made to the past as it once was actually lived but only to the linguistic traces of that world—such as its discourses and texts. With the basic element of fixity (the past as it was) out of play, a revolution in the epistemological infrastructure of history became possible.

The Negation of Traditional Ways of Truth Finding

The postmodernist revolution had to invalidate the assertions that (1) the past, as it had been actually lived, was accessible through evidence that had a direct link to the past, yielded facts, and could be reconstructed according to the rules of inference and causality; (2) selection and creative imagination were auxiliary not constitutive in writing accounts of the intricate web of facts; (3) an experiential core of human life, past and present, made possible the organization of the web of facts; (4) historians could through efforts at objectivity (understood as the attempt to gain detachment from the historian's context and its values) become to a sufficient degree a non-intrusive channel between evidence and historical account; (5) the meaning of past phenomena emerged from the reconstructed past itself, being hierarchical with more or less essential meanings; (6) the role of language in the construction of the historical account was mainly passive, and (7) both change and continuity shaped human life. For postmodernists, these suppositions were all based on the illusion of referentiality, the contentions that inquirers could "get in touch" with past actuality (the existential experience of past people) and proper methods could protect their findings from being distorted.

Practicing historians have always protested that such a picture of their theory of truth was an idealized one. Even Leopold von Ranke had recognized that the reflection of *wie es eigentlich gewesen* was never quite complete or pure. History cannot like other sciences be "satisfied simply with recording what has been found; history requires the ability to recreate."[44] Yet such fallibility need not compromise the historian's work beyond repair if the "impurities" and resultant failures were acknowledged properly and always remained open for correction by the collective judgment of historians. Incompleteness and perspectivism disturbed but did not negate the ideal of correspondence.

Poststructuralist postmodernists considered admissions of imperfections insufficient. Correspondence theories were irremediably and, above all, dangerously flawed. They presupposed the human subject of Western humanism, eventually fully emancipated and rational, who could control all. The complete grasp of the past was part of it. But, there could be no cognitive direct access to past existential experience. All that was left of the past were discourses and texts—linguistically mediated past experience. Indeed, the linguistically constituted world was the only one available to historians, and it offered no access to any objective referent (nonreferentiality). That made—it was thought—all claims to objective knowledge (and thus a unitary truth) impossible. They were illusions, easily manipulated to be instruments of power. Their origin lay in the longing for continuity, which so far has shown to be deeply embedded in the human condition but must be considered to be the root of oppression. Thus, the kind of changes in theory poststructuralist postmodernists strove for did not only affect technical features of historical methodology but basic suppositions historians held about human life and its dimension of time. The stipulation of nonreferentiality to an extralinguistic reality made not only possible, but mandated the abandonment of causality, the stable knowing and controlling individual, and the concept of an authoritative truth. In this difficult task the postmodernists received considerable help from antecedent changes in the thinking about human life and history.

PREPARATORY DEVELOPMENTS FOR THE REVISION OF TRUTH: DILTHEY, NIETZSCHE, HEIDEGGER

Traditional Hermeneutics and the New Conditions for Knowledge

For centuries, hermeneutics was used in historical inquiry to bridge the gap that existed between the "messages" from the past (gleaned from evidences of the past) and the reader of the "messages" in the present (living in an entirely different context). Firmly embedded in rhetoric, hermeneutics had been one of a few interpretive endeavors that made possible the proper "reading" and understanding of the "message." Its aim was the closing of the hermeneutic circle that linked author (in the past), text, and recipient (historian in the present). Success in that endeavor presupposed a sufficient commonality between the people of the past (the producers of evidence) and the present-day inquirer. Explanations for this commonality, bridging the distance, have varied. They have included perennially stable elements such as essences and structures (for example, recurrent patterns of development or a stable core in the human condition), the allegorical relationship between on the surface dissimilar contexts, and the stipulation of a transcendental subject that could stand outside of all contexts (the critical and objective historian). Above all, the older hermeneutics affirmed the traditional epistemology's reference to the past as actually lived. In history's case, the actual past could be reconstructed with a sufficient degree of certainty (truth).

An Early Step: Wilhelm Dilthey's Historical Hermeneutics

In the intellectual context of the late 1800s, permeated by vitalist thought (*Lebensphilosophie*), historians were increasingly deprived of their sovereign observer position and seen as being immersed in life. Thus, they were incapable of treating the world in the positivist manner as an "outside" object. The call for a history that tried to take account of the fullness of life also entailed a critical attitude toward primarily rationalist and empiricist (in the positivist vein) approaches to the past. Wilhelm Dilthey attempted to solve the pressing problem of how to find truth under the new condition.

The contemporary quest for a scientific history that was not patterned after the *Naturwissenschaften* but was an autonomous *Geisteswissenschaft* provided the setting for Dilthey's work.[45] Influenced by Friedrich Schleiermacher's previous widening of the range of hermeneutics beyond the understanding of single text passages to that of the whole text, Dilthey chose a hermeneutics that had as its central focus the *Erlebnis* (the consciously lived experience). *Erlebnis* constituted a unity of fact, meaning, and values that scientific history in the positivist vein could not grasp but the new hermeneutical approach of "understanding" could master. Such a *Geschichtswissenschaft* would rein in the exuberant richness of life and open it to analysis by means of permanent categories of historical understanding patterned after Immanuel Kant's critical categories. The hermeneutic circle between author and text—historian and the body of evidence—could be closed. In practice, an unhappy Dilthey ended up with a view of history as a sequence of *Weltanschauungen* (world views), each of which could be plausibly true, leaving the hermeneutical circle wide open.

Poststructuralist postmodernists would consider the attempts by Dilthey to close the hermeneutic circle misguided. They, who denied any referentiality beyond the linguistic one, saw in many of Dilthey's structuring elements no pure constructs but psychological constructs with a direct link to actual life. Also, despite the immersion of the inquiring historian into the field of investigation, the transcendental subject and the aim of a static truth with its empirical and evidential approach remained. Stability and continuity (now considered metaphysical concepts) were still present. Poststructuralist postmodernists, such as Foucault and Derrida, needed the transformation of hermeneutics into a "metaphysics-free" venture. In that quest they were much influenced by Nietzsche and Heidegger in whose works individuals and their thought were formed in direct encounters with the world.

Nietzsche and the Hermeneutics of Suspicion

An early attempt to bar the hermeneutic circle's closing through reaching an objective truth came in the so-called hermeneutic of suspicion. Consciousness, so far seen as only partially influenced by the context, came under the suspicion that its pronouncements of truth were in fact merely false fronts for interests far from the world of rationality. Hence, historians must expose the machinations at work in the deception and set things right in thought and, quite often, in life's practice. At the turn to the twentieth century, Marxists had long been familiar with the concept of a false consciousness, shaped in the interest of ruling classes and in contradiction to the prevailing modes of production and productive relationships. Freud had begun to speak of a consciousness completely submerged into the complex world of sexuality and the mechanisms to hide that. Yet poststructuralists could not be satisfied by such attempts, because in both cases the ideal truth with an authoritative voice was seen as merely hidden rather than as illusory.

Nietzsche's hermeneutics of suspicion would come much closer to the poststructuralist affirmation of truth not as an authoritative image of the world but as an instrument of the vital forces of life. Academic history, when it focused on the search for the objective truth, transformed history into a museal endeavor. The mere discovery of what actually had happened satisfied only a gazing curiosity, and the meaning and order it found provided only merely aesthetic pleasures. Such a history with a scientific approach also led to a historicism that valued everything equally and, thus, by relativizing all, destroyed history's role as life's guide. It also could not offer an escape from the subjectivist impasse because it actually fostered it.

The proper understanding of the past came from seeing it as diverse manifestations of the ubiquitous will to power that provided and directed life's energy. In the process, meaning and order were created, which reflected the interests of those who exerted the power. Truth represented only useful lies. That was far removed from the struggle of historians to contain interpretation within reasonable limits of verification. Poststructuralist postmodernists have negated those limits. Yet in their selective acceptance of Nietzsche's views, they have been silent on the limits to Nietzsche's usefulness for them. First, Nietzsche's will to power, as a phenomenon of ontic or ontological permanence and stability, fit badly into any world perceived of as a web of forces without fixity. Foucault, most heavily dependent on Nietzsche's work, would experience that problem most directly. Second, they praised Nietzsche the cultural critic but rejected Nietzsche the prophet of the Higher Man (*der Übermensch*). This "Higher Man" did not search for the truth, because he set *the* authoritative, although not absolute, truth by his life's example. For the masses, seen as inert, the "Higher Man's" pronouncements and actions spelled out the limits for the world in which they would dwell. Nietzsche's world was fluid only for the elite of *Übermenschen*.

Heidegger's Redefinition of Historicity

Poststructuralist postmodernism also would receive powerful stimuli from Heidegger's work. But since Heidegger experienced a *Kehre* (turn) in his work, they were not of uniform character. From the early *Being and Time* came support for the postmodernist intent to destroy the Cartesian program.[46] Heidegger's objections went to its core: the subjective consciousness (reason) as the master of thought and life. That meant to abandon the assertion of the transcendental subject in any form (the subject that could in thought transcend its particular context). The "I think" lost its central place in the center to the "I am" or the "I exist." Every human life was now a *Dasein,* marked by the individual's inescapable relationship with the strange world into which it was thrust and the anxiety caused by so uncertain a status. Life experience was a directly existential and not a purely cognitively mediated one.

The absence of the transcendental subject voided all attempts to establish a distance from the world. The "I" always remained immersed in the condition of radical contingency. The individual's inescapable immersion in the forever strange world needed a type of interpretation for which the context was no longer an impediment to knowledge but constituted the basic and formative condition (the being-in-the-world). Poststructuralist postmodernists could take comfort from the fact that the "I" with a stable identity had vanished. However, they could not agree with Heidegger's contention that a proper identity was established in the moments of fleeting authentic existence.[47] In them, the life of the *man* (German word for everybody, referring here to the routine life of unreflective people) was rejected and the one of keen awareness of each individual human existence was chosen.[48] Such an image of human existence denied to any discipline, particularly the sciences, the ability to bring the search for authoritative knowledge to closure. Only death put an end to the constant awareness of the *Dasein.* The hermeneutic (interpretive) circle would always remain open except, only temporarily, in the moments of authentic existence. Herein rooted Heidegger's argument against the objectifications by the sciences and the referential search for an absolute Being in the old metaphysics.

At first glance, historians and poststructuralist postmodernists should have welcomed that development. The human being had become a totally historical being—in the one case giving historical thought a preeminent role, in the other guaranteeing a postmodernist fluid world. But historians would find that the new historicity of the individual tolerated no general features and developments and excluded all possibilities for rational or empirical observations from the "outside" through transcendental maneuvers.

On their part, postmodernists would discover that the new historicity did not produce the world of unlimited options. Although thought was formed in seemingly uninhibited engagement with the world, Heidegger acknowledged the presence of some knowledge prior to the existential encounters. For Heidegger, the human being was immersed in a world that offered some effective but temporary certainty in tradition (prejudgments), which therefore could not be simply purged in the interest of either the historian's objectivity or the postmodernist affirmation of change's total dominance. All disciplines of inquiry worked with such an inescapable foreknowledge of the world, even the sciences. Of it, the central and certain one was the awareness, even dread of death (nothingness). History carried its mark in the human awareness of the finitude of life—an unwelcome but nevertheless factual linearity.

Still, Heidegger had rendered much support to the poststructuralist postmodernists' purge of metaphysics—of all that claimed permanence. And since his new historicity revealed the precarious, tension-filled and contingent quality of the world, it would facilitate a new type of analysis: deconstruction. As for hermeneutics, it had moved a far distance from being an instrument of text interpretation toward being an interpretation of the human condition that was created in the direct encounter with life. Its seemingly limitless horizon would be attractive to postmodernists.

Another Affinity: The Centrality of Language

From a poststructuralist standpoint, Heidegger's eventual *Kehre* (turn), after 1945, held another promise—the lifting of language to prominence—but also a disappointment in his focusing on Being (that which was common to all that ever existed but had been forgotten in modernity). For Heidegger there was no contradiction between the two. Language and Being were connected since language was "the house of Being." Being could be "grasped" as language, which pointed beyond the actualized world and was poetical and opaque. Hence, Heidegger wished to avoid the fatal error of thinking of Being as an "it," an object—as static present. Being held the answer to the question why things were as they were. But poststructuralist postmodernists could not assent to so totalizing and static a concept as Being and the ontological grounding of language in it. They also realized that Heidegger's approach gave human beings a privileged position: they could ask the question no other being could, that after Being. The roots of a new stable identity of beings (an identity not dependent on the context) showed here.

The same selective assent by poststructuralists would also be characteristic for Heidegger's concept of truth. Postmodernists would like its dynamic character. Truth could not be contained in objective statements by a transcendental subject but changed constantly in the midst of life, that is, in direct and originary interpretations. They would find congenial the stipulation that inquiry must concern itself with the ways and activity of interpretation (such as the language) not with its substance. That also meant to focus on the condition in which the interpretation happened. Heidegger saw a danger in the focusing on objects and their relations within a solid world because inquirers forgot about their central concern, Being. In Being there was the true freedom from the subjectivism that still had been clinging to the concept of *Dasein*. Just as through Derrida's *différance* would originate all differentiations that produced the world, Being anteceded all beings and all organized thought. As differentiated and objectified Being, beings were already secondary but they still seduced scholars to locate Being among them. This located all that made sense on the wrong level. Heidegger called this illusion metaphysics and saw in it the reason for the crisis of Western culture. But poststructuralist postmodernists viewed Heidegger's concept of Being as the longing for ultimate stability (a metaphysical concept), much like the traditional Logos, and parted company with him on that score. Being had no place in the fully fluid world for which they strove.

From Bergson to Heidegger the trend continued to eliminate as much continuity (stability) as possible from thinking about the world. The aim was a world of flux in which the special position of the human consciousness would be absent. Human beings were to be integral parts of the world conceived as a vast process. True reality was that which in a particular moment of the process emerged only to quickly disappear. For Heidegger it was a disclosure of Being, but for postmodernists a testimony to a world of sheer becoming. In the postmodernist venture to translate that eternal becoming into a theory of history Foucault and Derrida were leading proponents. However, all poststructuralist postmodernists shared the conviction that traditional historical theory and practice must be reconstructed not only by changing methods but also by changing fundamental assumptions (including that concerning the human condition).

FOUCAULT'S TRUTH: POWER MANIFESTED IN LANGUAGE

The Changing Roles of Reason and Power

Foucault's linguistic turn was less rigorous and systematic than that of other postmodernists, especially Derrida's. The importance of discourses would increasingly impress him, but so would the phenomenon of power. Indeed, the affirmation of power's ability to shape whatever went under the term truth stood at the center of Foucault's work. The discourses of truth changed together with the incessantly fluctuating power relationships. But power as a quasi-stabilizing force and ultimate referent also introduced a problem.

The loser in this changing perception of truth was reason. In the Enlightenment's concept of progress, power worked on behalf of reason to endow human beings with an ever-increasing capacity to cope with and control the world. Foucault inverted that relationship. As a series of thinkers had done since the Greek Sophists, he saw power and its exercise as shaping the world (of discourses), including the activities of reason and the resultant types of knowledge. Therefore, one no longer could portray history as a grand progress toward full rationality and, with it, truth. The history of truth seeking reflected no more than a sequence of temporary power arrangements with no overall direction or goal (including the knowledge of one truth), or set patterns. It depicted the games of power *(jeux de pouvoir)* in which reason played a merely supportive role.

Ordering schemes were not reflections of a world-immanent order but were produced by translating power relations into a seemingly rational order. The contention of objectivity could only exist due to deliberate or naive scholarly blindness to power's role. Henceforth, historians must demonstrate how truth claims operated as constructions useful to certain groups of people and thereby undermined such claims. That task had to be performed within the discursive world without recourse to "outside" referents, although the ontic status of power itself remained a stubborn and unresolved problem. Indeed, Foucault's whole career testified to his concern with the definition of the nature of power.

Truth as Construct of Power

The linguistic turn led to the proper environment for the new truth: a fluid, infinitely malleable world. Even Nietzsche's dictum that all the intellectual concepts and categories were really grammatical in nature proved insufficiently radical, because it still recognized the perimeters of a relatively stable grammar. These perimeters also had been wrongly taken to be features that mirrored the objective world when in reality there was no clearly ascertainable referentiality between the word and the world. Such referentiality had only been claimed to give legitimacy to that which was asserted. But content did not make for the authority of truth, power did. The traditional assertion of discourses with substantial truth value—those which referred to the actual past—affirmed only illusions.

Accordingly the historical account did not begin with evidence being shaped into facts. Foucault, the most historically minded postmodernist, did archival work for his early works on medical topics. But the traditional search for the web of evidence-backed facts, in reference to which past events and structures were to be described and explained, was soon replaced by the wish to depict all evidence as manifestations of power. Hence, Foucault's interest shifted to an inquiry into the formation of concepts—historical theory instead of historiography. There, specific configurations of power created specific facts.

With the discursive world negating a nonlinguistic referentiality to the actual past, there could be no "proper" or authoritative truth. The proper definition of truth rested on the supposition of a discursively constructed world of openness to all possibilities—one allowing for utter contingency. Here, critics pointed to the clearly nondiscursive nature of power and its fit into the linguistic world. The concept of power did undergo a decisive change over the years. But, in his early period of creativity, Foucault's thoughts on power still bore the traces of the hermeneutics of suspicion—power as a "distorting" force in accord with prompting interests. These were rather stable, if not perennial forces of a primarily political nature and as such rather traditional in conception.

How did Foucault envisage the proper inquiry into the past in a world of pure flux?

Foucault's Archaeology and Episteme

In his early and more structuralist works, Foucault used a way of inquiry he called archaeology. He defined the term differently from common usage. No longer did the term refer to an auxiliary discipline of history, the endeavor, as he saw it, of digging in the ground for objects of the past. It rather meant to dig below the surface of the discursive level not for the causes of discourses (such as ideas about and forces inherent in the objective world), but for the rules of discourse formation. They were to be found not in their pristine easy-to-perceive shape but "only in widely differing theories, concepts, and objects of study that I had tried to reveal, by isolating as their specific locus, a level that I have called . . . archeological."[49] No fixed inventory of rules could ever be established since these rules changed in time. Discontinuity governed all. As *epistemes,* quasi-systematic affirmations of power, they shaped society independent of human agency.

Epistemes resembled Lévi-Strauss's codes and could be found "behind" the phenomena. Thus, an episteme could be described as a unifying force. Epistemes also performed a differentiating function between cultures and the disciplines of knowledge. "By *episteme,* we mean, in fact, the total set of relations that unite, at a given period, the discursive practices that give rise to epistemological figures, sciences, and possibly formalized systems."[50] Foucault identified only three culture-shaping epistemes since 1500, although, by implication, there were more of them throughout history. While the term itself conjured up parallels to such terms as world view, *mentalité,* and *Zeitgeist,* Foucault claimed uniqueness for the episteme on the basis of its solely discursive reality. As such, it was located at a safe distance from traditional essences or foundations by conceiving of them as abstract structural patterns without substantial content. Nevertheless, their relatively lengthy durations gave them a quasi-metaphysical quality.

By necessity, the episteme, linked to the application of power, produced its exclusions, its "others." In the case of *Madness and Civilization* the repressed "other" was the phenomenon of madness (not to be understood simply as mental illness). Foucault tried to show that what appeared to be a "natural" separation between sane and insane was actually a deliberate construction enforced by society. In poststructuralist postmodernist terms, society, in and for its own interests, constructed these "others." The repression became manifest in the separation of the mad from society in clinics that derived their legitimacy from what was perceived of as ameliorative schemes. These were seen as part of progress and society was called emancipatory for it. In line with postmodernist thought, Foucault would claim no emancipatory credits for his own findings.

At the time of writing *Madness and Civilization*, Foucault went clearly beyond mere linguistic constructs to forces of an at least quasi-real nature. His thought showed the impress of Nietzsche's view of the struggle in Greek life between the apollinarian (rational, orderly, and harmonious) and dionysian (passionate, irrational, and emotional) approaches. Foucault's sympathies were with the dionysian. While in the later phase of Foucault's work Nietzsche's pair of world views faded away, remnants of his enthusiasm for the dionysian approach would remain important. His celebration of the experience of transgression would be the most telling trace. Best understood as the exploration of "negativity" (that which was beyond the limits drawn by society's order), it explained Foucault's sympathy for the works of such critics of rationalism as Georges Bataille and prophets of desire and suffering as the Marquis de Sade and Antonin Artaud. His desire for transgressions or "limit experiences" was a personal affirmation of the testing of the limits, prescribed by reason and its prevailing order, right up to the threshold of death. He even linked madness with death when he saw madness as the *"deja-la* of death," as making the fantasies and delirium of death present.

Foucault's Genealogy

Under the influence of Nietzsche's *Genealogy of Morals*, Foucault began to conceive of analysis as genealogy. He considered it to be the proper approach to the discursive world of endless becoming without beginnings and endings. Now the object of analysis was less the hidden rules for discourses but more the history of shifting power relationships. In this sense genealogy resembled history. But Foucault's new history as genealogy knew no continuity. Historians would have to deal with discontinuous and directionless power struggles to facilitate the understanding of cultural patterns and elements. With this shift to the more clearly discourse-oriented approach of genealogy, Foucault moved deliberately away from all remnants of the structural mode of thinking without ever abandoning it completely. Whereas he had seen madness and power as separate phenomena, one creating the other by exclusion, Foucault now spoke more of a paradoxically connected world. In it, the "same" and the "other" created each other continuously. The epistemes faded from this world of discontinuity with its phenomena of a fleeting tension-filled presence. Too often understood as totalities that constituted chronological entities, they dissolved into configurations shaped by forces sharing in the discontinuity of the world. Now the grounding of discourses was supplied by the social practices in which they were set. The only stability in history, albeit always a temporary one, belonged to contexts. Instead of searching for the illusory permanent and stable truth, the historian must concentrate on the unending task of ferreting out the power relationships that constructed views, ideas, and values and on laying bare the oppressions created thereby. None of that could and did sort out the "right" and "wrong" views, which would give the designation of *the* truth to any one of an infinite number of realizable possibilities. The historian's inquiry found only either dominant or oppressed discourses, produced by the never-ceasing discursive construction and reconstruction of the human world. But the tracing of the working of power behind the discursive formations would once more raise the still open question of the nondiscursive identity of power.

The concept of power employed in *Discipline and Punish: The Birth of the Prison* already showed a development toward a more fully fluid perception of power. There, Foucault demonstrated the often paradoxical working of power. Changes perceived as humanitarian improvements actually widened the possibilities for control and oppression. That made innovations hailed as emancipatory too often simply extensions of the reach of state power into new areas of human life.

Later, particularly in the history of sexuality, the power and knowledge connection emerged as joint to each other in a given and neutral union. Foucault marked it as P(ower)/K(nowledge) to signal that neither power nor knowledge must be thought of as ever standing alone. They could be supportive of and oppositional to the existing order. As a prime example for this ambivalence, Foucault would cite the modern state with its immense assertion of a new form of power: biopower. Progress in medical knowledge appeared as the power to keep everyone healthy. Yet inclusions and exclusions of people—by the definition of beneficiaries and "others"—were needed to accomplish the task. In this as in other cases, the discursive power exerted by the modern state was pervasive in all ordering activities, even in the organization of knowledge. Power was at work at every "site of life," not just in politics.

Modernity's teleological bridging of the gap between the "ought" and the "is" had been provided for by the progress that made the "ought to be" into the "is" in the perfect end state with its resolution of the existential tension. In stark contrast to that view, Foucault strove to define a fluid world from which all closure (continuity) was banned. In this fluid world, truth became ceaseless truth-construction, which legitimized no authority and hence could sponsor no oppression. The new fluid truth would affirm nothing consistently except ceaseless and aimless change. That was assured by the bipolarity of power itself. Power was a negative force when exercised as instrument for upholding the existing status, a positive one if it energized the opposition. Power enabled life to go on without illusion of aim or end. Foucault saw no possibility for any sociopolitical arrangements or an affirmation of a truth that would not produce an out-of-power "other." The full emancipation of the "other" had been the promise of progressive historians and utopians. Therefore, to search for truth involved the necessary opposition to whatever was established at a given time as truth. Change was truth, continuity untruth. What was said and stated did not matter; only whether it undermined or upheld the status quo did matter. Thus, Foucault could speak of his own works in terms of fireworks and bombs that did their jobs but in the process self-destructed. Such a truth fit properly into the totally fluid world. Epistemologically speaking, with a stable truth absent in the fluid discursive world, historical accounts could not be evaluated in relation to a "real" referent but only in their attitudes toward change.

JACQUES DERRIDA: A SYSTEMATIC ANSWER

Going beyond Saussure toward a Fully Fluid Linguistic World

In contrast to Foucault, Derrida never focused his attention on historical topics. Nevertheless his writings had a considerable impact on historical inquiry in as systematic a way as poststructuralists could deliver. In a change that established the smoothest possible fit between poststructuralist thought and its implied or stipulated totally fluid world, Derrida revised Saussure's theory of language or, as he put it, guided it to its proper conclusion. Derrida went beyond Saussure's detachment of language from the dominance of cognition. Although Saussure no longer had maintained the passivity of language in creating an image of reality, Derrida still sensed too much stability in Saussure's view of language.

Saussure had seen language as a stable, indeed static system since all that was dynamic originated and occurred in speech (parole). With a science of language as his aim, he needed language's stability. The historical aspect of the linguistic world was banned from language, which now was seen as a synchron and closed entity. The sign once more became secondary, this time to the system. That aspect was unacceptable to Derrida since it seemed to be a trace of metaphysics that impeded the breakthrough to a view of language compatible with absolute flux.[51] The sign had to be freed from the limits imposed by the system's quasi-stable totality. Instead, an endless process of scission produced meanings. Derrida would see in this free flow of signifiers the condition for a true antirealism. However, using a phrase coined by Jean-Paul Aron, critics would label Derrida's complete liberation of the signifier the beginning of the "hegemony of the signifier."

Differentiation: The Shaping Force of the World and History

Historians would be affected by Derrida's reasoning on behalf of the world of flux. The free play of signifiers in language fit perfectly to the postmodernist concept of the world as being in chaotic flux—aimless and meaningless before "inscription" (being written on). As an answer to the question after the cause for the multitude of named phenomena, Derrida used the linguistic principle of differentiation. So far, the "existence" of all phenomena of human experience and the distinction between them had been accounted for by their natures and essences. These accountings gave phenomena stable identities, and they could be ordered into clearly defined categories of the same. Derrida changed the identities of things and persons into purely linguistic ones. They were created by a process that separated the world of objects and persons from the as yet undifferentiated mass of infinite possibilities. That happened through a "process of scission and division which would produce or constitute different things or differences."[52] The process of "creating by setting apart," which Derrida called *différance* (his neologism), preceded all differences it produced.[53] That made différance, as the principle of differentiation quasi-ontological. "Quasi"—because Derrida would protest that différance was "neither a word nor a concept nor could it be absorbed into ontology and theology."[54] Différance operated as an irreducible principle for human consciousness and writing. The "presence" of anything was accounted for by différance.

Historians were affected by that stipulated différance since they needed to take into account Derrida's unique view of the process of differentiation. Rather than gradually revealing a preexistent reality, it constituted in an inescapable and originary process, a (textual) world of pure contingency and utter fragility. There, no being was ultimately identical to itself—that is, never even at least partially always the same—because that condition was infinitely "deferred." What appeared as the identity of any being at a given moment only looked stable but it was no more than a given stage in the ongoing endless transition from one identity to another.[55] Yet the differences produced by the linguistic relationships were not complete ruptures, because they pointed to a relationship between that which was affirmed and that not affirmed. Derrida's différance was meant to stress the fact that the temporarily not affirmed differed from that "present" not by being negated but only by being deferred. In the world of différance there also was no room for binary oppositions relying on rigid identities, such as true or false and facts or interpretations. The interlocked possibilities of the new world with its ever new combinations of signifiers (words) and the resultant new meanings did not tolerate them.

The play of différance guaranteed the total fluidity of the world without elements that were grounded in the sense of being exempt from that flux. In another context, Fredric Jameson has spoken of contentions of permanence as the "metaphysics of presence." Derrida saw it as deprived of its raison d'être by the denial of any referential knowledge. In the process of différance the concept of a more than temporary "real world" played no role.

An Ultimate Referent?

The differentiation process did affirm—intended or unintended—the existence of an indefinable whole that "preceded" the process. Thus, différance was linked to something encompassing that went beyond philosophy and theology. It was a priori to language and, because of that, inaccessible to language. Hence followed Derrida's injunction against calling the process of differentiation an objective process. Différance was linked to that unnameable undifferentiated state, and its working pointed toward it. It could be seen as a *Urprozess,* a process that partially disassembled and, thereby, made visible that unnameable whole. Just as in negative theology nothing can be said about what God is, only what God is not, so différance escaped all efforts of conceptual mastery by all the disciplines of inquiry, since they themselves were on "this side" of the linguistic divide. Différance worked in the linguistic world but had its roots beyond language. It was absolute alterity.[56]

Philosophically speaking, Derrida's unnameable whole constituted a sturdy and basic metaphysical element. As the fountain of constant construction but also of deconstruction, of "presences" and "absences," it knew no justification for negating anything, only for stating its temporary "absence." Hence the presence of différance demanded the constant advocacy of heterogeneity, multiplicity, plurality, and diversity—the mandate given by the radical "alterity."[57] The multitude of excluded or deferred "alterities" with their claims to equal status (of presence) prevented stable homogeneity. Every historical condition had a multitude of "absent" (deferred) counterparts. Human beings experienced that fact as the impossibility of establishing static and homogeneous conditions over any length of time.

Thus, the world was by necessity unstable and allowed for no permanence except that for the principle of constant differentiation itself. That principle's sturdy continuity could be tolerated because it was purely formal (rather than substantial) and antagonistic to its own permanence. Unlike the dialectical process in which the existing evoked its own contradictions and their conflict aimed at synthesis, the differentiation process had no such goal *(telos)*. It was aimless and endless. The discussions of the possible uses of history will show that Derrida would have to yield on the rigor of that view.

The New Historical Analysis: Deconstruction

Those who saw in *différance* the correct basis for viewing the world after the linguistic turn discerned in its related principle of deconstruction a mandate to change historical analysis radically. In the concept of deconstruction, Derrida provided the most coherent postmodernist means for the dismantling of conventional truth and its founding metaphysics. There was no special deconstruction for historical accounts, since they also were constructions of a linguistic nature. They, too, could and must be deconstructed like other texts.

Deconstruction was made possible by the internal dynamics of texts. Texts, historical and fictive, were constructs that reflected a long row of linguistic transformations energized by the principle of differentiation. Thus, historical accounts offered a dense reality produced by inscriptions and reinscriptions that produced meanings. Put in different terms, texts were composed of traces of various differentiation processes that assigned the temporary privilege of "presence" to some textual elements and "absence" to many "others." This built-in tension between presences and absences, as well as cohesion and contradictions, changed any text from a passive document into a rhetorical action. The text took on a life of its own, freed of its author's intentions or link to any referential content. Its dynamics derived from its internal tensions. Deconstruction demonstrated that the seemingly stable and solid text—a compilation of various text elements—constituted no more than a temporary neutralizing of its internal tensions. Hence it was necessary "to make enigmatic what one thinks one understands by the words 'proximity,' immediacy, 'presence' which for us mark our context."[58] Absent was the fact-plus-fact skeleton—the representational element—that upheld historical accounts and gave them stability and authority. Not surprisingly then, a historical text never had just one meaning but many. Thus the readers' interpretations in the act of reading superseded the once sought after authorial intent and meaning. They affirmed the desired plurality of meanings. The old hermeneutics, as the endeavor to ascertain the one correct meaning, had to be deconstructed. It, too, had been an instrument on behalf of presence, closure, and permanence. On its part, deconstruction was a means to reduce continuity and stability to flux. Once more, pluralism, heterogeneity, and diversity became the guardians against hegemony, oppression, and authority.

When the word text was used beyond the confines of written texts, culture turned out to be a favorite choice of application. Textual deconstruction became cultural deconstruction—deconstruction on a more complex scale but of the same character. Indeed, many poststructuralist postmodernists engaged in just such a deconstruction of Western culture. Stipulating that Western culture's hegemony and dominance over other cultures had been established by giving absolute privilege to the progressive discourse of history, the deconstruction of that discourse's supportive conceptual constructs became of prime importance. The aim was to demonstrate that the progressive argument on behalf of the Western tradition, based on objective knowledge, was really a linguistic construct created in a specific context. Then, Western culture would be shown to be a construct beset by tensions and fissures with no more stability and claim to a privileged position than anything else in the fluid world that différance produced.

From the premise that the world was one of absolute equality between that which was present and that which was absent derived the crucial poststructuralist postmodernist contention: the world of postmodernity would be one where differences could no longer lead to hegemony and oppression because of the impossibility to legitimize such behavior in the new world of différance. Deconstruction expressed that awareness and supplied the instruments of realization. Différance and deconstruction guaranteed the fluid world.

A MODERATELY LINGUISTIC APPROACH: JEAN-FRANÇOIS LYOTARD

In the most directly historical of his works, *The Postmodern Condition* (1979; English 1984), Lyotard's primary quest focused on the type of knowledge and truth finding proper for the postmodern society. One that acknowledged the world's total contingency and still would be useful as an instrument for the mastery of life yet would also be incapable of producing metanarratives.

Lyotard's views on the matter developed in phases. Early on, Lyotard remained close to vitalism with its celebration of the mysterious force of life into which rationality merged. He favored the actual and unique phenomenon that did not fit into scientific or historical systems. The specific form of affirmation came in a philosophy of desire that shunned a directly representational and authoritative truth.[59] Gilles Deleuze and Felix Guattari's works stated its case most prominently. While Lyotard's full assent was temporary, his later works still carried its mark.

In *The Postmodern Condition* he hued a line that crossed into both linguistic and representational areas, although his ultimate society of language games tilted toward the former. The postmodern society's agonistic struggle between different and incommensurable language games and the desired transcendence beyond logic (seen as search for stability) to paralogy (seen as search for instabilities) permitted no assertion of a binding or authoritative truth. Yet Lyotard came to dislike what he saw as too strong an anthropomorphic tilt in his views. Therefore, he would begin to speak of a world of phrase regimes. These phrase regimes were established by the different purposes that phrases served and the attendant sets of rules shaping them. By their nature, they established incommensurate differences and produced agreements (no wholes and unitary entities) only on a small scale and fleetingly as the kaleidoscopic configurations of a contingent world. All of that was properly attuned to Lyotard's passionate pluralism and would lead him to accent the *petits récits* (the small narratives). Anonymous creation and small scale (even micro scale) mattered for truth, not the substance of what was asserted. Eventually, when Lyotard's dislike of the anthropomorphic elements in his views became even stronger, he experimented with trying to erase all sharp distinctions between material and immaterial as well as subject and object.

REFLECTIONS ON THE NEW CONCEPT OF TRUTH

Basic Propositions and Questions

Did poststructuralist postmodernists succeed in their foremost intention—be it seen as ethical or political—to unlink truth from authority and its associated power? And what did it all mean for history?

Foucault, Derrida, and Lyotard each created his own design for the revision of the concept of truth, but they all prescribed to historians two basic presuppositions. The first of them stipulated that the proper understanding of truth required the negation of any claims to one authoritative truth. That, in turn, needed the negation of any attribution of "natural" inherent and stable qualities to persons and objects. These attributes, by virtue of their duration, were elements of continuity, they impeded change and legitimized power. "Natural" qualities—be they human nature or other essences—had no place in a postmodernist theory that must serve a human world now seen as marked ideally by endless and unimpeded change. Hence, all truth claims must recognize truth as multiple. Affirmations of universality, homogeneity, and uniformity must yield to those of pluralism, heterogeneity, and difference.

The second key tenet stated that the most potent source of resistance to change must be neutralized: the contention that historians could, in principle, gain cognitive access to a specific existential experience in the past (as once actually lived). Elements of a found or discovered past would constitute powerful obstacles to the envisaged totally open future in a linguistically constructed world of unlimited possibilities. The traditional assertions of an extralinguistically constructed access were the source of dangerous illusions of stability and continuity and wrong world views. The proper world of the historian, past and present, was that of linguistic constructions. Indeed, language as discourses and texts constituted the effective human world. There could be no "peeking" through a cognitive window at past actuality. That included the rejection of the historian's observations of objective and stabilizing features, including observations of recurrences and limits. Then only could the concept of truth be safely disassociated from oppression. Historical accounts would never again become the justification for the existing order.

Combined, the two presuppositions yielded powerful mandates to reshape the "doing of history." The execution of the mandates aimed straight at the two pillars carrying the truth referential to the actual past: evidence and objectivity.

As it had in poststructuralist narrativism, evidence lost its claim to represent a direct link to the actual past. In the world of discourses and texts it became solely a linguistically constructed message. The aim to represent "what actually happened" made no longer any sense. Evidence, once a guidepost to past existential experience, had no standing outside of the web of a historical account. The more so, since traditional objectivity also had turned out to be an illusion. The conditions stipulated for an objective observer, primarily a sufficient detachment from the historian's context, could never be realized. All assertions of order and meaning became free-choice linguistic constructs when before they had been "found" in a process that combined context-inherent and interpretative elements. Historians could not find in the body of linguistically mediated evidence any guidance to the true representation, only an invitation to choose one of many possibilities for construction, all of them of equal truth value. The standard in truth-finding could no longer be the closest (objective) approximation to the actuality of the past. The partially stable reality of life had disappeared. As for the traditional concept of objectivity, it was replaced by its postmodernist counterpart, the demand for "self-reflexivity." Historians must be ruthlessly honest in laying bare how their accounts were constructed. On that basis, all claims of an authoritative truth would be prevented.

The Key Struggle for Nonreferentiality

The new views on evidence and objectivity seemed to support the ethical and political aim of denying any authoritative truth, which alone made possible the desired abandonment of the oppressive ideals of universality, homogeneity, and "unicity." But problems for the necessary basic stipulation of a complete nonreferentiality surfaced in postmodernist theories as a difficult struggle for internal consistency. At the core of the difficulties remained the critical question of what actually made the linguistic world shape and reshape itself. Forces for a dynamics that had no connection with those of past theories and histories and were themselves not referents and, thus, quasi-metaphysical stabilizers needed to be found.

Narrativists had recourse to literary forms as stabilizers of historical accounts, but had left their exact nature as well as that of the narrativist dynamics unclear. Foucault chose power and wrestled throughout his career with its proper relation to the discursive world. Simply put, discourses were the expressions of power exerted. The shift from archaeology and episteme to genealogy, with its clearer discourse orientation, testified to different accommodations of power to the world of flux. Critics would point out that power, interwoven into all facets of life, could not be considered to be a purely discursive phenomenon. And as an existential force, power had a not-so-smooth fit with the fluid, discursive world. In addition, the stipulated ubiquity and dominance of power suggested a new reductionism, however carefully Foucault's argumentation concealed it. What did distinguish this reductionism from earlier ones was power's bipolarity. Unlike other "basic" forces, which usually had clear directions toward an end stage in a "good" human condition, Foucault's power could shift valuation from negative (in its attempts to establish and maintain systems of order) to positive (in its opposition to and negation of them). In that, the absolute standard for valuation in poststructuralist postmodernism became once more visible: the nonimpedance of change. Its formal nature avoided projecting any specific human condition as ideal. What happened in history did not matter, only whether it furthered or impeded change did. The claim to universality and continuity embedded in such an evaluation could be tolerated since it only aimed at change's own continuation. Truth beyond many, if not all contexts had become many truths of equal value.

Derrida's wrestling with referentiality occurred in the world of texts. These texts, including historical accounts, were no longer sturdy linguistic structures as witnesses to the conceptual mastery of the past and imbued with meaning by authors who had at least partially understood the objective world. Texts were fragile, constructed entities, beset by internal tensions, even contradictions, above all the tension between "presences" and "absences." The dynamics of history stemmed from these internal tensions. Again they conformed to a world, fluid, meaningless, and without authoritative truth that knew no stable meanings or order. Only meanings and order constructed by authors and readers yielded temporary contextual truths. Being fleeting and multiple, these meanings constituted truths that could not be misused as claims to authority (and power). Yet even sympathetic observers have located a perennial truth in Derrida's approach. All the constructions and dissolutions pointed to that unnameable "state before language," the totality of all possibilities, as the absolute ontological anchor.

Just as Foucault's power found its affirmation and negation in itself, so did Derrida's text. For Derrida, the theoretical affirmation of a fluid world (pure change) came via the concept of the all-pervasive and ceaseless process of differentiation (*différance*). Texts were both witnesses for it and obstacles to it. They temporarily represented stable elements (their negative aspect) but also facilitated by virtue of their tension-beset constitution their own deconstruction (their positive aspect). That made the text as bipolar as Foucault's power was. Historians, as all other scholars, aided but did not produce that process of deconstruction of all that seemed so stable. They were not the originators of deconstruction but only its agents. That raised the question after the ontological status of the process of differentiation as an ultimate reality or its manifestation.[60]

Yet the stipulation of a multitude of truths posed a serious problem. How could the absolute claim for the inherently beneficial qualities of pluralism, diversity, and heterogeneity be justified? One possible argument, the one based on their inherent goodness had been delegitimated. And so had any argument derived from past human experience. The linguistically constructed world offered no such valid lessons from history. Actually, the traditional study of the past would have shed doubt on the simple contention of the absolute goodness of heterogeneity without the benefit of a unitary element providing some limits for it. Thus, the moral and political goal of postmodernism could be formulated but not persuasively argued for in terms of the postmodernist theory of truth. It remained a theoretical postulate divorced from the existential reality of life.

Critics among historians have questioned the need for and viability of the poststructuralist postmodernist endeavor of a complete revision of historical inquiry with its attendant results. Some have rejected it as an example of extreme relativism—not new at all and having been previously rebutted. Modern historicism has sometimes been cited as a parallel phenomenon. Yet, while historicists did exhibit a clear relativism, they never denied an ultimate truth. Human beings were simply condemned to glimpse it from specific perspectives. The problem with historicism proved to be its ineffectuality in the practice of life. With its irreducible perspectivism about the human condition, it lacked moral or political bearings. The postmodernist program transcended by far the boundaries of traditional relativism, because its different truths were no mere perspectives on a possible ideal truth. Postmodernist views on truth reflected the absolute dominance of change and affirmed the limitless play of discursive formations or of signifiers. The full human existential experience needed to be reduced to discursive and textual artifacts. Critics would call such truth a fable or myth.

And there has been the ultimate problem. The ban of all claims to authoritative truth was inconsistent with the claim made for the exclusive and universal validity of poststructuralist postmodernist theory. Such a validity could not find any foundation after the reduction of the temporal experience to change—in a world of total flux. That theoretical inconsistency, together with others, left a difficult legacy to historians inclined to implement the postmodernist revisions. In poststructuralist postmodernist theory, the problem became clearly visible in the ardent debate on the poststructuralist postmodernist concept of truth as well as in the attempts to cope with the metanarratives and the proper uses of history.

THE DEBATE ON THE IMPLICATIONS FOR HISTORICAL THOUGHT AND PRACTICE

The postmodern world of complete flux, the very basis for poststructuralist postmodernist theories, had an ambiguous rationale. Yet the debate on its concept of truth hardly referred to the problems with the argument for non-referentiality. Historians have preferred to argue their case for and against postmodernism on the level of methods, approaches, and interpretations. On their part, postmodernists, too, have directed their attacks on the practice of history, leaving their own basic positions on the nature of the human world, particularly its temporality, implicit in their advocacies. Thus, the crucial theoretical presuppositions of poststructuralist postmodernism have rarely entered the debate in a direct manner. But they were always present and decisive. Largely unnoticed went the ethical, political, and cultural goals of the poststructuralist postmodernist endeavor as well as the crucial experimentation with the human temporal experience—the dimension of time in history. That also hid the credit poststructuralist postmodernists deserved for opening up for debate fundamental propositions of historiography. Awareness of that dimension of their discipline has benefited historians, as it gave the understanding of historical epistemology its proper depth. And it made plausible postmodernist concepts of postmodernity. That the challenge of postmodernism went to the foundation of life and history also explained why the ensuing debate has proved to be intricate, often opaque, but always fervent.

The Struggle for a Dynamic Human Condition in Hermeneutics

Changes in Hermeneutics. For centuries, hermeneutics had been understood generally as the art of eliciting the true meaning of texts. Thus, when Ankersmit characterized the replacement of the epistemological by the hermeneutical approach to historical inquiry as a decisive development in the ascendancy of postmodernism, historians had to take note. The statement was especially apropos if the term hermeneutics referred not to a still strongly cognitive hermeneutics (such a Robin G. Collingwood's) but to the continental hermeneutics (particularly Heidegger's). Poststructuralist postmodernists discerned in Heidegger's views of the world and the human condition history's most effective means to resolve its epistemological problems. When the inquirer was seen as being fully integrated into the web of life, knowledge emerged in the course of existential struggles. The change has often been characterized as the end of the Cartesian ego's dominance. The pioneers of poststructuralist postmodernism had welcomed that development, although Heidegger's hermeneutics showed tendencies that still posed problems for them: the search for an authoritative truth and ultimate continuity. They themselves would struggle with the persistence of continuous elements. Attempts to resolve the fundamental difficulty became part of the hermeneutics debate, too. The hermemeutic circle must not close in ventures based on a concept of truth that fit into the new view of the world.

Gadamer's Rescue of Tradition as Dynamic Continuity. Hans-Georg Gadamer's work offered an alternative to Derrida's deconstructionist views with their emphasis on arbitrary meanings and discontinuity. With its appreciation of the collective life and a moderate continuity, it would hold substantial appeal to historians sympathetic to the linguistic turn.

Heidegger's human beings were always in the process of forming themselves and their view of the world. They were shaped and reshaped as the *Dasein*. It was an anxious experience in a world that knew no proper closures in human life. Confronting the process of life and its ultimate end in death (nothingness) had to be accomplished without defusing the acute experience by means of constructs claiming permanence (metaphysics). Hans-Georg Gadamer agreed with his teacher, Heidegger, on the radical historicity of human beings. Our ability to think historically derived from the historical quality of life itself. Historical accounts were linguistic constructs because language was the only locus where all experiences of the world were mediated or, put in the vein of Gadamer, Being could be understood only through language. However, language here was not the abstract ability to communicate, governed by the individual's will and cognition, but a historical phenomenon since it constituted the collective experience of a particular group. It incorporated what Heidegger called "prejudgment"—an experiential knowledge that preceded any individual and collective existential encounter and theoretical thought. As tradition, it made possible the dialogue between past and present. Theoretically speaking, it represented a continuous element that was self-adjusting. While not seen as an element of *Festigkeit* (solidity or stability), it, nevertheless, set limits to the direction of the flow of life, negating Derrida's free play of signifiers.

Reflecting on that existential process yielded the only truth and meaning that counted. Hence the historian could not objectify history (give it an artificial stability) by abstracting it from life's ongoing process. No closure for the purpose of knowing the truth was possible. Neither could there be an escape from language. The truly historical consciousness remained truly linguistic in nature. Gadamer spoke of a *Wirkungsgeschichte* (a history that exists and is effective in the process of developing and not as a stable object of analysis or study).

Clearly, there were present in such a view elements of duration or "temporary permanence": tradition and an ever-so-vague totality of the process. That caused objections from modernist and postmodernist critics alike. They found the influence of the past as tradition disturbing. Jürgen Habermas sensed in tradition the presence of past coercion and oppression. Other critics pointed to the absence of criteria for distinguishing true from untrue statements. As expected, postmodernists criticized the elements of stability. Gadamer responded, in the postmodernist vein, by pointing out that the past was full of unrealized possibilities that through the medium of tradition became catalysts for change. Never completely known, thus not completely assimilable, tradition did not simply dominate but became a dynamic element in the "fusion of the horizons" (*Horizontverschmelzung*) between past and present that yielded the "new," the future—all of it visible in language (*Sprachlichkeit*). History could not be a static reenactment of the past. Rather the truth of historical accounts as that about life was a disclosure offered at specific points in time. Therefore, the truth that resulted from the endless dialogue with life was always provisional.

Thus, Gadamer's assent to postmodernism remained conditional. While the world had acquired some stable elements, the seeming "permanence" of tradition was not at all static (metaphysical) since it recognized the dominance of change.

For a Radical Hermeneutics. Some scholars were intent on preserving the early Heidegger's historicity of human life as the foundation of the poststructuralist postmodernist world view. Among them have been the proponents of (what they called) a radical hermeneutics (John Caputo, Roy Martinez, and their collaborators) who worked to buttress the cause of the completely historicized human being and its setting in a fluid world while preserving the possibility for fruitful inquiry.[61] They saw the new historicity—a matter of the whole human existence not limited to the area of cognition—endangered even in the works of philosophers seemingly akin to it, those of the older Heidegger and of Hans-Georg Gadamer. Just as Derrida did, they sensed in the works of both men elements of metaphysical quality, that is, tendencies to closure (stability). Their sympathies remained with the early Heidegger's "difficulty-of-life" model. Its world knew the tension-filled existential unity between the world and human beings. There the basic human experience was that of being "thrown" into a strange world—being adrift in the inescapable flux of time and struggling with life in the awareness of death (the dread of nothingness). With the neat juxtaposition of consciousness and an orderly, inherently meaningful world absent, human thought had to cope with constantly changing situations without reassuring stable anchoring points. Life's difficulties forced an interpretive engagement with the "facticity of life"— one full of contingencies. Accordingly, the favorable estimation of Heidegger by radical hermeneuticists changed when in his later life he shifted away from an existential analysis to an emphasis on Being—the grounding of beings. As for Gadamer, he stayed consistently *persona non grata,* because he granted continuity (in terms of tradition) a necessary, even constructive role. Radical hermeneuticists preferred Derrida's world shaped by différance.

These hermeneuticists strove to safeguard the direct human encounter with the world. "Facticity" of life demanded the absence of elements and schemata that alleviated or camouflaged the core characteristics of life— contingencies, paradoxes, ruptures, and discontinuities. The task of avoiding lapses into as much as traces of Being (the static being of all beings) such as essences, ideas, *arche,* or *ousia* would be a taunting one. In history it would mean the absence of an empirically arrived at database that could claim to have brought to a closure the never-ending production of meanings. The rejection of all stabilizing elements, even all consensus, also meant to remain unwavering in the negation of linear history with its telos. Never must radical hermeneutics yield to the nostalgia for meanings that were anchored in stable elements or views of totality. Meanings were produced *in* life experience for life and not *by* it primarily for cognitive purposes. All explanations as constructed meanings were destined to stay under construction. Hence radical hermeneuticists found Jacques Derrida's deconstructionism, as preparing the free play of signifiers, most affine.

An Endless, Slow Deconstruction. Hans-Georg Gadamer's hermeneutics had deviated significantly from the poststructuralist determination to consider pure change the effective warranty for the proper postmodernity. His digression received modified support from Gianni Vattimo's stipulation of the *pensiero debole* (literally, weak thought). An explanation must serve as a translation.

Vattimo considered not feasible the aim of a sudden deconstruction of Western culture. Instead he suggested a more complex definition of the West's cultural crisis and the way to overcome it. The *pensiero debole* involved a set of ideas, among them the finding that Western culture's foundations had become weak and postmodernists must strive constantly to assist that weakening process. Yet that struggle would not find a "clean" final solution in a world free of Western cultural influence. Such an assertion could constitute a sort of progress. One indication that the process would go on and on rather than end rather suddenly was the continuity built into language itself. It would keep the West's cultural world alive. In fact, in the very process of arguing against Western concepts postmodernists had to use the very language and conceptual world of that culture. On his part, Derrida had already acknowledged that dilemma but had dealt with it by calling such use ironic, designed to subvert Western culture. Vattimo accepted the inevitable ironic consequences, namely the prolongation of the traditional structures by the very acts of criticism themselves. Thus, the past would always be with us. No sharp break in Western culture and its history could be expected. Instead a constant weakening would continue and must suffice.

As a result, postmodernity would remain thoroughly in and of history. Globally speaking, Vattimo had no use for the view of pure "others" (the "native" cultures). He depicted the postmodern world as a "construction site" with the remnants of many cultures cluttering up the human world— all of them in the process of weakening.[62] The consequence was not only the fading of all claims to authoritative truth but paradoxically also of those to the absolute alterity of each culture. "Weak," it turned out, referred here to thought with a safe distance from all extreme claims.

A Historian's View. David Roberts suggested a variation of "weak" thought as the way to reach the poststructuralist postmodernist goal of a complete purge of metaphysics in a true world of change. This would necessitate the elimination of the postmodernists' own exemptions from the world of pure change. Most important of them were their claims to authoritative truth and its corollaries, such as the privileging of the "other." After the definite demise of the dualistic world (change intertwined with continuity) and the end of the dominance of the permanent over the temporary, history became the ceaseless process of human construction and self-reflection in a world shaped by "nothing but history."[63] A history that did "not posit metaphysical forms of totalization and closure, that does not claim to fix things for good, that entails a reflexive sense of historicity."[64] In that history, the process of life would run its course channeled only by its own constructed traditions. The competing claims of language and the world would be reconciled without recourse to metaphysics, sheer aestheticism, or nihilism. "Weak thought" would prevail, which affirmed nothing but the process of history.[65] However, when Roberts made authoritative truth claims for his postmetaphysical interpretation of history, he joined in the postmodernist paradoxical assertion that a world of ceaseless flux did have one all-important exception: its own authoritative claim to that permanence.

The elements of continuity and certainty in a moderately linguistic form returned as themes in the work of a number of scholars. They were sympathetic to history's extension of the processes of analysis and interpretation beyond the strictly cognitive approach. Properly done, history involved all aspects of human existence as demonstrated in Heidegger's encounter-with-life approach and Gadamer's collective process of meaning formation and transmission. In all of that, language had shown itself to be a powerful force. Nevertheless, the historical nexus, based on sufficient referentiality, preserved the connection between past, present, and the expectations for the future, involving the intentionality of the author and the fidelity to the past as it once had been lived.

The Debate on the Postmodernist Concept of Truth

The Charge to Historians Restated. As Foucault, Derrida, and other pioneers of poststructuralist postmodernism have made clear to historians, at the core of the poststructuralist postmodernist challenge to historians stood the demand that the presuppositions and ways of "doing history" must be adjusted to the world marked by the absolute primacy of change. The translation of the world, including human life, into one of ceaseless flux was to occur primarily via the linguistic turn, which, it was thought, made it finally possible to speak of a truth without stability for which nonreferentiality to the actual past was the key condition. Truth would be multiple, temporary, and strictly contextual, thereby depriving any assertion or action of legitimate claims to be the only right and lasting one. Historical epistemology would experience radical modifications, if not abolition.

The epistemologically stable link (via causality and proper evidentiary methods) of the historian's present to a stable past (as it had been lived) would yield to one shaped in accordance with the fluidity of linguistic approaches and linguistically defined truths. The stipulated access to the actuality of the past as once lived came to be seen as an illusion. No reference to the actuality of the past was possible since all that survived of it were linguistic constructs of what once was the present. Now, "'history' must be radically severed from 'past': the former is always calibrated with cultural contradictions, whereas the latter is much more a fluid notion."[66] Life must be seen as the limitless and directionless web of textual and discursive relationships. In it, only truths could be accepted that were strictly context-bound constructions.

Postmodernists frequently have characterized this change as the end of Platonic "foundationalism" in history. Such foundations were considered firm, if not permanent anchoring places for all accounts. Yet while historians have recognized stable elements in their truth-finding these have not been Platonic essences but empirically gained insights into recurrent structures and limits of human life. These elements have made visible sufficiently stable extralinguistic referents in the midst of seemingly incessant change. Postmodernists have declared even such empirical foundations illusory (metaphysical). The stipulation of a cognitively unbridgeable gulf, which separated words and worlds, would be the flashpoint for theoretical disagreements between historians and poststructuralist postmodernists. Thus, it was noteworthy that the difficulties Foucault and Derrida had experienced with genuine referentiality continued in all postmodernist theory building and in attempts to conform to such theories in creating historical accounts.

Ardent Postmodernist Advocacy. With so much more than a mere methodological rearrangement at stake, the exhortations aimed at historians to accept the postmodernist revisions have shown a sense of urgency that even transcended the one with which the New Historians of the late 1800s and early 1900s called on their colleagues to become fully modern. The New History had wished to enhance history's new status as a distinct inquiry, particularly as a separate academic discipline. Postmodernists would have a different concern. Patrick Joyce praised poststructuralist postmodernism for putting into doubt "the sanctity of 'history' as a distinct form of knowledge predicated upon the autonomy of the social."[67] Others have found traditional history theoretically too unsophisticated, or as one scholar put it, still dwelling in "a world of the flat-earth-variety."[68] And again others perceived history's redirection toward postmodernism as a necessary adjustment to the new context. "We live in the postmodern age wherein the old modernist certainties of historical truth and methodological objectivity . . . are challenged principles." Therefore "history must be reassessed at its most basic level."[69]

The rejection of demands for radical change in historical inquiry came from historians, however much they differed in their views, foci, and arguments. They agreed on the destructive effect of the denial of a possible referential, authoritative truth and of the theoretical tenets derived from it. Historians also protested that, contrary to postmodernist contentions, they have never claimed to have attained the final truth about the past but only that such a truth must remain the ultimate although probably never attainable ideal. Good historians always have been aware of the fallibility of their findings—due to error, insufficient data, risks taken in interpretation, and the experiential background of the historian. They have affirmed, however, that the cumulative results of proper perception, cognition, and imagination, expressed in the symbolic forms of language, could lead to a sufficiently proximate knowledge of the past as it had once been lived. For that, a collective effort of cooperation and critique was necessary.

Alun Munslow juxtaposed the typical postmodernist rejection of traditional truth as a mere "ersatz truth," which resulted from the arbitrary closure of historical inquiry. Its underlying concept of reality as "being out there" was a self-deception. Instead, "history may be defined as a language-based manufacturing process in which written historical interpretation is assembled or produced by historians."[70] An ardent proponent of an unconditional postmodernism, Keith Jenkins affirmed the centrality of the issue of truth when he argued that the postmodernist challenge must aim at the very foundations of past historiography—the assertion of Truth. The capital letter T connoted *the* authoritative statement on the past. The primary aim had to be "the dissolution of the referent into representation which, for many lower case historians [those adhering to the empirical method] signals the dissolution of their history by postmodern means." Jenkins maintained that those concerned about the role of truth in history did not understand that epistemology had never enabled us to know the actual past and will never do so. What historical accounts have offered as truth have only been "useful fictions" enforced by power. As he put it, "there is nothing definite to get out of it [history] other than that which we put in it."[71] The assertion of one truth was an instrument for intimidation and domination. At times, Jenkins was even blunter when he found that might made right. In more restrained terms, Hans Kellner criticized historians for behaving "as though their researches into the past, as though their writings were 'about' it [the actual past], and as though 'it' were as real as the text which is the object of their labours."[72]

Voices of Opposition. Critics of postmodernist theory maintained just as firmly that without an effective search for truth, rooted in referentiality to the actual past, and an effective cognitive element all intellectual endeavors were beside the point. Richard Evans, reflecting the sharp edges of the debate, spoke of "intellectual barbarians at the disciplinary gates" who denied even the possibility of access to an extralinguistic actual past.[73] According to Arthur Marwick, postmodernism portrayed history as "worthless" and for Lawrence Stone it caused a crisis of history. Gabrielle Spiegel, despite her empathy for the linguistic approach, found that the "dissolution of the materiality of the verbal sign, its ruptured relation to the extralinguistic reality, entails the dissolution of history, since it denies the ability of language to 'relate' to (or account for) any reality other than itself."[74] As will be seen, some Marxist critics would be equally adamant.

In 1987 and, then, in 1994, Gertrude Himmelfarb offered her critique of the dissolution of all that was stable into a fluid world only temporarily stabilized by linguistic constructs or by the Foucauldian affirmation of power as arbiter of truth. The dissolution of the actual past into an indeterminate chaotic flux, in which neither a human being as stable agent nor a world as objective context existed, created a tabula rasa. Onto that blank slate, "historians can impose upon the past their own determinacy."[75] These changes corroded historical veracity so that history could be written as one liked it. In line with her long-standing opposition to all relativism and theory-based historiography, she reaffirmed the essential elements of historiographical praxis: the centrality of the search for one truth about an actual and rationally accessible past, reliance on documentary evidence, carefully delimited interpretations, the assumption of meaning and order inherent in past reality, and affirmation of an accessible extralinguistic reality. Truth about the actual past must remain the aim of the historian's activities although historians knew how fraught with danger the process of truth finding was.

Perez Zagorin also reaffirmed the traditional mastery of the past through the use of empirical methods as well as the assertion of an ordered universe understandable by rational means. He denied the postmodernists' claim to a superior understanding of history that he considered a nonunderstanding. Postmodernism, by excluding an accessible past reality condemned itself to be a purely aesthetic endeavor concerned with endless analysis of texts and no interest in contexts. Particularly corrosive was the exaggeration of the role of language in history into more than the medium for the findings of historians. Its mediating role could be fulfilled better without the radical change the poststructuralist postmodernists advocated.

The traditional concept of truth affirmed by the critics of postmodernism added up to an arrangement of methods, approaches, and attitudes that was marked by a cautious trust in ascertaining the nonlinguistic reality, rationality, openness to revisions, limitation of claims for findings, and deemphasis of the subjective. As for the dimension of time, they dealt with it in its fullness—granting the equal importance of change and continuity.

These critics of postmodernism have denied that the stipulation of a world dominated by change had been or could be successfully translated into a theory of history. One argument for their judgment has been the implications of the new concept of truth for action on behalf of the desired postmodernity. That truth could not be used to provide enduring and universal legitimation for the postmodernist agenda: to condemn univocality, the exclusion of "others," and truth as servants of special interests. Neither did it give authority to condemnations of the present academic history as a phenomenon of "reactive capitalist/bourgeois culture" (Sande Cohen). Nor did social activist scholars welcome unreservedly the new interpretation of truth. Some of them observed the reduction of the activist potential of knowledge when, for example, even science was reduced to rhetoric.[76]

The Debate on Evidence and Objectivity. Two pillars upheld the traditional theory of truth: evidence and objectivity. The one delivered the crucial link to the past as once lived. The other aimed at negating the influence of life's context on the historian. Together they held out the possibility of at least an approximation to a true account.

In the debate on evidence, postmodernists used by now familiar arguments against any link to the actual past via evidence. They changed the status of the evidence or, as historians often spoke of it, of the sources. The critical process leading from evidence to facts (statements made on the basis of sources also involving interpretation) would be blocked by declaring all evidence to be not direct traces of the past but linguistic constructs of and about that past—be they narratives, texts, or discourses. Or, to put it into historical terms, there were no primary, only secondary sources. Historians must realize the impossibility of facts understood in the traditional sense, since the past has come to us with discursive constructs or narratives of past people "imprinted in the evidence."[77] No ever-so-sophisticated methodology could sort objective "facts" from linguistic constructs and then reconstruct the past from accumulated facts because historians were working in a cycle of discourses or narratives—those constructed by the people of the past followed by those constructed about the original ones. With even that which historians had seen as evidence of objective contexts having become a purely linguistic phenomenon, historians must replace the fetishism of facts (the "factualist/empiricist idea") with a pure constructivism.[78] Direct reference to the actual past through objective remainders was an illusion.

The difficulty with an epistemology lacking referential truth as its standard would show when postmodernists had recourse to quasi-standards. Jenkins, for example, condemned traditional historiography as a bourgeois ideological construct against which postmodernists must wage a relentless attack. However, the rejection of the traditional approaches to history (mixed empirical/interpretive ones) on the basis of a distinction between good and bad ideologies used a standard problematical for poststructuralist postmodernists. It fell back not on purely formal but on substantive arguments that were off-limits to them.

Ardent defenses against such challenges to history's ways of truth finding were mounted by many historians. A systematic and continuous criticism of the devaluation of evidence came from Geoffrey Elton, who already in 1967 had battled the relativism of E. H. Carr. The critical focus on relativism of any kind and degree remained the same in his *Return to Essentials: Some Reflections on the Present State of Historical Inquiry,* published nearly a quarter of a century later (1991): relativism of any kind and degree. Keeping the postmodernism debate strictly on epistemological grounds, Elton and other critics repeated their conditions for a sufficiently authoritative historical truth. They were the critical study of evidence combined with tight restraints on interpretations.

Gertrude Himmelfarb agreed. She had shared with Elton and other historians the dislike of social science and theory-oriented histories. These were too far removed from past reality, which had its specific, always contingency-beset order and was elucidable only by rigorous study of the evidence. Perez Zagorin spoke for many social historians on behalf of the traditional mastery of the past through the use of empirical methods. These and other critics insisted that without the guidance of objective evidence all interpretations were possible. But the chaos historians feared, as a result, one advocate of a radical postmodernist approach celebrated as a source of hope. "History now appears to be just one more foundationless, positioned expression in a world of foundationless, positioned expressions."[79]

Traditional history's second epistemological pillar has been objectivity. Since Thucydides, historians have affirmed objectivity though being always aware of its precariousness. The possibility of objectivity's ideal realization had been maintained only by naive historians and, later, in a more sophisticated way, by those who advocated history as a pure science. Optimal rather than perfect objectivity, one contributing to the sufficient degree of proper correspondence between account and reality, had been the actual aim of practicing historians. Only then could emerge from the evidence the order and meaning inherent in past life. Yet in the present age of skepticism, even such limited claims for the feasibility of objectivity came under suspicion. Thus, Peter Novick's well-known assessment of the American historical profession targeted its blatant failings in the realization of objectivity and came to the relativist conclusion that there was "no king in Israel."[80] But postmodernist theory denied even the feasibility of historians achieving an objective stance. Such an attempt has been called naive, spurious, and negligent of the insight "that historical accounts were subservient to various powers and interests."[81]

The majority of historians has not been ready to write off objectivity. Elton was an uncompromising advocate for this majority as he held firmly to the possibility and necessity of striving for objectivity, however fallible. The rejection of objectivity in the search for truth "leads straight to a formless nihilism which allows any historian to say whatever he likes."[82] Postmodernism was an especially destructive nihilism. In his defense of objectivity, Zagorin pointed out two often forgotten aspects of objectivity, interpretive discipline and collegial critique.

The postmodernist rejection of objectivity as a remainder of an outdated truth finding used a second justification. With the dissolution of the self-identical individual into the linguistic stream of life, historians had become integral parts not masters of the world of discourses and texts. There could be no longer a juxtaposition of observer and observed in which objectivity could play a role. With it had disappeared the tension originating in the conflict between subjective interpretations and the objective meaning of the past. Now objectivity meant to join one's subjectivity to that of others in affirming the multiperspectival nature of knowledge. As a new kind of "objectivity," historians had to practice self-reflexivity, that is, to assess critically and openly the process of construction used for producing their accounts. Such a truth, devoid of any consensus seeking, would hold no temptations for illusions of stability (closures).

Two American historians provided examples for different reactions to the postmodernist rejection of traditional objectivity. Thomas Haskell argued against the widely voiced view of objectivity as based on the pretense of the historian's isolation from the given context. He appreciated the postmodernists' attention to language but protested against their depiction of objectivity as an illusion based on a pretended indifference and passivity (in order for the historian to be the sensitive antenna for a nonexistent inherent order and meaning). Objectivity resulted from an "ascetic self-discipline" that enabled historians to resist the temptation to write what was pleasing, unrealistic, ill-scrutinized, bordering on propaganda, or to ignore opposing viewpoints. Historians, still with firm identities, must practice self-control, detachment, and fairness, the deliberate standing back to see their own and the different viewpoints together—despite their own positions, even enthusiasms.[83] This posture validated the traditional search for truth and the historian's continued agency in life and analysis. By implication, objectivity also was necessary for a democratic society's discourse.

A divergent stance was taken by David Harlan, who agreed fully with the postmodernist rejection of the traditional concept of objectivity. Impatient with what he saw as academic historiography's lack of creative imagination, especially on values and social vision, Harlan referred to objectivity as the "dull-witted monarch, who despotically ruled the discipline of history since the late nineteenth century."[84] Postmodernists would add to that the phrase "with evil intent." They would also agree with Harlan's contention that "the irony is not simply that after two hundred years of searching we have yet to come up with the hoped-for set of objective criteria; it is rather that we do not *need* them (emphasis in original)."[85] Yet Harlan's willingness to abandon the objectivity ideal really stemmed from his contempt for the prevailing historiography that he saw as engaged in an illusory methodology-obsessed and action-inhibiting search for truth. Against that he put the hope that the postmodernist world of flux would be the optimal condition for the reinvigoration of the liberal social imagination. However, such an assertion collided with the postmodernist injunction against all privileged truth. The deconstruction of objectivity could not be used as a preparatory step for the realization of an authoritative activist ideal. Harlan's attempt to affirm the postmodernist views but to preserve an element of permanence in the flux pointed once more to the built-in conflict between the postmodernist stipulation of multiple truths and the legitimation of purposeful action.

For postmodernists, objectivity was part of a history that was passé. It was part of the pretense of history to solve complex problems in a sophisticated way, when in reality it kept the "ramshackle phenomena" of present historical inquiry alive. The historical nexus would best be helped not by straining for an illusory objectivity but by helping to "to construct imaginaries of radical emancipation." Compared "to the kind of historical knowledge of the past provided by empirical historians . . . a postmodern *posthistoire* future seems a desirable possibility."[86] Such a vision meant for historians (an admittedly quite diverse group) the abandonment of the restraints imposed by the objective context and by the findings of historians of the past. "If poststructuralists are correct that we cannot fathom the original meaning of the texts offering us a window on other human experience, we will remain imprisoned in the present." If this were all that postmodernist theory could deliver it was no "small wonder that historians draw upon their practice of reconstructing the past in order to resist this verdict."[87]

■ 17 **THE METANARRATIVE CONTROVERSY**

THE ARGUMENT AGAINST THE HISTORICAL
METANARRATIVE: LYOTARD, FOUCAULT,
DERRIDA, BAUDRILLARD

The General Argument

The Motive for Rejection. Since the 1980s, the term metanarrative has replaced the formerly used phrase philosophy of history. The prefix *meta* (Greek for beyond) indicated a narrative that overarched other narratives. Like a philosophy of history, it linked smaller historical accounts together to a single narrative that stretched over long periods of time, if not all of history. Yet the use of the term metanarrative indicated more than a mere change in terminology. It signified the ascendancy of a way to make sense of history in accord with the postmodernist concept of truth. Philosophers of history had seen their task as the discovery of the overall meaning inherent in past events by discerning the permanent structures and forces at work in them. Metanarratives were seen, like all concepts and narratives, as linguistic constructs, which disclaimed any link to objective schemes of order and meaning. Such a link was blamed for all claims to a privileged position, illegitimate in terms of the poststructuralist postmodernist concept of truth.

Logically, the revision of the concepts of truth and truth finding occupied the very core of postmodernist thought. Chronologically, however, the rejection of the metanarrative preceded that revision. Disappointment with progressive, including Marxist, metanarratives provided the trigger for postmodernist thought. Indeed, the rejection of the metanarrative was not based on the wish to demonstrate some flaw in the epistemology of progressive thought but on the one to indict progress on behalf of a new truth. Lyotard expressed that when he concluded "the crisis of the modern ideals concerns the ideal of emancipation itself, that of the Enlightenment. In two centuries we have learned that the technical development, the increase in prosperity and knowledge, the progress of the avant-garde, the gaining of democratic freedoms does not necessarily lead to the universal progress of humankind."[88] Instead, the human catastrophes ascribed to the metanarrative of progress made that and any other metanarrative dangerous illusions. Hence Lyotard defined "*postmodern* as incredulity toward the metanarrative," although the blunt word rejection would have described his intent better.[89] This call for the rejection of the metanarrative raised the general question concerning the proper scope and kind of meaning, especially a unitary one, historians could affirm in their accounts.

The Limits to the Postmodernist Critique. In pressing their argument against histories of a universal or quasi-universal scope, postmodernists should have critically confronted not just progressive but also two other types of philosophies of history or metanarratives that have dominated historical interpretation in Western culture.

The prevalent metanarrative in the ancient period relied for its unity on the perception of an inherent tendency of states and cultures to follow the cycle of ascendancy, acme of power and prosperity, and decadence. The narratives of particular states, cultures, or civilizations had their unifying bond—their metanarrative—in that universal and "deeper" dimension: the teleological pattern of the life cycle, here energized by a variety of forces. Later, the cyclical pattern played a subsidiary role in medieval history as the four-empire theory, was fully revived in the Renaissance period, shaped into a complex system by Giambattista Vico, and given new prominence in the twentieth century by Spengler, Toynbee, and others. In their criticism and rejection of metanarratives, postmodernists have virtually ignored the cyclical paradigm. They would have found congenial its affirmation of the relativity and uniqueness of cultures in the aimless sequence-of-cultures pattern.[90] But the view of cultures as totalities with clear identities and the teleological nature of the (cyclical) pattern would have been unacceptable. And there was the incompatibility of poststructuralist postmodernist hopes for a dynamic postmodernist age with the grim image of the cultural cycle's unavoidable stage of decadence and subsequent static posthistory.

Postmodernist critiques of the metanarrative also did not focus on the second model, the late ancient and medieval Christian view of history with an even clearer universal and singular development. In this case, postmodernists accepted modernity's verdict of that model's outdatedness, by virtue of its ontological features: the governance of history by Divine Providence and the ultimate permanence in a different ontological sphere.

Postmodernists focused their criticism exclusively on the third type of metanarrative: the progress view of history as the master matrix of history's meaning. Their opposition manifested itself in the searching for and purging of modern concepts with a perceived metaphysical (that is continuous) quality. All meanings were to be ephemeral, infinitely pliable, multiple, and, while at a far distance from being stable and inherent, quasi-stabilizing linguistic phenomena. Without appreciable links to the material contexts or spanning long term segments (continuity), they displayed none of what has been contemptuously labeled the "metaphysics of presence" (Fredric Jameson)— a claim to durable validity derived from mere presence. This was a denial spurred on by the postmodernist supposition that all versions of progressive history carried the mark of the Enlightenment's fatal mistake: the retention of reason as the central and permanent shaping force. As traditional critics had pointed out, the metaphysics of God was reshaped by the *philosophes* into one of Reason, transformed by Hegel into one of the Absolute Spirit, and transfigured by Marx into one of economic justice. This residual metaphysical element provided a "deeper" level of existence that was more durable and powerful than the historical one. In it originated the *telos* propelling history toward an end stage of fulfillment. The postmodernist world of flux was not compatible with such an affirmation of continuity. The ideal world of ever-shifting constructed meanings could not accommodate any element of continuity beyond the briefest constructed one. All else evoked the suspicion of an incomplete purge of metaphysics and raised the specter of authoritative truth with its perceived dire consequences.

Traditional versus Postmodernist Rejections of the Metanarrative. Often overlooked in postmodernist arguments against the metanarratives has been the long-standing hostility of most historians to philosophies of history. For historians, philosophies of history were untimely syntheses in which final conclusions were drawn before the empirical database justified doing so. Historians also objected to the radical reduction of complex matters to the working of one or a few basic forces.

However, the postmodernists' rejection of the metanarrative did not focus on the gap between evidence and statements. That objection was made irrelevant by the different status of evidence in the postmodernist concept of truth. Central to the rejection of the metanarrative was the condemnation of metanarratives as too dangerous. These narratives had served as bases for the oppressive ideological attempts to reconstruct the world that have caused so much suffering. This ethical/political argument against philosophies of history resembled closely that of some modernists.[91] The agreement came on the reason for the condemnation of the metanarrative and involved especially the neo-positivist philosopher Karl Popper. An exile from the Nazi threat, he considered metanarratives (which he subsumed idiosyncratically under the term historicism) as too dangerous for their totalitarian tendencies and argued for more reason, logic, and empirical evidence as proper remedies. But postmodernists counted these very remedies among the forces of modernity implicated in the ills of the twentieth century. The progress view was not to be rejected for its faulty reasoning but for its inherent tendency to legitimize oppressive behavior and institutions. Progress was inescapably evil since it knew only one development and one end. Force had to be applied to shape all of life in the already-known image of the future. Just like other metanarratives that of progress relied on a metaphysics of permanent forces and patterns for achieving continuity in history. This progress legitimized oppression and the exertion of power on behalf of authoritative truth.

When poststructuralist postmodernists put forth different arguments against the metanarrative in general and that of progress specifically, they faced the task of formulating the conditions for historical entities without having recourse to meta-, grand, or master narratives linked to a presumed inherent order.[92] Their proposals varied in specifics but agreed on the central aim to banish any continuity not marked as constructed. The new historical accounts would be devoid of those (metaphysical) claims to privilege on the basis of permanence or continuity that had been the origin of murderous ideologies. In these accounts, with their celebration of the dominance of change, the existential tension would not be diminished or resolved by a new and presumably perfect order. Instead the goal must be a change of attitudes, especially the abandonment of all quests for a new stability (with its new privileged views and groups). All the affirmation must be given to ceaseless change in the fluid world. The tension was to be reduced constantly.

Lyotard's Winding Path to *Petits récits*

The Influential Call to Action. Early in his career, Lyotard formulated the postmodernist programmatic exhortation to display "incredulity toward metanarratives."[93] All along, the motive for the exhortation remained the profound disappointment with progress. "Now we must note in general, that the historical development goes on and on and brings none of the hoped for emancipations."[94] At one time, the progressive narrative had spread a powerful message of hope and by virtue of it had overshadowed every other historical narrative. Now, that progress could not deliver on its promise of development upward from ignorance, oppression, and superstition (non-rational causes of misery) toward the perfection of a rationality, people saw its real nature and found it morally objectionable. This condemnation included the Marxist version of progress, which Lyotard at one time had tried to reform.[95] His firewall against the metanarrative was the contention of the incommensurability of all historical perspectives. In line with the required plurality of truth, no totalizing and universal views of history could be tolerated. There were to be no more "orgies of theories, discourses, and political movements" of a meta-scope.[96]

Another Triadic View of Human Development. Surprisingly, Lyotard's *The Postmodern Condition* knew an overall scheme of history, which, like other postmodernist historical accounts, had a three-stage overall structure (harmony in unity, the turbulent historical period, harmony in diversity) that even seemed to give postmodernist historical accounts a progressive "good" ending.

An early—innocent and natural—stage in human development was characterized by a harmonious unity between narrative and social bonds. The narrative affirmed the forms and rules of traditional society as timeless and had sufficient authority to act as the bond of social unity. As for legitimation, the narrative's performance sufficed. In that society's organic community, the existential tension that in the historical period made human life so turbulent remained strictly limited since change and continuity were still routinely aligned to each other.

The second stage (theoretically the historical, but practically the modern one) began with a secular version of the (biblical and Hindu) story of the Fall: the end of organic unity came with the rise of scientific knowledge and its discourse. Its narrative replaced the traditional narrative when it usurped a role beyond its task of supporting the existing order and, thereby, destroyed the natural bond between narrative and social order. Before, narratives had been anchored in the traditions and customs of the society, were noninstrumental, and aimed to report and denote rather than prescribe. The scientific narrative or discourse represented not just one of many possible variations in the collective discourse, but, with its entirely different view of the world, it claimed exclusive rights in the process of shaping society. Instead of the traditional narrative's plural proofs, one proof only counted—the scientific one. Or in Lyotard's terms, there was only one legitimate language game in society. And there was no way out, since the claims of tradition with its developmental or historical approach had been banned. The scientific world view had no specific context to which it was bound. It had no limits in time and space, but was destined to be the dominant force everywhere and forever.

What Lyotard called the "pragmatics of scientific knowledge" no longer found its base in the self-legitimation of society. The legitimation of its authority rested in a truth value abstracted from the social group and its bonds. Plural proofs of truth yielded to one proof of truth only. The legitimation for scientific knowledge and its discourse came from the perceived progress itself—a self-legitimation. At the end of progress stood a society that accepted scientific knowledge for shaping its discourse. Yet such an expectation was based on a special narrative: the metanarrative of progress.

Prompted by his disenchantment with progress, Lyotard formulated his program for the delegitimation of progress. His call for a general "incredulity toward the metanarrative" was meant as the first step in the destruction of the dominant position of scientific knowledge. That knowledge would then have to face up to its limits and its desertion of truth in favor of "performativity," which shaped all questions asked and answers given. Performativity referred to such criteria as "the best possible input/output equation." Lyotard's postmodernism grew out of this "context of the crisis of narratives."[97]

With the rejection of all metanarratives—not only of progress—began Lyotard's third age, the postmodern one. In his case, the break in the interpretation of truth finding did not seem so sharp as in Foucault's and Derrida's work. Lyotard viewed the postmodern age as developing out of the modern period, sometimes even considering it as a phase of modernity. Modernism could be rectified by revisions, which would strip the scientific narrative of its excessive claims and make it only denotational and not prescriptive. The result would not be undisturbed tranquility but a society of coexistent languages engaged in an agonistic struggle of language games or, later on, of phrase regimes. Each of these games had its own rules incompatible with the others. Flux without any dominance would prevail and prevent new hegemonies founded on claims to represent true knowledge. Even the striving for consensus was dangerous as it did violence to the heterogeneity of language games.

As for narratives in the postmodern age, they would need to be restricted to those of small scale—*petits récits*, as Lyotard called them. These "little narratives," where the historical nexus between past, present, and the expectations for the future had tight limits as to space and time and therefore lacked the grand narrative's claims. They were the key elements of the future society and its analysis. Postmodernist critics have found Lyotard's rejection of the metanarrative not sufficiently credible since it did not repudiate forcefully enough the claims of empirical or scientific knowledge. In a more general way, other critics questioned whether the historical development Lyotard described was not based on so sturdy a continuity as to make his account resemble closely a new metanarrative—this time legitimizing postmodernity. Lyotard eventually pursued other interests with inquiries into the problems of semiology, the problem of justice, and the proper relation between immaterial and material reality.[98]

Foucault's Metanarrative of Power

Temptations and Resistance. Foucault wrote works that by their subject matter constantly tempted him to conform to a progressive metanarrative. He tried not to yield in his opposition to a continuous narrative, specifically rejecting suggestions of ameliorative tendencies in history. He also strove to expose the presence and instrumental role of permanent (metaphysical) elements and their privileged positions. He even avoided the term "total history" made prominent in the 1960s and 1970s by his contemporaries, the historians of the *Annales* group. These scholars knew totalities with a diachron dimension in their studies of long series and others with a synchron quality, such as the concept of *mentalité*, in the quest for grasping the totality of life at a given time. Foucault objected to assertions of both types of totalities. For him, too, any concept of a total history spanning across centuries or all of society harbored the fatal temptation to think in terms of grand developments with their oppressive tendencies.

Like other postmodernists, Foucault was especially critical of progressive and evolutionary views of history. His predisposition against a smoothly linear course of history had been reinforced by the works of some historians of science. Gaston Bachelard, Jean Cavailles, and Georges Canguilhem had emphasized discontinuity in the formulation of concepts of development as well as in shifts in discursive practices. Foucault made it one of his major principles.

If all claims for totalities as substantial wholes were negated by showing their rather arbitrary construction, a new type of historical record, even historicity, would result. All metahistory would be replaced by "mere" history, in which temporary discursive configurations appeared and dissolved in quick succession in the infinite flux of life.

Foucault found the realization of his program difficult. His early *Madness and Civilization* (1964; English translation 1972) tried to demonstrate the constructions of the phenomenon of madness in various periods of Western culture. Foucault's rejection of the metanarrative came in his refusal to view the modern treatment of the mad as the result of a process of amelioration—as progress. History knew no long- or short-term telos, center, or cumulative development. However, Foucault would not be completely successful in staying the course in banning long-lasting elements and totalities. The phenomenon of madness itself (that which was constructed in specific forms) still remained a permanent element across the discourses concerning it. And the periods, differing from one another by ways in which they constructed perceptions of madness, represented clearly defined entities without crossover elements—totalities in all but names.

Foucault's determination to elide permanent elements or processes was fused, in his early works, to the hermeneutics of suspicion. The construction of madness followed the pattern of Nietzsche's duality of the apollinian and dionysian aspects of Greek culture. The repressed reality was the dionysian element, so contrary to harmony and order for those in power but also so necessary to a full human life according to Nietzsche and Foucault. The latter never accepted the emancipatory interpretation of *Madness and Civilization,* propagated by opponents to contemporary psychiatry in the 1960s and 1970s (R. D. Laing). The claim that the mad were the really sane was never Foucault's. He was not interested in "liberating" the mad. The modern ways of coping with madness were means of control, too, although more subtle ones.

The tendency to perceive totalities also was not always successfully avoided in Foucault's dealing with the concept of *epistemes,* which played so significant a role in his early work. The epistemes performed a foundational role in the differentiation between the disciplines of knowledge and between cultures. He asserted that "in any given culture and at any given moment, there is always one *episteme* that defines the conditions of possibilities of all knowledge whether expressed in theory or silently invested in practice."[99] Epistemes were constructed configurations manifested in cultural phenomena and gave temporary contextual continuity to them. Even, Foucault's periodization of Western history since the Renaissance was based on such unity through epistemes. Their too-close proximity to totalities of a "real" kind (a quasi-essence) became the reason for their abandonment in Foucault's later work.

The struggle against progressive (ameliorative) tendencies did not diminish in his later works. In *Discipline and Punish* (1977), Foucault denied modern penal practices any superiority over those of the past. The diminution of crude corporeal punishment was paid for by new types of tighter and more forceful coercion that cast their net of disciplinary practices wider and wider. And while Foucault always found the concepts of sexuality of Western culture too limiting, in his works on the history of knowledge and sexuality he rejected the view of the history of sexuality as the story of emancipation. He argued that the sexual repression theory (including the version that spoke of suppression in the interest of economic production) presupposed a "right" approach to sexuality and made sexuality a mythical force to be freed. Foucault saw sexuality purely in terms of behavior and its control—one of the bodily experiences related to pleasure. He demonstrated his views in an analysis of the practice of Christian confession, which for him was the transformation of sex into discourse for the purpose of control.

The Centrality of Power, Again. One force prevailed in all of Foucault's work: power. Early on, power still represented a primarily negative force. Power relations produced a "false consciousness" of the world through enforced distortions. But that fact could be exposed and in the course of time, remedied. Thus, such a process pointed at a truth hidden by machinations and, with it, to a metanarrative of emancipation in the realization of truth. Foucault proceeded beyond the hermeneutics of suspicion toward the view of power as simply a given force. From this permanent (albeit purely formal) feature of the human existence there was no escape. The whole web of human relations was pervaded by it. Therefore, its absence or special presence could not be a goal of any discourse. Instead, power as a bipolar force fit more harmoniously into Foucault's world of discourses with its arbitrary transformations of one discourse into other discourses. Power's manifestations in life could be hegemonies as well as oppositions to them. Its tendency to closure, that is, to stabilize relations in favor of some individual or group, posed a constant threat to the world of flux. But its contrary tendency to fuel opposition constantly restored the flux. This ongoing interplay did not lead, as the dialectic had, to a proper resolution. History showed no more than a sequence of attempted or realized hegemonies and their eventual destruction. But did such a view not represent a metanarrative of a cyclical nature with a wavelike shape? In that case, the permanence of power had the effect of drawing Foucault's postmodernism back into the very realm of the historical metanarrative. In addition, Foucault recognized an important element of continuity: the enforcement of order and discipline proceeded from brutal and open enforcement to internal and hidden controls. And there were the ages: Renaissance, classical, modern, followed by that of ultimate insight into the human existence, the postmodern. These ambiguities about the metanarrative would pose a special problem for Foucault's ambition to design a postmodernist political action program.

Derrida's Rejection of Metanarratives

Deconstruction of the Metanarrative as Text. Without addressing the problem of the metanarrative directly, Jacques Derrida formulated general critical arguments that were destructive of metanarratives. These narratives have based their claims for the universality and unity of all of history on permanent nonlinguistic foundations and essences. Among these foundational propositions was the crucial one that the text did represent a nonlinguistic reality. But metanarratives only evoked the illusion of objective unity, stability, and universal validity, when in fact there was no access to meanings and types of knowledge about the world outside of language. Derrida reminded everybody that "*there is nothing outside of the text* (emphasis in original)."[100] He spelled out in the principle of deconstruction both his objection to the metanarrative and the techniques for dismantling its claims to represent a reality beyond itself and to derive a privileged position from it.

Derrida's key argument against the deceptive solidity of the meta-narrative emphasized that the term "text" pointed the careful reader not only to that which was "present" in the text but also to that which was "absent" from it. That "other" was the excluded one, who by implication was always an oppressed one. The absence could result either from a conscious suppression—where the "other" was forcefully integrated into the "same," that meant to fit it into the known categories of the system—or simply from an omission. In that concept of the suppressed "other" Derrida found the ethical rationale for opposing metanarratives. They tended to preserve their continuity and, thereby, they tended to prolong the suffering of the "other."

In textual analysis, deconstruction located in the absence of the "other" the origin of the dynamic tension, the spur to change. In the purely linguistic "reality" that the historian investigated, the inescapable and paradoxical in-terlinking of "presence" and "absence" denied to any text (always a deceptive assertion of a solid "presence") the quality of being a stable and autonomous entity. In simpler words, all that we perceived as reality, including economic, social, historical, and institutional structures, was no more than a discursive and unstable network. There could be no reality in terms of stable identi-ties of persons, objects, and forces. They were tension-filled indicators of the linguistic differentiation process. This process gave meaning to words by the shifts in the relationships of words to other words and represented the irreducible reality. In such a world, there was no place for authoritative narratives and discourses, certainly not for the traditional metanarratives.

Deconstruction of the Unitary and Universal Narrative. Traditional histori-cal metanarratives—particularly the progressive ones—claimed to reflect the work of the Logos, which, as the ultimate self-identical (an a priori ontolog-ical) force, gave intelligible order to the world. Derrida called this approach logocentrism; a term he preferred to that of metaphysics. It established the existence and dominant role of the Logos as the ultimate ontological layer of permanence. Why then metanarratives? Because "logocentrism and the metaphysics of presence" were expressions of "the exigent, powerful, sys-tematic, and irrepressible desire" to put an end to the differentiation process with its endless production of meanings. That desire aimed at finding an ulti-mate and stable reality (the "transcendental signified").[101] Derrida opposed all such attempts to find a stable irreducible ultimate behind or below all phenomena, most directly those of Hegel and the varieties of Hegelianism.

But not even the views of his kindred in philosophy, Heidegger, escaped. The latter, too, strove to free philosophy from metaphysics (or in Derrida's terms, logocentrism). But, until late in his life, Heidegger searched for a linguistic expression that had an immediate and perfect link to Being (the ultimate unity of all beings). Derrida saw in such a longing a dangerous nostalgia. Beyond language there was only a realm of "nonconcepts" and "undecidables."

Logocentrism has prevailed in Western culture since the ancient Greek philosophers. The progressive metanarrative, a teleological logocentrism, offered the (illusory) assurance of future permanence following the full emancipation of reason. Then, contingency together with the fear of chaos would be permanently checked and the existential tension resolved. Derrida was confident that he had supplied in deconstruction a theoretical framework to postmodernists who wished to deprive the logocentric view of its privileged status—in the case of history, the metanarrative.

In theory, the Derridean view of history knew no preferences among cultures, since all of them were dangerous grand scale attempts at closure. His argument also could not but lead to the contention that each culture experienced necessarily its own "other" that challenged, changed, and eroded it. Therefore, all cultures must experience deconstruction. Historians would assist in that deconstruction by demonstrating the tension-ridden unity of metanarratives. Yet, so far, Derrida and other poststructuralist postmodernists have focused exclusively on the deconstruction of Western culture's understanding of the world and history. Derrida maintained that Western culture's logocentrism, with its attendant ethnocentrism, created an especially numerous and oppressed "other" that argued against that culture's "presence." Hence Western culture had become particularly harmful to the "other," be it the Third World or those harmed in its own society, when it attempted to order the world according to the expectations of progress.

The Auxiliary Struggle against Phonocentrism. For a brief moment, a quasi-progressive element seemed to assert itself when Derrida claimed the priority of writing over speech. But the claim to priority was not argued for primarily in terms of time, despite Derrida's startling statement "I shall try to show later that there is no linguistic sign before writing."[102] He advanced the claim because he considered the present secondary position of writing relative to speech a major cause of logocentrism. The argument rested on the contention that in the logocentric Western culture speech gained its superior ranking due to the representational mode of thinking. Spoken words were held to be in closer proximity to those mental processes that made reflections on reality possible. Spoken words enabled phonocentrism. "When words are spoken the speaker and the listener are supposed to be simultaneously present to one another; they are supposed to be the same, pure unmediated presence. This ideal of perfect self-presence, of the immediate possession of meaning, is what is expressed by the phonocentric necessity. Writing, on the other hand, is considered subversive in so far as it creates a spatial and temporal distance between the author and the audience; writing presupposes the absence of the author and so we can never be sure exactly what is meant by a written text; it can have many different meanings as opposed to a single unifying one."[103] All that writing was credited with was the mere phonetic transcription of speech's words. This privileged position of speech made Western culture inescapably ethnocentric and, by implication, also oppressive to the "other" and hence ethically wrong. But Derrida maintained that "this phonocentric necessity did not develop into the systematic logocentric metaphysics in any non-European culture. Logocentrism is a uniquely European phenomenon."[104]

In sum, against the perceived logocentric relationship between consciousness, speech, and writing, sponsored by phonocentrism, Derrida put the assertion that writing did have priority over speech. That alone could lead writing out of the position of a secondary channel for transmission of concepts from consciousness. Language would then have the full autonomy that even Saussure had not given it—the necessary condition to destroy the hegemonic position of logocentrism and with it the progressive metanarrative. Then only could essential transcendental signifiers such as God, a stable self, reality, and freedom be abandoned.

Although Derrida modified the rigor of his assertion, critics have pointed out that if the assertion of the priority of writing could neither be based on temporal nor on logical grounds, no other priority could be cited. At best, he could plead for a contemporaneity of speech and writing, which, however, would not be corrosive of logocentric and representational thinking. And the metanarrative's fate would have to be weighed on a different scale.

A Contrarian's View: Jean Baudrillard

In the years before his views became rather eccentric, Baudrillard agreed with the common postmodernist view that modernity represented a characteristic mode of civilization. Its major trait was the opposition to tradition, historically speaking to all anterior cultures. Yet, modernity "in the process had itself become oppressive."[105] Postmodernity, the third of the stages after premodernity and modernity, would correct that. In it, the reductionism of Freud and Marx would be rejected and the full reality of the present would be included in the analysis of consumer society, mass media, and modern art. The world created by these and other features had a powerful transforming power. Here, Baudrillard's assessment of postmodernity came close to that of the structural postmodernists. The conditions of life created by mass production, communication, and consumption would lead to total stagnation. Its impact had yet to be completely internalized by people.

Thus, Baudrillard's postmodernity offered a basically stable world without hope for amelioration that must be accepted stoically or passively by people. The new world only had the simulated dynamic of a disco with its rapidly flashing lights. In a startling turn, what had been a poststructuralist postmodernist analysis acquired a structural postmodernist prognosis. In Baudrillard's argument the observer could find Henry Adams's prediction that the rapidly increasing speed of innovations would lead to the state of entropy and Nietzsche's prediction of a fundamentally bored populace experiencing the endless recurrence of the same.

On other occasions, Baudrillard employed concepts that conformed well to poststructuralist postmodernist thinking, above all that of simulation. The latter played a key role in his view on the development of the understanding of value. The early stage with its symbolic exchange, that lacked abstract measuring standards, was followed by the stage of mercantile value with its emphasis on production of goods (still of objects). A most important change occurred in postmodernity and its society of simulation. In it the symbolic exchange involved elements of life previously not accounted for as mercantile values. Above all, the postmodern world of simulation knew only signs without referents.

Reflections on the Postmodernist Rejection of Historical Metanarratives

A review of the poststructuralist postmodernist rejection of the metanarrative provided another reminder that postmodernist struggles against the metanarrative and totalities were not moved primarily by epistemological considerations. They were moral protests against developments in the twentieth century. Lyotard, Foucault, and Derrida subjected metanarratives to withering critiques for the crucial support they rendered to hegemony and oppression by dominating all other historical narratives and repressing dissenters. Thus, postmodernists would see in the progressive view little more than a legitimation for exploitation inside of Western culture and for colonialism outside of it.

The brunt of the blame came to rest on the view of history as progress. A judgment that often overlooked its proper limits. First, much of the horror had been caused by fascism, a movement that was hostile to the Enlightenment and the progressive view of history. Thus, the condemnation of both of them would have to be at least modified. Second, the existence of the metanarrative could not be held against practicing historians since they have in general been opposed to grand views of history, such as progress. Historians criticized the loose link between a sound evidentiary base and interpretation. Third, postmodernists have mostly overlooked the fact that their oppositional impulse originated in their ethical disenchantment with what they saw as modernity's unkept promises. Hence, their protest had some of its roots in the very values and ideals of the Enlightenment.

Furthermore, in accord with the postmodernist preference of change over continuity, historians would have to also condemn the grand historical nexus of progress. By postmodernist logic all historical nexuses had to be rejected as they all contained the illicit recognition of elements of nonconstructed continuity. That put in question even nexuses that conformed to Lyotard's call for the *petits récits*. In them, too, concepts of grander reach were present—such as the sense of justice so prevalent in his called-for *petits récits*, although the specific configurations of justice were incommensurable.

Yet the strategy of negating all stability and continuity, however short of duration, was not so easily accomplished or, put into postmodernist terms, closures were not so easily banned. They proved to be elements of human existence formed and supported by a strong longing for them. Every historical nexus testified to that. Despite their firm determination to avoid such nexuses, neither Foucault, Lyotard, nor Derrida quite succeeded in their attempts.

Foucault replaced the metanarrative of progress with a random sequence of conditions of life. History, far from being the progress toward the perfect rule of law, showed how "humanity installs each of its violences in a system of rules and thus proceeds from domination to domination."[106] Opposition to closures destroyed established power systems only to create new ones in the process. The quest for power (an existential phenomenon) established as well as destroyed closures, giving history a directionless wave-like pattern.

At first glance, Derrida knew not even that much. The ideal human history would show the free play of signifiers, which produced endless reinscriptions on the scroll of human life. Yet in his later pronouncements, Derrida yielded considerable ground in the direction of a substantial development. He spoke of the preferability of democracy and a development toward the "democracy of the future" that presumably would be fully congruent with the world of flux. And he restored the word emancipation to legitimacy, although defined as a process without the telos of a stable state of perfection.

In a remarkable irony, Lyotard, who created the famous phrase of "incredulity to the metanarrative" did, in his own work, not at all observe his own injunction. And Baudrillard's views amounted to a new metanarrative.

The rejection of the metanarrative in the context of the poststructuralist postmodernist world exclusively dominated by change has been difficult to realize. Metanarratives in the form of progressive schemes could be easily deconstructed. But the declaration of the unimpeded dominance of change as the preferred reality necessitated the abandonment of the complex, endless intertwining of change and continuity in favor of the sole reality of change. This abandonment amounted to the end of history in a posthistory where human beings would not ever fall prey to illusions of closure in the hope of resolving the existential tension. Human ambitions and strivings would have to abandon any substantial goals of a better, if not perfect order in return for the absence of the vicissitudes caused by closures. The posthistoric period would not be a static stage of a resolved existential tension but one in which people must engage in a never-ending process of resistance to certainties and illusory solutions in which they themselves are liable to succumb. At that point, a case could be made that with such a sequence of radically different ages the metanarrative had not really been deconstructed but had only undergone another metamorphosis.

THE ONGOING DEBATE ABOUT THE METANARRATIVE

The Issue of Meaning and Order in History

The issue of the metanarrative has been part of the wider issue of meaning and order in history. Therefore, it mattered that the postmodernist rejection of the metanarrative occurred in the poststructuralist postmodernist world of constant flux. Once more, this time in the case of the metanarratives as large-scale meanings and order schemes of history, postmodernists felt compelled to dismantle what they considered dangerous buttresses of metaphysics. Both order and meaning must be seen as constructed phenomena, infinitely pliable, multiple. The human existence did not yield meanings; meanings constructed human existence. Or as John Toews put it, postmodernists practiced "the reduction of experience to meanings that shape it." He perceived a new intellectual hubris, "the hubris of wordmakers who claim to be makers of reality."[107]

Lyotard's agonistic language games or phrase regimes, Foucault's world of the discursive presence of power, and Derrida's world as texts were to provide the properly flexible setting. In it, historians could no longer discern a clear order and meaning in the past and use it to construct a nexus. The objective world as well as the individual with a powerful consciousness and a clear self-identity had disappeared. In Foucault's world, discourse and power blended into a unity—anonymously shaping meaning and order. In the Derridean vein, the text became the central "agent" of history, albeit one with multiple meanings. With its "indeterminacy and hence instability and fluidity" the text lacked the clear meaning that once was seen to reflect the author's intent guided by the sources.[108] Readers on their part were emancipated from finding the proper meaning of the account. They had become cocreators of ever-shifting meanings. Meanings and the order they indicated were truly multiple.

Such a complete rejection of the traditional view of meaning in history found determined opposition among historians. They rejected the postmodernists' depiction of historians as presumptuously all-knowing and all-powerful despots over their accounts and pointed to the limitations by evidence and objectivity. The rejection of the author's role in shaping meaning (representing human agency) made the production of meaning "impersonal, operating 'behind the backs' of language users."[109] As for readers, they had always understood historical accounts in their own contexts and to some degree recreated the texts. Yet this activity did not make the readers' interpretations identical with the past represented. As for the autonomy of the linguistic dynamics from human consciousness and intentions in general, it was rejected and the historian's important role affirmed. However, as was seen, on the issue of the metanarrative the battle lines between historians and postmodernists were blurred. Both groups, for their own reasons, distrusted metanarratives. As a result, the debate on the metanarrative took on a strange shape.

A Great Issue and a Slim Debate

Ardent Opposition. As in all other cases, the postmodernist rejection of metanarratives came in terms of the new understanding of truth. For Alun Munslow such narratives were an illegitimate and dangerous extension of the scope of historical construction of meaning. Keith Jenkins put the rejection of metanarratives or, as he put it, the replacement of *History* by *histories*, in terms of a purge of the traditional ideas of order and meaning. These ideas, thought to be Platonic essences, were really constructed by social and economic interests without lofty and permanent foundations. He admitted that *History* (the metanarrative) had also been effectively criticized by traditional, empirical historians. But Jenkins argued that they did so in the spirit of a "for its own sake" history, which was another illicit attempt to neutralize the revisionist power and intent of history.

In an affirmative manner, the logic of the postmodernist stance on the metanarrative has been stated by Robert Berkhofer's critique of the metanarrative. He defined the metanarrative in an inclusive manner. "The Great Story, or what others might call the 'metastory' or the 'metatext,' applies both to the larger context of partial histories and to the whole past conceived as history that justifies the synthetic expositions of normal historians." That quite properly directed attention to the presuppositions underpinning all historical accounts. In doing so, Berkhofer shaped his critique of the metanarrative as a special application of the general postmodernist theory of truth to historical accounts. He concentrated his deconstruction on the traditional assertion of access to an ascertainable referent or, in this case, the Great Past. That Past implied illicitly "a 'whole' or 'total' past that can be understood and constituted as history"—an entity that had some inherent meaning, that could be found rather than constructed.[110] Great Stories were synthetic constructs for organizing historical narratives, no more. None had better claims to truth than any others. Unwanted consequences of that position showed when that view seemed to deny a "true" position also to the accounts of the Holocaust (whose facts Berkhofer did not doubt and considered horrible) and to those in terms of class, race, and gender (he affirmed). Any privilege of truth accorded would presuppose an account firmly linked to an objective referent. Yet when the rejection of the metanarrative, by force of logic, accepted the destabilization of all certainties, the role of that narrative in the world of activism became problematical. Thus, as salutary as the rejection of metanarrative and certainties was in reference to the grand Western ideologies of the twentieth century, it turned out to be less useful when applied on a global scale, especially in the aftermath of decolonization.

Ambiguity in the Postcolonial Deconstruction of Progress. The postmodernist antimetanarrative argument found a new stimulus as well as a seemingly congenial context in the decolonization of the world after 1945. In that context, deconstruction proved an ideal tool for destroying the progressive narrative perceived to be an instrument of Western imperialism. However, this usefulness of the deconstruction soon found also its limits in the process of state building.

Edward Said's *Orientalism* (1978) offered a deconstructive reflection on Western colonialism. The book dealt actually with the phase of colonialism via its investigation of the influential concepts of Orient and Occident. Orientalism, seen as a typical product of the Western formation of the image of "others," used a schematized Orient (the "East"). It ascribed arbitrary common characteristics to mid-eastern cultures, such as the preference for a static existence, dark sexuality, and mystical tendencies. This discursive image, set against that of the rational Occident, was steadily solidified in a large body of scholarly works.[111] Adhering to Foucault's stipulation of the inevitable connection of knowledge and power, Said saw that detrimental image as a guiding, although sometimes contradictory element in colonial domination.

Yet Said's account encountered characteristic problems in the use of postmodernist concepts. He sympathized with the new scholarship that eliminated the anthropologist as outsider gazing at alien cultures and deciphering them in Western terms. But while he rejected the Western concept of objectivity as part of an insidious Western epistemology, he accepted only partially Foucault's world of discursive formations and Derrida's impersonal textualism. He preferred a new humanistic world of empathetic people, capable of some detachment in the conduct and analysis of life. And Said indicated that relatively stable, even traditional identities would be part of it.

Robert Young's *White Mythologies: Writing History and the West* also emphasized the value of postmodernism's deconstruction of the Western metanarrative in the context of decolonization.[112] In addition, Young found the concept of the "other" globally useful, as it, due to its purely formal character, could be universally applied. Therefore, his ultimate focus was once more on the detrimental impact of Western culture on the Third World. "White mythologies" shaped the thought of other cultures. Especially influential was the progress view of history that provided the rationale for the conquest of wide parts of the earth. By its application, the "other" was rendered invisible as people became more and more like Westerners in a global application of the epistemological principle of making the "other" the "same."

The Foucauldian world view with power at its center and the Derridean elaborations on the "other" as well as on the equalization of logocentrism with ethnocentrism (particularly Eurocentrism) had proven useful in the liberation struggle. But in the building of new states and desired firm ethnic identities postmodernist theories proved detrimental. The emerging countries wished for firm collective identities and totalities (groups as realities) and for a development envisioned as emancipation. Continuity became once more desirable when the new entities tried to access their long silent "true" precolonial pasts. The search was for lost traditions in the interest of stable identities.

A number of scholars, especially Keith Windschuttle, have criticized the use of deconstruction by critics of Western culture. Windschuttle found it remarkable that the deconstruction of the Western metanarrative has pointed out the oppression of the "other" in Western colonialism, but no parallel deconstruction of other cultures and their oppressive relationships to their "others" has yet been attempted. This lack of a parallel deconstruction exists even though, for example, in the Americas some of the pre-Columbian societies had built powerful empires that cruelly oppressed and brutalized many people.

A Postmodernist Look at Time. Considering the importance of the postmodernist revision of the temporal dimension of human life—be it the change and continuity dichotomy or the progressive linear concept of time—the discussion of that topic has been surprisingly sketchy. After all, poststructuralist postmodernists had stipulated no less than a new world of exclusive contingency or discontinuity. Ankersmit and others were therefore acting in the postmodernist spirit when they rejected historical time—which they equated with the linear time of progress—as an invention of modern Western civilization. Yet no direct discussion of the role of time in postmodernism generally and the metanarrative specifically ensued.

Elizabeth Deeds Ermarth attempted to give the rejection of the modern (linear and progressive) perception of time a theoretical base. She saw modernity's progressive image of time as related to reason's dynamics and telos. Shaped by the Cartesian rational and control-minded subject, it depicted a unitary development. Now, the break toward postmodernity—"an inalienable shift of cultural dispositions"—made visible the character of temporal concepts as constructs rather than as given categories.[113] Hence it was possible, even mandatory, to deprive linear time of its dominance. The transition to a rhythmic time perception could begin. Events did not happen *in* time, but time itself became an integral part of historical contexts, which differed in its rhythms. In contrast with the abstract linear time, rhythmic time was in close touch with life, emulating its different speeds, perspectives, ruptures, and understandings. Free of the grip of an overall telos, and the past with its outdated restraints, and open toward a future of spontaneous creativity, human time was no longer properly characterized by Descartes's "I think, therefore I am" but by Ermarth's "I swing, therefore I am."[114] Historians must accept that "historical [linear] time is a thing of the past."[115] Rhythmic time segments in individual and collective life could still follow one another chronologically, but they were no longer part of a unitary development.

Still, Ermarth's views did not fully support the reduction of the dimension of time to mere change, although they were in accord with the postmodernist attempt to purge metaphysics with its essences, stable identities, and laws of history. Rhythmic time, rather than replacing linear time, can be seen as referring to the varied time experiences human beings have in the framework of the inescapably linear course of human life—a linearity that remained the governing mode of human time, one marked by the constant intertwining of change and continuity. Thus, Ermarth's work pointed toward a fuller understanding of how the dimension of life has to be understood. That and not the postmodernist partial view of time would step into the place of a simplistic linear progression.

The Silence of Historians. In contrast to the rejection of the metanarrative's centrality for the postmodernist challenge and its undoubted relevance to and connection with history, historians continued in their reluctance to enter into a debate about the metanarrative. There was no incentive to do so, since for once historians and postmodernists agreed on the rejection of the metanarrative, although for vastly different reasons. Historians objected to the insufficient evidentiary base of metahistories while postmodernists accused metanarratives of being grand illusions used as instruments of oppression.

Historians understood that the postmodernist objections to historical meta-narratives were corollaries of the postmodernist theory of truth. Hence they answered the postmodernist challenge in the general debate about truth finding, a more familiar and congenial territory. One that also was more important in coping with the postmodernist challenge.

In historical practice, recourse to a not-so-new large-scale entity would lead the debate on the metanarrative into the field of cultural studies and in the vicinity of anthropology. The task waiting there was the transformation of a traditional concept into a postmodernist one.

AN INNOVATIVE VARIANT: THE NEW CULTURAL HISTORY

The New Large-Scale Concept: Culture

So far, the metanarrative debate had been conducted in strict dependence from the progress theory. Postmodernist arguments were formulated in reference to it, with all the limitation that implied for the creative potential, especially for the poststructuralist postmodernists. Change came with what some have called the anthropological turn. Its centerpiece was the acceptance of culture as the key concept for large-scale entities. That acceptance required the postmodernist reconstruction of a concept with a history of meanings stretching back over 250 years. At the core of the revision stood the affirmation of the world of dominant change and of nonreferentiality. As the historians turned to anthropology, that discipline took its version of the linguistic turn.

The Shift from the "Social" to the "Cultural." By 1980, a telling competition between two prominent terms became increasingly visible in the social sciences and history. The terms society and social began to share their places of prominence with culture and cultural. Then, in many works, they were replaced. The development was seen as a major one, often referred to as the cultural turn. Some scholars even sensed "a kind of academic cultural mania."[116] The change produced fervent, often hostile debates. Much of the debating was the result of the link between major tenets of the emerging new cultural history to those of poststructuralist postmodernism. Both intellectual currents aimed at the dismantling of the strict empiricism and strong materialism in the social sciences.

The use of the word "new" in connection with cultural history pointed to the already lengthy career of the term "culture" in Western intellectual life. The concept of culture emerged in the eighteenth century when, in the minds of prominent scholars, the dominant Christian perspective on the world yielded part of its place to secular ones. At that point, culture connoted a special refinement in human life, particularly through and in art, intellectual life, and music. Culture ennobled human life. A century later, Jacob Burckhardt's *Kulturgeschichte* became prototypical for histories focusing on culture understood in that sense. With time, scholars would claim more influence for culture, until as an internal force it came to be credited with shaping states and other large collectives. Already in the late 1700s, Johann Gottfried Herder saw in culture the expression of a group's soul. In the following century, modern nations relied on culture for defining their unity. Later, philosophers of history replaced states with cultures or civilizations as units in their theories of history. Spengler's *Kulturen* each had its own "soul," and for Toynbee civilizations were different fundamental responses to the challenges by their environment.

Culture as manifestation of the refinement of humanity found a most powerful support in the progress view of history, eventually enhanced by evolutionary ideas (Lewis Henry Morgan's anthropology). While the sense of culture as process of refinement has been retained into the present, powerful negations of it have emerged. Franz Boas had suggested an anthropology with constructed entities. For Marxists and Radical Historians of the 1960s, the suspicion of being a tool of exploitation and oppression adhered to culture (understood in terms of "High Culture"). Independently, the globalization process brought both a practical and theoretical awareness of the diversity of the world's population. Gradually, evolutionary schemes of cultural development, mostly in terms of a civilizing process in the Western mode, faded in importance. In line with this development, postevolutionary anthropologists had shifted toward less historical interpretations. Culture was defined simply as the sum total of what a certain group of people did and thought. Cultures were interpreted as structural and functional systems, primarily shaped by traditions (sets of meanings and habits) and the material circumstances of life. In the 1950s and 1960s, Claude Lévi-Strauss's structuralist anthropology gave this type of culture a nonmaterial basis: relationships among its parts which accorded with a "deep" code. His contemporaries among historians, the *Annalistes*, embraced anthropology. They affirmed cultural units when they championed *mentalité* as the mental space within which members of a collective operated. The sense of unity remained, albeit one less tight than the "deep" code.

Then, since the 1960s, culture once more experienced a redefinition. It set anthropology on a course toward to a special prominence in human studies, rivaling philosophy and history. The increasingly intercultural issues of a global world assisted that development. The new anthropology derived much of its vitality and sense of purpose from its participation in the linguistic or semiotic turn and a generalized poststructuralist postmodernist mode of looking at the world. Agency shifted from individuals or collectives to language and semiotics as the world assumed the quality of total flux. With it, anthropology seemed to ascend to the status of the key discipline for studying human life everywhere, not just in exotic places. Ironically, that ascension led to a severe crisis in the discipline as the very tenets of the new anthropology appeared to negate the rationale for studying other cultures.

The Transformation of Culture on Semiotic Terms. Historians would most often encounter the new anthropological model through Clifford Geertz's work. Leaving behind his once strong advocacy of social science methods, Geertz moved to the humanistic side of the scholarly spectrum. He revived Max Weber's concept of the human world as a web of meaning created by human beings in their individual and collective lives. And he accepted the postmodernist preferences for change, at least as far as it was useful for his new concept of anthropology. The decisive shift accentuated interpretation, appreciation of the local and the unique, and the new hermeneutics with its inescapable total human immersion in life. Culture became a text, the decipherment of which owed more to the methods of literary criticism than to science. Geertz focused his attention on symbols, especially on rituals and their readings. In a shift eventually characteristic for the new cultural history, he observed and analyzed human actions not in terms of causal effects but rather in those of meanings.

As it had been in all of modern anthropology, the main focus remained on the concept of culture. But Geertz did not aspire to reshape cultural anthropology in the image of another grand theory of culture. Such theories with their systematic constructs were fallacies that reified culture and were simplifications when they stipulated reductionist wholes founded on one or the other material base. In line with anthropology's turn, Geertz affirmed that "the culture of a people is an ensemble of texts, themselves ensembles, which the anthropologist strains to read over the shoulders of those to whom they properly belong." Obviously, Geertz did not consider this definition of culture as text to be reductionist. Scholarly inquiry would be guided by Geertz's succinct declaration: "It is explications I am after, construing social expressions on their surface enigmatical."[117]

As his method of presentation and analysis he chose what Gilbert Ryle had called "thick description," which aimed to make enigmatic things (particularly human actions) intelligible by discerning the meanings conveyed in them. Thick description made the material contexts and consequences of actions dependent on their meanings. Human actions were messages to their "readers." In analysis, the term thick description referred to the "working through" the multiple layers of meanings involved in actions (such as rituals) to demonstrate the informal logic of actual life. Here, the sought-after precision of empirical research yielded to "cultural analysis [that] is (or should be) guessing at meanings, assessing the guesses, and drawing explanatory conclusions from the better guesses, not discovering the Continent of Meaning and mapping out its bodiless landscape." The anthropologist must "uncover the conceptual structures" of the people observed in their actions and must bring out those which were generic to that group against the background of other possibilities.[118] Case studies did not yield laws or other fixed generalizations but only material for thick description of the local and the unique. The latter interpreted the flow of social discourse and found, at the most, clusters of meanings. In the end, the aim is still "to draw large conclusions from small, but very densely textured facts."[119] But consensus of findings was not the proper goal of anthropological work. Truth emerged in plural form in debate, not in monological systematic theories. Hence Geertz agreed with the poststructuralist contention that research was not the search for ever deeper truths or one Truth.

Geertz delivered a model of culture that in general fit postmodernist preferences. Cultural phenomena were neither rooted in permanent essences or foundations nor were they secondary to socio-economic realities. They were human constructions, fitting the postmodernist fluid world. That model has had its critics. Postmodernists among them have discerned a concept of the whole—a totalization—in Geertz's codes of cultures, even traces of preferences for High culture. Both of them needed rejection. Traditional scholars affirming the pragmatic value of history have pointed to the purely aesthetic nature of Geertz's concept of culture. The concept's utility was restricted to the observation of cultures since cultural elements were incapable of being agents of change or, in technical language, performative. The lack of guidance for action was for these critics too high a price for a purely semiotic world.

Put into the broadest terms, the accent in new cultural studies shifted to the nonmaterial side of life, specifically to the view of culture as discourse or text. The task would be to make social and economic structures become utterly malleable entities in the web of signs and symbols. As a result, the new cultural history of the 1980s and 1990s was expected to end the long-standing subjugation of history to the material side of life. The task entailed epistemologically the acceptance of the end of referentiality to the actual past.

The concept of culture had taken the combined linguistic and post-structuralist postmodernist turns and assumed the characteristics of a web of meanings. These meanings, as statements that made sense of the world, were no longer, as in social history, rather stable features gleaned from the observation of an objective world or rooted in permanent foundations of human life.

Yet the notion of an entity "culture" survived, although some scholars were not entirely comfortable with it because of its "essentialist" implications.[120] Culture was to be a strictly formal system—constructed, contextual, flexible, and, for many scholars, autonomous from the praxis of life. Meanings became signs that, however, pointed at no ultimate meanings—stable signifieds. Culture like language was ever shifting. Historians would analyze meanings as the signs that pointed to other signs.

The Problematical Dynamics of Culture as System of Symbols

How Does a Semiotic System Change? The now semiotically conceived culture still knew structure as the regularized use of symbols. But the sign and its signified (that which the sign referred to) did not leave the semiotic domain. When new cultural historians used terms such as ideologies, world views, identities, discourses, or rituals as examples, they implied no nonsemiotic reference. Yet with the tendency of cultural systems to favor continuity in habits, customs, and rituals the new view of culture needed a dynamics that matched the poststructuralist postmodernist insistence on the dominance of change. While the structural aspect took care of the maintenance of a system of meaning, the question of change, here referring to the matter of the production and transformation of meanings, remained vexingly open.

Social historians had relied on meanings gleaned by the observer from the network of objective relationships among objective entities (persons and things) using empirical methods of inquiry expressed in language. The tendency had been to ascribe much of the thrust in social change to the material side of life. In the new cultural history, the entities with inherent meanings and of significant duration had yielded their place to constructed and unstable ones of a purely linguistic nature. But could cultural change be accounted for entirely within the system of signs and symbols, or did ties to the actual life with its mixture of the material and nonmaterial play a significant role after all?

In search for answers, some historians were influenced by two cultural sociologists: Marshall Sahlins and Pierre Bourdieu. Both tried to mediate the seemingly stark opposition between sturdy structures and the needed flexibility for the practice of life. Geertz had tried to expunge structures of a permanent nature (actually those of appreciable duration and continuity) in favor of the fluid semiotic world, thereby undermining traditional concepts of truth and the utility of history. Sahlins gave cultural structures and categories the character of processes (albeit very slow ones) so as to bridge the gap between structures and practice. Standards and beliefs (the structural elements) could now more easily change and interact with the specific contexts. Culture was not just the product of a dominant material aspect of life but it was a participant in the full interaction of life—an agent at one moment and recipient at another moment. Bourdieu stressed to an even greater extent the dynamic of life and returned the concept of agency to structural systems.

Still, Sahlins's and Bourdieu's ideas were auxiliary to rather than causative for the variations brought by historians to the model of culture. There it was important that historians had always tried to observe the proper balance between change and continuity and between semiotic and the material elements. Technically speaking, that approach had safeguarded the performative quality of the "old" cultural history.

The problem of change in the new cultural history revisited the poststructuralist postmodernist problem of referentiality in the context of two related questions. Where, in the absence of elements of the past's full actuality were the standards for interpretation and construction of meaning in a culture seen as an autonomous system of signs or symbols? And where, in the absence of actual steady contextual connections, was the legitimation for speaking of a cultural system? Both of these questions were involved in the problem of how cultural history could account for change strictly within the bounds of a semiotic system. The problem had implications far beyond theory. Critics would sense two important weaknesses in the concept of a purely semiotic world: the unresolved problem of referentiality and the passivity of the semiotic model in regard to history's utility for life. Or, in the preferred way of speaking, what was the nature of the connection between the semiotic world and social practice?

Autonomy versus Mutual Transformation. Some scholars saw possibilities for an "internal" dynamics that generated change from inside the system. Of the various suggestions, one was for the stipulation of a system that lacked tight cohesion. Such looseness made it possible for the system, due to its insufficient cohesion, to harbor its own contradictions and tensions, thereby, spurring on change. Another suggestion relied on a system with arrangements of symbols that produced meanings open to different interpretations and, therefore, were apt to spur multiple changes in the system. "Symbols connote different meanings . . . [they] are polysemous."[121] Thus, signs could produce their own unexpected symbolic consequences. Another view, albeit one that already reduced the autonomy of the semiotic system markedly, had recourse to human beings as agents who by design transgressed the systemic limits, even subverting them. In this view social practice (including human agency) and semiotic system seem more intricately linked than a strictly autonomous system could permit.

Historical analysis changed together with these alternatives. As long as it could deal with cultures as autonomous symbolic systems, the task of analysis seemed simple. The "objective" world was now the one of signs or symbols manifest in texts (be they actually written materials, rituals, ceremonies, or simply relations). The systematic or regular use of signs and symbols revealed meanings and whatever was involved in the emergence, duration, and fading of meanings. Historians must locate these meanings and "thickly describe" their web so as to explain the cultural dynamics. However, the complexity of historical analysis increased when the semiotic and the material influenced each other even to a small degree.

Without the insistence on a reductionism of all and everything in culture to the purely semiotic, the matter of cultural change became a question of the relative influence of the symbolic and that of other aspects of human life. The social sphere, symbolically mediated, could then be credited with a measure of influence, although the semiotic was still considered the ultimate reference. The relative strength of either aspect of life varied according to specific circumstances—resulting in configurations of both long and short durations. Such a dynamic web accorded well with the new cultural history's preference for the local and unique. And the definition of human life as a web of meanings was not necessarily canceled by the recognition of its material aspect. Culture's system of signs and symbols would give and receive in the web of meanings. Or as William Sewell put it, social practice would echo in the semiotic system. Others, such as Ann Kane, would speak of recursivity or of a mutual transformation.

The Varied Practices of the New Cultural History

The debate about the autonomy of culture as a semiotic system has involved the ubiquitous problems of history's referentiality and usefulness. Answers have depended on the status ascribed to the semiotic. Strong advocates of a new cultural history have taken the formal system of signs to be the wellspring of all—"the irreducible sphere of being"—not in a metaphysical sense but as the end of all chains of nominalist reasoning.[122] Signs or symbols were the only grounding reality for meanings. The persuasive answer on the feasibility of such an autonomy view would have to come from historical practice. There, the struggle for a view in accordance with life turned out to be not one in terms of some perceived theoretical autonomy but in terms of a precarious balance between the semiotic power of giving meaning and the material side of life's sturdy concreteness. The price paid would be the abandonment of the rigid autonomy of culture as a semiotic system. Such a modification of the new cultural history, away from radically semiotic interpretations, hinted at a rapprochement with traditional historiography.

Several ventures, at various distances from the semiotic, explored the dimensions of culture. They have ranged from an adjusted social history (*Alltagsgeschichte*) to a deliberate turn to the unique and local (microhistory) and to a freewheeling connection among elements of the cultural system (New Historicism). Finally, a blend between narrativist, poststructural postmodernist and traditional historiographical elements produced cultural narrativism as an influential genre. They all shared a distrust or at least a distaste for histories of a linear type.

Alltagsgeschichte (**Insufficiently Postmodernist**). A prominent theme of the new cultural history has been the postmodernist recovery of the "other." In their search for the complete web of life, the new cultural historians turned their full attention to those forgotten in the grand scheme of things. That concern was judged to be missing from social history because it supposedly could not shed its enthusiasm for a history shaped by grand general structures and forces. Yet, since the late 1880s, social historians have contradicted that judgment—to a degree. They have intermittently, as Lucien Febvre put it, spoken on behalf of those "unknown men doomed, one might say, to do the donkey work of history."[123] The *Annalistes* had done much to recover the stories of the so-far hidden. Then, in the 1980s, a group of dissatisfied social historians created the so-called *Alltagsgeschichte* (history of the everyday).[124] In deliberate contrast to the prevailing social history, these historians dropped concerns with generalizations on a large scale and their quantified forms.[125] The center of attention was the routine life of common people, their working, eating, housing, vacationing, et al. The explicit purpose was it to make visible the consequences of that which formed the subject matter of grand scale history for the daily life of common people. Much like in traditional historicism the account of a specific context should speak for itself, without the creation of a unifying scheme. But a systematic progressive emancipatory desire—foreign to postmodernism—showed nevertheless in dealing with suffering, social and economic inequities, and restrictions. Affinities to postmodernism could be detected in the diminution of the role of large-scale social structures, the refusal to affirm any central group, force, or feature, and the rejection of social or political exclusion. However, in a fundamental difference, historians of the *Alltag* used social science methods that affirmed referentiality to past actuality.

Microhistory. Beginning in the late 1970s, another group of historians strove to break free from the social history that emphasized long-term processes, structures and forces (macrohistoric elements).[126] In the inquiries of these microhistorians, the postmodernist "other" received attention not because of its ethical implications for society but as witness to life's contingency. Individual and small-scale collective experiences, highlighting the multiplicity of meanings in life, moved out from under the shadows of grand systems into the spotlight. The principle of stressing that which was individual and unique held true also for sources. "A close reading of a relatively small number of texts . . . can be more rewarding than the massive accumulation of repetitive evidence."[127] Such use of often unconnected and isolated pieces of evidence could reveal reality (Carlo Ginzburg's "evidential paradigm"). As for these connections, Ginzburg himself has struggled with the competing attractions of morphology (relating features from different cultures on the basis of formal affinities) and history.

Nevertheless, insights of a more general character could be gained. Thus, the miller in Carlo Ginzburg's *The Cheese and the Worms* pieced together his own system of meanings (in his case, a cosmology). He reconstructed an "obscure, almost unfathomable, layer of remote peasant traditions."[128] The true relationship between popular culture and the dominant culture became manifest. The former could no longer be seen as the mere result of a passive modification of the prevailing world view but was best viewed as a creation on its own merit. In the resultant plurality of cultures was reflected the contingent character of life. But the question of what microhistory with its stress on the unique, local, unexpected, unsystematic, and outright offbeat could contribute to historical knowledge remained open. Or as Edward Muir put it, "How can historians concerned with trifles avoid producing trivial history?"[129] Answers have referred to the mentioned unearthing of long obscured subcultures, the complementarities between microhistory and macrohistory (without fusion) and the bridging of the gulf between the present and the now strange past. As for links to poststructuralist postmodernism they were manifest in the rejection of grand systems and the affirmation of contingency and discontinuities. So, however, were disagreements over the postmodernist assessment of the traditional use of evidence and the affirmation of referentiality.

The New Historicism. In the 1980s, a so-called historical turn occurred in literary studies, initially those of early modern Europe. The New Historicists, with Stephen Greenblatt as seminal scholar, called for seeing literary works no longer aesthetically in isolation from their contexts but historically as integral parts of changing contexts. But the historical context to which the works were to be linked was not the one with relatively stable ideas, beliefs, and practices but a world of fluid meanings and order. Literary works were shaped by that world and shaped it in turn. Early on, Greenblatt himself had emphasized that all expressive acts occurred in a network of material practices and even acts of critique were beholden in language and otherwise to the existing culture.

Literary works had been led out of their elitist, aesthetic isolation in order to change the ways they were studied and understood. In the world of New Historicism, any aspect of culture could be connected to others, even randomly, without limits. Therefore, it has been said that "New Historicism has a portmanteau quality." The theoretical result was the enabling of the inquirer to "seize upon an event or anecdote . . . and re-read it in such a way as to reveal through the analysis of tiny particulars the behavioral codes, logics, and motive forces controlling a whole society."[130] The practical result was the ability to find the "other" as the then not present. Critics could charge that such choices were leading to arbitrary pastiches and montages.

An attempt to rein in such freewheeling connections came in the stipulation of a limiting code, which for Greenblatt ultimately resulted from human practices. He defined the code as "a set of interlocking tropes and similitudes that function not only as objects but as the conditions of representations."[131] Collective beliefs and practices acquired in the tropological system a basis for being defined, constructed, and analyzed. But its siting in the fluid world brought to New Historicism the problem of nonreferentiality. If the cultural world were discursively or textually constructed, did New Historicism escape the aesthetic realm? Could the primarily synchronic study of relationship between phenomena shed light on developments? New Historicists have suggested the interplay between containment and subversion (really a version of continuity and change) as generator of developments. The New Historicist solution also experienced problems similar to those of Foucault's power. There was no ascertainable link between findings, activism, and truths.

The Role of the Cultural Narratives. The new cultural history with its search for order in life's meanings would find a promising approach in the recourse to narratives. In the search for order in the web of meanings, accounts that have been called "cultural narratives" played a significant role.[132] They did seem to be especially well suited for the purposes of the new cultural history as they ranged over a wide spectrum of people, avoiding the concentration on what was now called the elite; were on the whole sympathetic to the "other" of older traditional accounts; incorporated new kinds of interpretations, linguistic and anthropological; and recognized meanings as decisive elements of history. However, this also made cultural narratives another testing ground for nonreferentiality.

Of the large number of cultural narratives, a sample of some well-known ones will exemplify the genre and its characteristics. Early on, Emmanuel Le Roy Ladurie, in *Montaillou: The Promised Land of Error* (1979), consulted records of inquisitional proceedings not to learn about the Albigensians in general but about how their beliefs were applied, modified or simply misused in the routine lives of commoners.[133] The result was an image of the collision of existential drives, wants, rational reflection, quest for power, and sacred longings, all within a supposedly uniform system of meanings. The cultural system showed a surprising richness and malleability. Meanings were reconstructed in the contexts of individual lives. And in *Carnival in Romans* (1979) Ladurie presented "a deep probe into the geological stratifications of a dated culture."[134] The account of that Carnival in 1580 described a ritual of both Christian and Pagan nature with its meaning transformed by the religious wars of the period. Ritual and reality blended into each other and so did the local and the general French contexts. The story of a private affair, *The Return of Martin Guerre,* offered Natalie Zemon Davis the opportunity to explore the possibilities inherent in an anthropologically oriented cultural history. On the surface a story of passions and deception, the account told much about life, attitudes, rules, infractions, and punishment—in short about the world of meanings in a section of sixteenth-century France. And in her *Fiction in the Archives,* Davis focused on the world of the "other"—people in trouble with the law—through the letters of remission from supplicants.[135] She treated the processes involved as rituals from which much could be discerned about contemporary life. As cultural history, the work reflected the new appreciation of language (the formalistic writing) but still displayed a sturdy sense for the past existential experience (the actual content of the petitions).

Robert Darnton chose a variety of sources to ferret out "not merely what people thought but how they thought."[136] The deep resentments of the journeymen could be "read" (deduced) from the symbolic messages "sent" by the story of the Great Massacre of Cats, the violence, hunger, and the crudity of the contemporary society from the fairy tales, the suspicious attitude toward disorder in a hierarchical society in the files of a police inspector, and the world view of intellectuals from the symbolic tree of knowledge. While Darnton strove for a "history in the ethnographic grain," he exercised the traditional caution of historians in assessing the narratives as to their tellers, their motives, and their contexts.[137] The semiotic world and the actuality of life were fused in a complex way that defied all reductionisms, including those of psychoanalysis. The aim of it all was not to produce a cognitive map of life in eighteenth-century France but to illuminate segments of that life's web of meanings.

Judith Walkowitz's study of crimes against young women in Victorian London could serve as an example for the special attractiveness of cultural narratives to feminist historians.[138] In highlighting the fate of unfortunate young women, the account presented an array of meanings given to events from male, female, suffering, and dominating perspectives. But the world of meanings never lost touch with social and economic realities and their con-stellations of power. In that, it was typical of many other cultural narratives with its pragmatic sense for the complexity of life in which the intertwin-ing of meanings with existential reality constituted a major element. The practical value of the narrative was not neglected either (performativity).

In these works, the "other"—the oppressed—"resist" the existing order and historians must read the stories accordingly.

The Identity Debate. Since the 1980s, many books have been published, papers read, and discussions held on topics concerning the new cultural history, including cultural narratives. The periods and themes treated have had an extremely wide range. So voluminous has the work been that the promises and the problems of the new cultural history could best be highlighted by exploring one of the most prevalent themes: identity. From the standpoint of poststructuralist postmodernism the concept has been troublesome. Its inevitable implication of stability (continuity) in the term stood at an odd angle to the world of complete flux. Yet even in that world, identity—uncomfortable a subject as it might be—proved unavoidable. In traditional historiography the concept's combination of change and continuity has been aligned with a world marked by the same combination. In the case of human beings, the centrality of the strong individual in Western culture demanded a sufficiently stabile identity. But in the new cultural history, identity had only a linguistically constructed, contextual quality and all inquiries into it would be focused on the process of its construction, maintenance, fading, and reconstruction.

In the identity debate, the human self remained an important topic, yet approaches to its construction differed widely. Sexuality offered the possibility (although not unlimited) to construct masculine and feminine genders, as well as gay and lesbian identities. The body and what it meant for identity became an important topic of debate, especially in feminist history. The "reality" of group identity was ardently contested. Were class, ethnicity, or race entities significantly reflective of special features or conditions of the material world or human physiology, or were they pure cultural constructs not dependent on materiality at all?

The debate on identities stretched well beyond the self to virtually all the entities historians encountered. Antagonisms amongst people were often seen in terms of the construction of (imagined) enemies. Even geographical entities experienced the identity problem. "Creating" China, "imaging" Germany, and the "imagining" of continents (megageography)— each of these activities referred to entirely constructed entities. In the end, scholars and authors were not alone in constructions. The "writing of . . . " was accompanied by the "reading of . . . " which emphasized the readers active role in constructions and reconstructions of identities.

All of that work tried to maintain the prevalence of construction in identities and to shun that which could suggest stable elements. The mandate of the dominance of change was to be strictly observed. The utter flexibility of constructed identities brought forth an infinite possibility to relate everything to everything with the consequence that much of history began to resemble a construction site for identities—endless and aimless. Such a history satisfied purely theoretical preferences but caused problems for history's utility. Susan Pedersen has put forth her reservations in the case of a conference on British Empire studies. There the struggle of identity formation by various groups could have led observers to "conclude that the British Empire was nothing more than a great staging ground for the elaboration of 'Britishness,' in which groups of rather self-absorbed British men and women could experiment with different identities without doing much harm to anyone."[139] In contrast, Pedersen regretfully noted, the materiality of the world, especially politics, remained an ignored reality.

■ 18 **POSTSTRUCTURALIST POSTMODERNISTS ON THE INDIVIDUAL AND THE UTILITY OF HISTORY**

COULD HISTORY STILL BE USEFUL?

The question of history's usefulness has all along been one about the degree to which the present could benefit from the past for illuminating human existence and its problems. The historical nexus suggested that history could yield useful answers. Ancient historians had tried to discern lessons in history that would stand the tests of life, especially those of political life. Medieval chroniclers had found guidance in history's events toward discerning Divine Providence. Much later and in a secular vein, Lord Bolingbrooke and many others saw history teaching the timeless lessons of philosophy through specific examples. Doubters have all along questioned such usefulness.

Advocates of a "history for history's sake" stance, who tried to isolate the study of the past from the nexus, have denied that such utility should or could be of concern to historians. Now, poststructuralist postmodernists asked questions about the instructive role of the past and foresaw a world from which the guiding elements for the historical nexus had disappeared: a limited authoritative truth, a sufficiently stable and intelligible human condition, some inherent order and meaning visible in recurring features, a self-identical individual, and the intertwining of change and continuity. In the world of endless and directionless flux, human beings would neither need nor be able to create historical nexuses of any consequence. The important lesson of history told of the illusions of the past, including the progressive view of history and its false elevation of the human being to its central position. Postmodernists raised once more the question of what in their world was meant by the utility of history. The answers given would be of great importance to movements of social, political, or cultural activism, in particular Marxism and Feminism.

THE DECONSTRUCTION OF THE INDIVIDUAL AS HISTORICAL AGENT

Historians and the Diminished Status of the Individual

Foucault and Derrida replaced the self-identical individual (one with a good measure of autonomy and stability) with one constructed by its linguistic or rhetorical context. Hence the diversity of human beings was no longer seen as variations of one common nature. The latter fell under the injunction against permanent universals and essences. The new linguistically constituted individual neither could nor wished to discern meaning from a stable core.

As was the case with other changes, this one, too, had seen some preparatory steps. They had been taken, ironically, by the same modernity that always has been seen as celebrating the individual. In the nineteenth century—the so-called Golden Age of history—Hegel had reduced the human being to a scripted actor in the vast drama of the World Spirit's movement toward fulfillment. Marx had defined it as a product of socioeconomic conditions that cooperated in a set course toward economic emancipation. Nietzsche saw the individual emerging as a product of the will to power in the struggle for domination. Freud had limited the human being to a sexually driven being who was engaged in a mostly futile struggle to balance the demands of the id and those of society. In history, the advocates of the New History (Henri Berr, Karl Lamprecht, and Frederick Jackson Turner) aimed at a history that deemphasized the individual's role when they, too, ascribed the real determinative influence to grand forces. With the individual as an anonymous part of a collective, the individual human being was vastly diminished as an effective agent in history.

The poststructuralist postmodernists found all of these diminutions insufficient and called for a radical denial of the human being as an effective historical agent. In that endeavor they got support from what one observer has identified as "the revulsion against the self" so clearly manifested in some of the influential literature since 1960.[140]

The "End of Man" and of Western Humanism

Their opposition to structuralism notwithstanding, Foucault and Derrida would concur with Lévi-Strauss in his expectation of the "death of man."[141]

For Lévi-Strauss the autonomous subject with some control over itself and the world was an obstacle to a new science of human life, but for the postmodernists it became one to their world of total flux. These postmodernists aimed at "dehumanizing" or "decentering" the world of culture. All human identities became constructs—"positionings" some called it. The new social order and the intellectual world would be marked by the absence of the even partially autonomous self. This purge of all definitions of the human identity that relied on stable elements also meant a rejection of any form of emancipation of the so-far repressed "true" individual self. The linchpin of Western culture was to be removed.

Foucault's Verdict

In Foucault's works, identity forming was defined in terms of the force—power—that shaped all order, which at first was a structural one and, later, primarily a discursive one. Only as just another construct among the discourses of power or desire could the human being be moved out of the privileged center it has occupied in Western historical discourse. In later years, especially in his books on sexuality, the individual recovered some facility to construct itself, somewhat apart from the impact of prevailing discourses of power. That change was, however, never fully worked out.

Occasionally, Foucault argued that the Enlightenment had brought about a detrimental change from a discursive-friendly pre-Enlightenment to the modern era—hostile toward free discourse—in which language was confined to the role of a mere medium. In that world in which language had been the purely auxiliary instrument of consciousness, that which Foucault called the "constituent" subject (the one with a stable identity) thrived and could not be dislodged. Only postmodernity, with a radical affirmation of the linguistic world of full discursivity, facilitated the dissolution of the self-identical subject. In it, the constitution of the human being would happen in and by the specific discourses of a period without recourse to a powerful consciousness or a stable subject. With its position as a stable entity being effectively undermined, the "end of man" will have arrived.

Thus, Foucault could call the autonomous individual, Western culture's central phenomenon, a one-hundred-fifty-year-old invention that would disappear "just like a 'crease' being ironed out of a crinkled shirt."[142] Or, put differently, "man would be erased, like a face drawn in sand at the edge of the sea."[143] Although he referred to "man" as understood in the modern period, in practice his judgment encompassed the whole span of Western culture from Plato to modern philosophers and scientists. The assault must be one on Western humanism as a main buttress of Western culture and its prevailing historical thought.

Derrida's Deconstruction of the Individual

Derrida, too, spoke of the linguistic construction of the human being. For-mer ages had not understood that. There had been the ancient period's fascination with character representing a human nature with variable com-binations of fixed traits; the medieval view of human beings as unalterably sinful but also created in the divine image; and modern human beings seen as destined for full realization of their inherent rationality. In the tradition of Western humanism, all of them affirmed an individual that was at least partially autonomous. Historians, too, treated people as having stable selves and showing sufficient commonality (sameness), persisting over time. Much of the use of history for guidance in life relied on such a self.

Derrida cited two arguments for deconstructing the "self-identical" subject. The first pointed to the intractable dilemma besetting the work of modern consciousness. The quest after the fully objective truth came up against the awareness of the impossibility to obtain such a truth because of the unavoidable subjectivity. Derrida's deconstructionism aimed beyond finding yet another in the end unsuccessful way to circumvent the epistemological block. In that context, the total deconstruction of the notion of a self-identical human being was called for.

The second and presumably weightier argument against the stable, self-identical subject was the ethical one. That subject had stood at the center of modernism and, thus, was complicit in the catastrophes of the century. In the solid self with its stable unity and fundamental sameness rooted the enduring hegemony over the "other." Human beings must come to under-stand their identities not by recourse to a source of stability that yielded to them a constant core of sameness (such as a stable human nature) and thereby legitimized the exclusion of the "other" (anything outside the de-fined being). Rather, much as the twists of one's hand shaped and reshaped the pieces in a kaleidoscope into ever new arbitrary configurations so lin-guistic constructions did with human identities. The latter were unstable, arbitrary combinations of elements without fixity that were effective and could be understood only in their ever changing discursive contexts. Such human beings would remain totally open to "alterity" (otherness) and, in a sense, to their own overcoming.

Derrida has pleaded that he "never said that the subject should be dispensed with. Only that it should be deconstructed. To deconstruct the subject, does not mean to deny its existence." The subject was, in Derridean terms "inscribed in language" or resituated into language.[144] Derrida spoke here really of a reality effect (an "as if" impression) of subjectivity, while the actual and stable subject had vanished. The effects of the erosion of the central role of the conscious and active individual in Western culture mattered because the "end of man" constituted a primary feature in the desired unraveling of the general construct called Western culture.[145] History as this culture's image in time would find its appropriate end.

Lyotard's Cautious Redefinition

Lyotard's work played a more moderate role in the postmodernity debate about the nature and role of the individual. In the interest of breaking the hegemony of certain features of modernism he joined in the postmodernist condemnation of the link between consciousness and sign (word). That link had provided the basis for the representational view of knowledge and, with it, for the Enlightenment's rational and activist individual. Lyotard's esteem for the linguistic aspect of life led him to perceive the individual as located at the "nodal points of communications."[146] The "nodal point" identity did permit the conception of the human being as an empty placeholder to be filled with contextual meanings. But Lyotard's main interests were systems and how their narratives were linked to social practices. Thus, the individual did not hold his interest for too long. Neither did his later tendencies to soften the distinctions between material and immaterial phenomena rekindle the search for the proper identity of the human being.

Farewell to the "I"

What had been a centerpiece of Western culture vanished in poststructuralist postmodernism. The individual who struggled to cope with life by finding the true order of the human world became not only a redundant but a harmful figure. Deprived of its at least partial autonomy from the context, the individual merged into an impersonal web of linguistic relationships. German scholars have spoken of an *Abschied vom Ich* (farewell to the I). To history that mattered because the human being lost its status as a significant historical agent. With the major obstacle to a world of total flux removed, poststructuralist postmodernists now had to demonstrate whether and how their view of history would be able to guide, support, and justify the actions that human beings had to take. In light of the ethical and political motive for postmodernism a proper answer was crucial.

CAN POSTMODERNIST VIEWS OF HISTORY JUSTIFY ACTION?

Foucault: Power as the Spur and Resistance to Action

The reconciliation of theory with life's practice posed special and in the end unresolvable difficulties for Foucault. His lifelong endeavor to find an answer focused on the phenomenon of power and the institutions of domination it had sponsored throughout history. In the end, he would find that power was no mystical or abstract force but resulted only from the behavioral wish and ability to dominate.

Ironically, that centrality of power was fostered by Foucault's enduring distrust of power. For that, scholars have given psychological reasons such as early conflicts with his father, the experience of being made an outsider as a homosexual, and the resultant attitudes of defiance of conventions and rules. While these were worthwhile considerations, it mattered more that his desire to defy established power turned in his theoretical work into his determination to find ways to destroy hegemonies. Indications for that came in his fascination with madness, violence, punishment, and sexuality—all seen as constructs susceptible to serve as occasions for suppression. And, until late in his life, the ideal of transgression or limit experiences, understood as transcending the limits drawn by society, was a driving force. Such a perspective on life doomed Foucault's institutional affiliations: his brief membership in the Communist Party of France and his flirtation with radical Maoism after the Days of May in 1968. The tight organization and institutional discipline of political movements did not fit Foucault. Neither did their affirmations of an objective order. All of that left Foucault, who, after 1968, became a more committed political activist, in search of the proper rationale for political action.

Whether power was working behind the scenes (as episteme) or as an integral part of all aspects of life, particularly knowledge (P/K), the question posed was the same. Which advice for action could be derived from a history destined to remain forever an aimless domination-opposition-domination sequence, with none of them being preferable to the other? The democratic answer that proper action must aim at giving power to the many proved to be of no avail. The many, once in possession of power, also would establish their domination (with the inevitable exclusion of others) and, thus, necessitate renewed opposition. At points, Foucault seemed to indicate that the management of power and political activism in a strictly local context and the resultant *petits récits* offered the optimal solution. Yet that affected only the scope of the exertion of power and nothing else.

Occasionally, Foucault would lapse into quasi-emancipatory arguments, such as his fight for the rights of prisoners, that besides being conducted as a struggle against oppression took on illicit emancipatory characteristics. Such lapses into a progressive historical perspective did not prevail. More typically, Foucault voiced sympathy for the views of the New Philosophers, especially André Glucksmann, who suggested perennial dissent and opposition, particularly from and to the Past Masters. Foucault agreed with them on the only choice for scholars as activists. In a world where history told of the endless sequence of oppressions and oppositions, activists must oppose without pause and exception all established exercise of power. The "good" fight was not directed against any specific set of dominant ideas and institutions, but against the legitimacy of any regime of domination. That seemed to counsel, as a Berlin graffiti of the 1990s suggested rather crudely, *keine Macht für niemand* (no power for nobody). That tenet had a definite pessimistic ring. Because of its denial of any possible use of power for "better" purposes than sheer domination, Foucault's approach was labeled conservative by Marxist critics. A more fitting characterization of Foucauldian history would be a variation of a Greek myth. Sisyphus had been condemned by the gods to push a boulder up a hill with the promise of relief once the boulder had reached the top. But the boulder would roll downhill again and again just inches from the crest. The postmodernist intellectual must act like Sisyphus but without his vain hope for ultimate resolution. Opposition that ended up in establishment was condemned to begin its work over and over again.

The Story of History as Successive Assertions of Power

Foucault's views fit well into the world of flux, which tolerated only relationships that were formal not substantial. Power derived its meaning only from the domination/subjection relationship and not from the discourses of ideas or ideals on behalf of which it was exerted. What had been considered important in history—that which cultures affirmed in their ideas, concepts, institutions, and actions—had lost its place to the mere fact of power being exerted. All assertions of power on behalf of existing conditions were detrimental and needed to be combated. The substance of the conflict did not matter. The existential tension between the "is" and the "should be" or "wished for" was not so much resolved as constantly dampened down by the affirmation of change. Change was left as the only permissible permanent element.

History remained the aimless and endless sequence of dominations and their dismantling. There could be no liberation and emancipation from power relationships, certainly not in terms of a teleological history. In that new historical world, even the postmodernist enlightenment on the workings of power could not change anything. Domination and its injustices were perennial features of human life against which activist intellectuals struggled as tragic heroes without hope for a new "good" order. History's lesson was stark and simple: to remain stoically in opposition to that which was existing—to deny it continuity.

Derrida's Rationale for Action: The "Other"

Derrida's approach to activism derived from his view of a human world in which permanence was granted to the principle of constant differentiation itself but not to its products. That principle's continuity could be tolerated because it was purely formal (rather than substantial) and antagonistic to any permanence for its own products. Differentiation had a perfect fit to an aimless and endless world.

Yet, as was seen, every action, even writing, established a "presence," that is, a condition in which one state of affairs was preferred to a different one, the "other." But in the world created by the working of *différance,* to be "absent" meant not to be nonexistent, but only to be temporarily crowded out (deferred). Indeed, any object or person of however solid-seeming a presence was beset by the tension between itself (being "present") and that which was "absent." The dynamics created by that tension acted as the agent of incessant change. All order and its affirmation amounted to a suppression of the "other." By its very existence, regardless of its kind, every order violated heterogeneity.

Therefore, the proper activism in the world created by différance must aim only at keeping unchecked the constant retrieval of the suppressed "other." The motivating force for action could not be the claim that the "other," once retrieved into "presence," would be ethically better. Indeed, once dominant, it would create new hegemonies and privileges. Regardless of their substantial content, all ordering concepts harbored the intent to limit or even halt the play of signifiers. They were equal in their tendency to be oppressive. The suppressed or deferred "other's" claim to affirmation could not rely on any substantial argument on its behalf but only on the claim that it was not "present" at the moment.

The assertion of the claims of the "other" solely on the basis of its temporary "absence" was necessary since there were no extracontextual or extralinguistic standards available for such ethical judgments. History could not demonstrate more than that. Derrida's ethics was a formalistic one: the differentiation process was the ultimate "good" and deconstruction its agent. "Deconstruction is, in itself, a positive response to an alterity which necessarily calls, summons or motivates it. Deconstruction is therefore vocation—a response to a call."[147] In short, before the first reflective thought appeared, an "other" elicited a response to itself. A call of an ethical nature was heard though it did not have an ethical system to guide it. Even the ethical sense was no more than an inscription on the matter-of-fact equality of all discourses. It described how the world operated and not why it was desirable to act accordingly. The priority of the "other," which seemed an ethical even political demand, was a given.

Derrida's action program aimed at what Karl Popper called an open society but conformed to a linguistically constructed world. Its guiding principle was the "free play of signifiers" set against the powerful desire for closure.[148] In the face of the dangers posed by closure—restriction, oppression, privilege, and hegemony—such a free play onto which could be inscribed strictly temporary meanings was seen as the sole hope. Although differentiation and différance still produced an "other," they were merely formal processes that worked on behalf of plurality and heterogeneity and lacked any substantial arguments on which hegemonies could be established. Derrida would argue that, while even postmodernists made for "presences," these presences were open to constant change and thus reduced the violence to the "other." The true violence was caused by attempts to endow that which was "present" with a stable identity (closure).

All of that made Derrida both a stoic and a prophet of hope. A stoic since he had to accept the tension between that which was "present" and that which was "absent" as a permanent condition. All possibilities of the linguistic world were active at any given time, either as the temporarily asserted or as elements undermining it. "Presence" and "absence" were synchronously "real." Thus, "violence remained in fact (almost) ineradicable."[149] Little more could be done than to accept that condition, which critical observers could well interpret as affirming the traditional view of a permanently imperfect human condition despite constant attempts of remediation by the assertion of change. Nothing of lasting import happened in history as human beings could not transcend their conflict-laden suspension between that which existed and the "other."

ACTIVISM WITHOUT THE GUIDANCE OF THE PAST

As an endeavor with an ethical, social, and political concern at its core, poststructuralist postmodernism could have been expected to show a high degree of interest in so-called lessons of history. But with the assertions of the nonreferentiality of human knowledge to the actual past and of the complete dominance of change over continuity as basic mandates, the definition of the new historicity's usefulness became a difficult task.

The single most important of history's lessons—for poststructuralist postmodernists perhaps the only one—derived not from the traditional historian's quest for knowing the actual order and fate of specific past contexts. Its results were now irrelevant. Lessons for the creation of theories or of efforts to establish the proper social and political order could now be deduced from the dominance of change over continuity and the futility and undesirability of all strivings for closure. These insights had not been available to people of past periods. Formerly, lessons of history had been derived from the historian's intricate endeavor to decipher the web of past human activities and thoughts. Gaining them was made extraordinarily complex by the acknowledgment of the interweaving of these activities and thoughts with the temporal experiences of change and continuity. Hence, declaring change to be dominant seemed to simplify radically the task of deciphering and gaining guidance from the past. Life's reality proved otherwise. The difficulties encountered in matching the postmodernist theories of action to the practice of life testified to that.

At times, postmodernists sounded as if the human agent were the decisive feature. After all, a new enlightenment about the true human situation had to occur, spread, and be made effective for the postmodern world to function. But postmodernists had made the individual's status completely pliable so as to fit into the fluid postmodern world thereby minimizing the individual's role as historical agent. True efficacy of "action" was ascribed to Foucault's anonymous hand of power and to Derrida's equally anonymous process of differentiation. Of human beings was only asked that they not hinder in the praxis of life the working of power on behalf of change and the free "flow" of différance. Derrida even implied a quasi-authoritative standard when he indicated that societies could be judged by the degree of tension between that which was established and the "other." High tension pointed to a tyrannical assertion of "presence" and low tension to a relatively milder, though still unacceptable oppression. Foucault and Derrida could not but be aware of the ambiguity embedded in both of the dynamic principles, power as well as differentiation. They destroyed discursive orders or texts and, without aiming to do so, created new ones. Thus, both power and differentiation's disposition to negation proceeded to stimulate the undoing of the results of their own work. That was needed in order to neutralize the strong human longing for closure to which postmodernists quietly conceded here the status of a continuous and strong counterforce.

This ambiguity or bipolarity in the dynamic forces resulted in different perspectives on human action. Foucault's solution turned out to be a simple one: a conscious Sisyphus-like effort at permanent opposition. Derrida's guide to action centered on his concern for the "other." That, too, led to incessant action by virtue of the inevitability of ever new "others."

Deconstructionist criticism as effective activism pointed out the fragility of all constructed order schemes—their inner tensions and contradictions, which eroded their seeming stability, solidity, and legitimacy. In doing so, deconstructionism produced an ethical "effect" as it highlighted traces of the "other" in a given text—be it a book or a culture. It would evoke the respect for the "other," which represented the one and only acceptable permanent norm for action. No other "ought-to-be" mandate could be constructed. However, in his most recent work, Derrida even acknowledged the ideal of emancipation but only as a process of the endless discovery of the "other" and not as a telic force.

The inconclusive outcome mattered less—it was foreordained—than the light the debate shed on Derrida's view of activism. The ideal direction of that activism, the establishment of unfettered change—with no guidance from the past—could best be described by the Derridean phrase "the impossible possibility." For Derrida's world with endless violence to the "other" (according to him, the inevitable "other" inevitably violated), lacking any hope for permanent emancipation and for a *telos* or ideal order in the free play of signifiers, death seemed the only solution to the existential tension. And both Derrida and Foucault did speak on occasions of death in that way.

RESPONSES TO THE CHALLENGE

The body of work critical of postmodernist concepts concerning history's use as a guide in life and theory has remained fairly small. Historians were loath to touch the issue since it seemed to harbor temptations to transgress the proper limits of "doing history." Part of the criticism focused on the issue of order and meaning writ large—the metanarrative. Yet most historians saw it as their main, if not exclusive task to reconstruct a specific past in its actuality. That did not make them necessarily partisans of the often derided "history for truth's sake only" school because the theoretical framework of historical accounts always was anchored in historical nexus building that tinged all historical writing with the pragmatic brush. The nexus involved the use of the past. On their part, historians have criticized postmodernism's inability to assist civic life by supplying values for its support. As special evidence for postmodernism's estrangement from life, Himmelfarb cited its inability to condemn or even affirm the reality of the Holocaust. She also pointed to the dissolution of the individual's stable identity as responsible for the low status of political history and the lack of any moral basis for political action.

Lyotard, Foucault, Derrida, and others had wrestled with this problem of action in a world of indeterminacy from which the at least partially autonomous individual had disappeared. Advocates of postmodernism among historians had to face the problem's historiographical manifestations. Among the few who did so with confidence, Keith Jenkins took his cue from Derrida in developing a postmodernist position. Derrida had ended up defining the ethical decision situation in the manner of Sartre's existentialism. There the individual found itself alone in deciding on a course of action, rejecting help from any historical nexus or ahistorical ethical system. The individual being who made an "authentic" choice was fully aware of the condition of solitude. Jenkins worked with the Derridean version of authenticity, the concept of indecidability. Ethical decision making guided by established schemata fettered the future with all the restrictions of the failed past. Therefore, in the place of the "lessons of the past" must step the "rich 'imaginaries'"—the not yet realized promises of the future. Jenkins wondered whether history should still be considered of any concern. Critics could point out that even in the denials of the usefulness to history, the latter returned, albeit, in a purely negative role. Historical accounts told how to avoid vicissitudes by excluding oppressive and tyrannical tendencies from the "imaginaries." Another, even more surprising concession to lessons from the past was the use of the terms "emancipatory" and "democratizing" as guides for postmodernist thinking. They sounded reassuring but relied definitely on notions of nexus and an objective past.[150] Such ideals admitted a surprising degree of closure. The postulated sharp distinction between detrimental stability and beneficial change kept haunting postmodernist theory's application to history. The element of closure and exclusion seemed impossible to ban when ascribing even a trace of usefulness to history.

In a different but still instructive manner, the difficulties of postmodernist theories also afflicted David Harlan's argument against the usefulness of the historical nexus. History, as "one of the primary forms of moral reflection" must strive beyond simply knowing the past toward "rethinking who we might become by rethinking who we once were."[151] Historians must see the futility of formulating the expectations for the future within the perimeters of the past because the course of human development was not linear and cumulative but discontinuous. "History is a line we ourselves must rig up, to a past we ourselves must populate."[152] With the past no longer "a graveyard of dead contexts" to be symbolically reconstructed, it did not stand in the way of unlimited possibilities for the future. In the end, as was seen, Harlan's vision of the future did contain a substantial vision gleaned from the past—a liberal democratic one. Such an implied order and meaning of the future resided at a considerable distance from the Foucaldian endless chain of dominations broken by oppositions or Derrida's chain of texts bespeaking a longing for the absolute never to be indulged in by closures. Harlan participated in the postmodernist dilemma when his envisioned content affirming future did not fit well into the indeterminate world of endless and inherently aimless flux.

As an intellectual endeavor with ethical and political motives, poststructuralist postmodernism encountered great theoretical difficulties in finding in history any basis for moral and political action. The problems, caused primarily by the stipulation of nonreferentiality, were addressed by three historians who were critics of postmodernist theories of truth but were willing to listen to postmodernist ideas and formulate a nuanced response with a special focus on their impact on the public sphere. Joyce Appleby, Lynn Hunt, and Margaret Jacob, who differed in many ways from one another in their works, published their *Telling the Truth about History* in 1995, which "confronts head-on the present uncertainty about values and truth-seeking and addresses the current controversies about objective knowledge, cultural diversity, and the political imperatives of a democratic education."[153] As historians who wished for historiography to buttress—albeit critically—a pluralistic democracy of justice and freedom, they assessed the controversies generated by postmodernists over "national history, scientific integrity, and the possibility of achieving truth and objectivity in human knowledge of the past."[154] Their review of the history of historiography laid the groundwork for a reaffirmation of the basic assumptions in traditional historical epistemology. To that purpose, the authors distinguished clearly between a productive and a complete skepticism. The latter, including postmodernism, "is debilitating, because it casts doubt in the ability to make judgments and draw conclusions." A democratic society, as did all others, must rely on a potentially knowable and useful nexus between past, present, and the expectations for the future. For it, historians must engage in a vigorous search for the truth about the past (the life actually lived), which meant to remain open to the questions raised by postmodernists and concede ambiguities in the existing historical methodology without ever abandoning its validity. Neither the individual nor society could do without affirming "that truths about the past are possible, even if they are not absolute, and hence are worth struggling for."[155]

The discussion on the public use of history continued in works that focused on the application of postmodernist theories to the action programs of powerful mass movements, especially Marxism and Feminism. Their relationship to poststucturalist postmodernist theory offers many insights into complex problems that arise at the juncture of theory and life's praxis, particularly the one of social and cultural activism. Thus, their experiences with postmodernist theory have been of paradigmatic importance.

PART 4

**POSTSTRUCTURALIST POSTMODERNISM AND
THE RESHAPING OF SOCIETY**

19 WHAT KIND OF MARXISM IN POSTMODERNITY?

THE CONTESTANTS AND THE HISTORICAL SITUATION

Marxism's Handicaps

The contest of ideas between Marxism and poststructuralist postmodernism has been especially tumultuous because its issues were of large proportions, involved sharply antagonistic positions, and touched many lives directly. Marxists defended their versions of the progress theory, which had a theoretical structure honed in decades of conflicts, discussions, and revisions. Against them, poststructuralist postmodernists put an antiprogressive theory to end all systematic theories, especially those marked by a telic linearity. At stake in the struggle was the elaborate and dogmatic Marxist scheme of history affirmed by the Second International (1889) and subsequently refined and revised by theoreticians and regimes. According to that orthodoxy, changing production relations shaped history. Its teleological course displayed a fixed sequence of periods leading from primitive communism to industrial capitalism and onward to an end stage of fully realized economic justice. Such an objective, causally structured, and predetermined development could find no place in the postmodernist world of discontinuity, linguistically constructed entities, and ceaseless, nonredemptive change.

Although the Marxist side of the debate never lacked skilled defenders, conditions in Western society and culture did not favor it. When poststructuralist postmodernism came into its own, the crisis of confidence in modernity had also engulfed Marxism. The sense of certainty and hope that Marxism had engendered in millions of people was eroding under the impact of political and social developments. Signs of this erosion went beyond theoretical second thoughts in some individuals and small groups who, over many decades, had tried to lessen the rigid systematic of orthodox Marxism. Examples reached from George Lukács, Antonio Gramsci, and scholars of the Frankfurt School to the Budapest and Belgrade groups. In general, they advocated a Marxist theory more closely attuned to the full human condition and less to grand theory. Their voices proved less persuasive than the image of repressive practices in the countries where orthodox Marxism prevailed □ **169** as official philosophy of history and the order of life: The brutal imperialism apparent in the suppression of national dissenting voices (East Germany, Hungary, and Czechoslovakia), and the appearance of the New Left. Equally harmful was the unexpected vitality of capitalism. Finally, the collapse of the Soviet Union after 1989 signaled to many the end of Marxism.

The diminished hope placed in Marxism and the challenge of postmodernism created a situation for contemporary Marxism that Martin Jay has likened to that of bourgeois culture in the late 1800s. "The spectre of detotalization and disintegration, which haunted bourgeois *fin-de-siècle*, has returned to chill the socialist movement . . . of our day."[1] Many Marxists identified postmodernism as part of the specter and criticized it as the product of "an advanced form of an intellectual malady."[2] A few others have assessed the role of poststructuralist postmodernism more benignly as a standard for the modification, even the replacement of Marxism. They spoke of the problems in Marxism as a crisis limited to certain tenets of "classical Marxism" or as one of the recurrent renegotiations of Marxism.[3]

Signs of a Radical Postmodernist Critique

Due to the historical nature of Marxism, its views on history have been at the center of the ensuing debate. In it, a large segment of Marxist scholars have rejected any postmodernist influence. For them, postmodernism represented a decadent bourgeois phenomenon tied to the late stages of capitalism. They doubted that any significant concessions could be made without destroying the Marxist theory of history. Rather, they suggested a reverse adaptation— postmodern conditions should be defined in terms of Marxism. At the opposite end, scholars such as Ernesto Laclau and Chantal Mouffe, who have often been tagged "post-Marxists," have argued for a complete revision— a deconstruction—of Marxism on postmodernist terms. Crucial Marxist tenets concerning history, such as the dominance of economic phenomena and the resultant transparent, universal order of the world, must be abandoned in the new world of flux. Laclau and Mouffe celebrated that change as the necessary liberation of Marxism. Critics saw in that abandonment of objective entities and their ordering power the loss of the fundamental base for arguments against capitalism. Postmodernism lacked any foundation for social action. In between the two opposite stances a wide spectrum of scholars has tried various degrees of adaptations.

THE DECONSTRUCTION OF THE MARXIST VIEW OF HISTORY

Basic Disagreements

The collision of Marxism and postmodernism showed most clearly in the debates on the human world's order. For Marxists, the complex web of human phenomena had found a clear and universally valid organization in a dual institutional structure. The economic sphere with its modes and ownerships of production (manifestations of the struggle to control nature) provided the structure that determined all other activities and institutions (the superstructure). Depending on the version of Marxism, the determinism was more or less rigid. The perceived goal of the course of history was the establishment of the just economic institutional order that would be reflected in the appropriate superstructure. At that point, the proper truth would replace the ideologically charged illusionary truths of the past. Actual life and ideology would finally be one. The existential tension was resolved in a human existence where (in principle) the wish for change had met its end in the proper continuity.

Poststructuralist postmodernists rejected this view of the human world completely. They objected to the Marxist's reliance on objectively "real" entities, their hegemonical relations (primary economic structure/dependent cultural superstructure), objective forces working in a dialectical way, a unitary and universal development, an immanent telos, and an end to all change in a just world. Marxist structural stability, with its objective entities and forces, did not fit into the postmodernist fluid and decentered world. Especially troublesome was the foundationalism that gave a privileged position to economic structures. Society was no more than a contingent, momentary state of social relations, which themselves were discursive constructs. Even the end stage with its ideal economic order and unbroken continuity was a hegemonical concept. Equally objectionable was the Marxist reliance on the dialectical view of development with its aim of an ultimate synthesis. All closures were relapses into the old ways of thinking about history in terms of unity and totality. Ceaseless change must replace the ideal of an ultimate end. Its striving for absoluteness and universality made Marxism complicit in the horrors of twentieth-century history.

But should the fact that "guaranteed philosophical and epistemological underpinnings of the [classical Marxist] theory do not stand up" be reason for abandoning even those Marxist tenets that should be retained?[4] A nuanced response to the call for the rejection of key tenets of Marxism came from a group of British Marxist historians who strove to adapt Marxism to the new post-1945 world.[5] Independently of, but somewhat parallel to postmodernist theoretical considerations, they widened the scope of Marxist social history—approximating the inclusiveness of cultural history—without abandoning the objective character of social forces or the supremacy of economic forces among them.

Different Views on the Dynamics of the Human World

The course of history has for Marxists been determined by the imperfect adjustments to each other of the modes of production to the ways of production.

Throughout the past, such adjustments in the modes of production have lacked the full justice toward which the inherent telos guided historical development. Human beings, acting as members of a class, were the agents for the realization of that telos. In the modern struggle between exploiting and exploited classes, the proletariat was the decisive class. The mechanism advancing the ultimate goal was the dialectic form of resolution in which the given order was opposed by that which, as part of the given, had failed to gain justice. The established power generated its own opposition. In the course of the struggle a synthesis (accommodation) emerged. In Marxist history these syntheses represented temporary way stations on the road to the full economic and social emancipation of all.

The deconstruction of this view of history by postmodernists was intended to be complete. The economic determination of life was attacked as a simplification that forced change into predetermined channels—an inappropriate stabilization of the fluid world. The rejection also encompassed the status and role of the proletariat with its decisive role. The last of the class struggles would be fought and won by the proletariat. Yet in the postmodernist view, all struggles were discursive struggles without objective (ontologically founded) dimensions. Hence the concept of the proletariat produced by objective conditions was an outdated remainder of an ontologically stable world. Its very stipulation violated the injunctions against the claims of being objective, real, and privileged. The Marxist expectation of the proletariat's self-abolition at the point of full human emancipation from exploitation did not make it less objectionable a concept. Postmodernity's fluid world knew no binary oppositions but plural discursive entities in endless contestation.

Thus, those who wished to adapt Marxism to postmodernist thought have merged the proletariat into the plurality of opposition groups, reflecting the world of many and ever-changing "others." The proletariat had a strictly contextual, not a universal importance. Its reality, too, was only discursive. "If the unity of the class is created through the process of symbolic representation, the unity of the class is itself a symbolic event and belongs consequently to the order of the metaphor."[6] Such abandonment of a key feature of Marxist views on history roused strong opposition. André Gorz rejected the transfer of the proletariat's historical role to other, more ephemeral groups. Such downgrading was one more step in the transformation of Marxism into an aesthetic enterprise that obliterated Marxism's role as a guide to action.

A response to the negation of objective structures and forces, specifically that of class, was given by E. P. Thompson. In his *Making of the English Working Class*, he abandoned the narrow explanation of class as an automatic result of objective economically determined relations.[7] The working class(es) rose within specific historical conditions of which economic circumstances were indeed preeminent. The gestation of class consciousness was a creative construction of meaning by the people who lived in a certain context.

The Issue of Periodization

Even Marxists who have dealt with postmodernism sympathetically have not concurred in the rejection of social or historical totalities. "Without a conception of the social totality (and the possibility of transforming a whole social system), no properly socialist politics is possible."[8] With history seen as an objective whole, Marxists have used much erudition to find the proper chronological segments of human development. After 1945, the unexpected vitality of capitalism proved a spur for revisions of prevailing Marxist periodization schemes. And postmodernism's prominence as a cultural phenomenon posed the urgent question after its proper place in Marxist schemes of historical development. Answers linked the new capitalism, perceived to be less predictable, with poststructuralist postmodernism. Each of them made the schemes of periodizations more flexible than they had been in orthodox Marxism. But the thinking in terms of clearly identifiable periods remained intact.

Rather than viewing postmodernism simply as a symptom of decadence, Fredric Jameson fitted postmodernism with its "depthlessness," decentered subject, and overwhelming contingency into a modified periodization scheme inspired by Ernest Mandel.[9] An ample measure of economic reductionism was retained when postmodernism became the cultural expression, even "the dominant cultural logic of late capitalism."[10] As market capitalism became monopoly capitalism and, then, global capitalism the dependent culture changed in step from realism to modernism and, then, to postmodernism. The latter mirrored a looser and more "confused" capitalism with its total commodification of life. In Jameson's scheme postmodernism was history's tool to destroy mature modernism. As a historical agent, postmodernism helped erode the stable elements in high modernism, such as the hierarchical distinction between low and high culture and the authority of firm standards. Although Jameson largely approved of postmodernism, one must not overlook that for him Marxist historical thinking was primary, and postmodernism represented only an expression of a certain stage of capitalism. Ephemeral as it was, postmodernism could not shape the course of history. Most certainly, it was not the harbinger of history's end. Some Marxist critics found Jameson's synthesis "cogent" but *marxisant* rather than Marxist.[11]

A second example came with David Harvey's re-periodization of capitalism. For him, too, periodization expressed the actual order of history and was not a construct without strict objective limits. But Harvey found economic and cultural developments less rigidly linked. Rather "we see postmodernism emerge as a full-blown though still incoherent movement out of the chrysalis of the anti-modern movement of the 1960s."[12] Unstable aesthetically, it "celebrates difference, ephemerality, spectacle, fashion, and the commodification of cultural forms." Capitalism on its part made a "transition in the *regime of accumulation* and its associated *mode of social and political regulation* (emphasis in the original)." The rigid Fordist-Keynesian regime of accumulation yielded to one more unstable, uncertain, and flexible. Since societal, economic, and cultural regimes paralleled one another, postmodernism had a justified temporary place. In this as in Jameson's case, postmodernism represented a shift "capable of theoretization by way of the meta-narrative of capitalist development that Marx proposed."[13] However, in Jameson's and Harvey's works the tensions between Marxist claims to universality and totality and the postmodernist flat rejections of them were not resolved. The two scholars did not yield on the former, regardless of internal or external contradictions remaining in their adapted schemes. That held especially true for the dominance of the economic sphere. Neither did Eric Hobsbawm in his series of books on modern history abandon Marxist thought, although he used it flexibly.

Other Marxists were willing to yield more ground to postmodernism. Among them were those who simply wished to deemphasize the diachron orientation of Marxism by adding the spatial dimension to the temporal. The latter had dominated in orthodox Marxism's reasoning to the detriment of the synchron spatial dimension. The consequence has been an over-emphasis on Western developments and a neglect of the diversity of the global world. A strictly historically oriented Marxism was no longer sufficient in the stage of modernized capitalism. "Marxism itself had to be restructured to incorporate a salient and central spatial dimension."[14] The theorization of space must be at the core, not just at the periphery, of Marxist thought. Old Marxism had shown traces of spatialization in its imperialism theory. Jameson had spoken of the need for new social cartography (a cognitive remapping) of the now decentered global network of the third stage of capitalism.[15] Marxism must follow in the tracks of capitalism, which in order to survive expanded its reach spatially. Taking into account the decentered condition of the global world and the fluidity derived therefrom would save historical materialism by adjusting it to the "new, postmodern culture of space and time."[16] That argument pleaded for a Marxism in which space had equal status with time—the geographical with the historical—in the interest of a realistic universality. Hegemony, oppression, and emancipation would take on their full meanings.

However, most Marxists were not willing to diminish the Marxist historical view of human development and rejected major concessions to postmodernism. The very flexible scholar Dick Hebdige drew a line of defense around the economic basis for all phenomena and the central role of the proletariat in his Gramsci-influenced Marxism with the concept of hegemony at its center. The attitude also marked the attitudes of some of the New British Marxist historians. Hobsbawm did not yield on hierarchically ordered objective structures and forces in his otherwise updated Marxism. Without these elements, that which had made Marxism attractive as a view of life was lacking: the hope for an end stage of at least greater economic and social justice and the inherent telos pointing history into that direction.

About History without an Ultimate End and Hope

Marxist reformers sympathetic to postmodernism saw the close link between modernity and Marxism as detrimental, since postmodernist criticism of modernity immediately affected Marxism. Could one produce an "updated" Marxism from which were absent the perceived fallacies of modernity? The polar oppositions between the postmodernist and the Marxist world views made the realization of that project extraordinarily difficult, perhaps impossible.

In pursuit of that goal, no ingredient of Marxism was more important than the idea of an inherent aim of all historical development: the end stage with a just social order with no more class struggles. Power would largely be functionless and so would ideological struggles, because ideology would cease to be an instrument of exploitation. In temporal terms this meant the resolution of the existential tension in the triumph of continuity. Such a stable end stage came closer to the views of the structural postmodernists than to those of the poststructuralist postmodernists. For the latter, it represented the extreme transgression of the injunction against closures—the same objection they had voiced against the ideal end stage of the Enlightenment's progress theory. The Marxist hope of an end stage must be supplanted by the acceptance of endless change.

A Marxism as the "the road to nowhere" or a "journey without destination" stood in sharp contrast to the old Marxist longing for the final fulfillment. While the denial of any end to history fit well into the ideal of a fluid world, it abolished powerful incentives and standards for action. Marxists discerned a purely aesthetic endeavor. At best, Foucault's constant opposition to and Derrida's endless deconstruction of the existing order remained. Hence many Marxist theoreticians demanded that the telos of history must not be abandoned in return for the perceived benefits of a purely contingent (some would use the word chaotic) world. Agency could only be sustained by a directional, persuasive if not inspiring hope. Furthermore, Marxism as action-inspiring theory needed "real" not constructed forces driving developments in the proper direction.

Still, some Marxists strove to give Marxism a stronger affinity to postmodernity and were willing to deconstruct Marxist theory. A significant part of that deconstruction would be directed at the Marxist scheme of history. On the basis of the postmodern world being purely contingent, even chaotic, these Marxists distinguished a "redemptive" from a "democratic" Marxism.[17] Others would use the contrast of utopian and non-utopian Marxism. The redemptive or utopian Marxism had no place in a postmodernity that was seen as "modernity without the hopes and dreams which made modernity bearable."[18] Changes in Western culture prescribed the deconstruction. The most prominent voices in this regard were those of Ernesto Laclau and Chantal Mouffe. Their advocacy championed a Marxism that fit the postmodern fluid world: one without the "evident truths." Prominent among the latter was the projected perfect end stage.

Laclau's and Mouffe's approach found few outright followers. Critics pointed to "the 'double void': double, because empty, equally, of theoretical substance and of any genuine practice, that is, normative specificity or direction."[19] Marxists could rely only on the indeterminacy principle in the search for an entirely new radical democracy.

Christopher Norris offered an example for a more selective adoption of postmodernist concepts. He rejected the denial of referentiality with regard to truth, yet exempted Derrida and his textualism from that rejection. That surprising exemption relied on his perception of an opening in Derrida's otherwise rigid textualism. He cited Derrida's defense of an ultimate separation of philosophy from literature that for Norris prevented the engagement with ethical, political, and epistemological issues from being seen as an undifferentiated textual free play. This meant the gaining of a foundation for political (Marxist) action on behalf of reform. Raymond Williams put it more bluntly when he stated that "a Marxism without some concept of determination is in effect worthless."[20]

A different assessment of Derrida's work emerged from a brief French exploration of the relationship between Marxism and the postmodernists. Although it yielded no solution, the episode provided insights into Derrida's, perhaps even the general postmodernist, dilemma in ethics and action. In the early 1980s, French Derrideans, particularly those on the political left, engaged in a fervent debate on the usefulness, if any, of Derrida's views. Those who thought that these views could be useful took two contrary positions. One suggested that deconstructionism should be made a tool for activist (in this case, Marxist) policies. The other called for Marxism itself to undergo a deconstructionist inquiry and transformation. Many were not convinced at all and the debate faded after yielding a major conference and a short-lived Center.[21]

Advocates of a moderate adaptation of Marxism to postmodernism were numerous. Convinced that postmodernism was seriously wrong, they, nevertheless, looked for a theoretically feasible link between the logics of necessity and contingency. They admitted that the postmodernist critique of modernity, to which Marxism was now linked, had been effective. "Increasing rationality cannot guarantee increases in freedom, and to that extent the 'utopian' modern project is in trouble. But that should not give rise to disillusionment and despair, nostalgia, frustration or panic. Little has actually been lost, beyond excessive faith, misplaced hope, and unrealistic expectations."[22] Marxism was to be seen as a political venture full of risks, not the fulfillment of a predetermined destiny. Neither had modernity itself offered much security since science and technology could not guide political actions securely. Thus, those were not justified who wished to flee from modernism by radically deconstructing all its manifestations, including the traditional form of Marxism. Instead, some Marxist reformers have spoken of a radical democracy with greater economic justice as the appropriate aim of history. In accord with that, preference went to modifications in the manner of the British Marxist historians where social theory and empirical evidence cooperated by critically stimulating each other. However, such an approach affirmed the access to material reality and collided head-on with the crucial postmodernist denial of referentiality seen as absolute necessity for a totally fluid world. This fundamental divide in the views of the world and their application to life has dimmed the prospects for experiments in combining Marxism and postmodernism.

A MARXIST VARIANT WITH POSTMODERNIST THEMES: THE FRANKFURT SCHOOL AND HABERMAS

In its over four decades of creative activity, the Frankfurt School's transformations have linked it through some views, concerns, concepts, and criticisms of modernity to postmodernism, although such affinities were hardly welcome. Key commonalities came in structural postmodernism's projection of an end stage marked by a monotonous and seemingly unbreakable routine and in poststructuralist postmodernism's insistence on the salutary dominance of change. But rather than pointing to direct influences, the affinities were witnesses to shared broad shifts in Western intellectual life.

From Philosophy of History to Theory of Culture

In the 1930s, members of the Frankfurt *Institut für Sozialforschung,* particularly Max Horkheimer, Theodor W. Adorno, and Herbert Marcuse initiated a fundamental critique of modern society, which they always identified with a liberal and capitalist order.[23] But, already in the late 1930s, especially after the ideologically disenchanting Hitler-Stalin pact of 1939, the Soviet Union, too, became an object of that critique. In this early period, the aim had been the construction of an overall theory of social change in the Hegelian and Marxist vein with a less rigidly determinist interconnection between material and ideational aspects of society. Marx and Freud were accepted as respected guides rather than as the dominating masters of orthodoxies.

Then, in the 1940s, with Adorno and Horkheimer residing in the United States, they realized that their quest had crystallized into the question of "why mankind, instead of entering into a truly human condition, is sinking into a new kind of barbarism."[24] In a crucial shift they turned from a traditional philosophy of history (seen now as a *Geschichtsmetaphysik*) to a systematic historical examination of culture. Culture ceased to be a secondary phenomenon that reflected the economic base (as in the superstructure concept of orthodox Marxism). Instead, it represented the broad and diffuse area of mediation between the conceptual realm and life.

The Valuation of Change over Continuity

The basis on which Adorno and Horkheimer evaluated change and continuity differed considerably from the purely formal affirmation by poststructuralist postmodernists. The latter thought in terms of a conceptual realm that was a purely linguistic construct with no effective link to the material life. Horkheimer and Adorno disagreed not on behalf of a positivist representational theory of cognition but on behalf of one that relied on the complex interweaving of language, concepts, and material contexts. That view made possible statements with a claim to truth value, which transcended the limits of tolerance of poststructuralist postmodernists. The ability of Critical Theory to elaborate insights useful for remedial action depended on the formulation of such statements. Adorno's mediation technique showed how the particular (a context) and the general (a dynamic force) created each other in a new dialectic. Here, too, the result was a world of flux, this time not produced by a linguistic reductionism but by effective and conscious human action. Choices in it were not created by the arbitrary realization of endless possibilities (poststructuralist postmodernism) but by a never ceasing rational critique of the existing context. The resulting world knew emancipation, though not as a realized ideal state of affairs but as an ongoing process of critique.

When the historical Enlightenment failed to produce a dynamic emancipation it became the object of sharp criticism in the *Dialectic of Enlightenment* by Horkheimer and Adorno.[25] For them, the new barbarism visible in the catastrophes of the 1930s and 1940s was due not to a sudden resurgence of the irrational but to objective developments that drove Western culture relentlessly toward it. The authors supplanted the well-worn explanation for them—a not-yet-sufficiently developed human enlightenment—with a more sophisticated but also more ominous historical one.

History, once more in the often used postmodernist triadic form, had first seen the separation of reason from nature and myth, then the development of an ever greater promise of critical reason, and, finally, the fateful misdirection toward a new mythical stage, this time produced by reason itself. The parallels to structural postmodernism were striking.

In the mythical period, human beings existed in a state where reason had not yet clearly separated from nature. Myths represented early attempts to order the cosmos, while still leaving human beings integrated into the world. The characteristic image of the world was that of the recurrence of the same—"the principle of immanence, the explanation of every event as repetition, is the principle of myth itself."[26]

Then the myth-destroying work of critical reason commenced. With the replacement of mythical images by rational concepts began the demystification of the world (akin to Weber's *Entzauberung der Welt*). The replacement of the world of animism by the world of rational construction continued until, in the modern period, reason as scientific rationality gained exclusive dominance over explanations.

The historical Enlightenment marked the high point of hope in reason but also the point at which the fateful reshaping of reason began. Just as some structural postmodernists had seen it, reason's crucial critical facility weakened steadily as a complex process turned critical into technical or instrumental reason. The latter, aiming at greater control and domination, escalated the original and necessary separation from nature into one of ever deeper alienation from it. In the interest of certainty and effectiveness instrumental reason tended to limit the methods, depth, and range of exploration and established permanencies in the interest of special groups. Here Critical Theory noted that the relationship of reason to other human ways to relate to the world was marked by relentless antagonism. This held true especially in regard to reason's counterpart, *Sinnlichkeit* (sensibility), which was repressed. Epistemologically speaking, truth became a matter of abstraction and numbers, while the truth seeker, fully emancipated from nature, held total control. When all challenges from the natural and social world had been stifled, rationality of a certain type became the absolute sovereign. In the world of numbers and facts, the human beings could feel to be in absolute control while not noting their absolute alienation from nature and society. Or, to put it into postmodernist terms, the story of rationalization in its bad form had replaced all other metanarratives. Hence the misdirection of the historical process and, with it, the crisis in Western culture.

The deeper alienation could not be alleviated in the world constructed by instrumental reason. Only critical reason could discern in the given reality, the "other"—here referring to that which was not at all or not yet fully realized. It alone could, in the language of the Frankfurt School, negate the given.

Critical Theory's Postmodernity

In the later works of the Frankfurt School there was an awareness that the third phase of human development had begun—a new mythical one. The hopes for emancipation with its salutary change faded as "enlightenment reverts to myth."[27] Although never called postmodern, that phase resembled in its central feature structural postmodernism's postmodernity. No joyful empire of reason and freedom would emerge but instead an age with a tightly organized and static order. Its claim to full truth and, thus legitimacy for the existing order, was treated as being beyond the reach of challenge.

But just like the poststructuralist postmodernists, Frankfurt scholars refused to see such a static society as the proper destination of human development. An endless stage of the same could not sum up the whole of history since it hid the reality of history as suffering and gave no voice to the victims. The impressions of truth and harmony were falsely created by the suppression of critical reason, the very source of all negation and opposition to the existing liberal and capitalistic order. Unlike the structural postmodernists, the Frankfurt scholars knew a counterforce to the postmodernity of an endless continuity of the same. And in contrast to the poststructuralist postmodernists, they did put against the static world not a chaotic one with a purely constructed order but a fluid world that did not exclude objective and inherent meanings. And the mandate for action was clear: to restore reason, having been temporarily waylaid, to its critical status.

The shadow cast on Western culture was that of *Verdinglichung* (objectification most blatantly as commodification) which also figured prominently in structural postmodernism. In the world of dominant *Verdinglichung,* negation, as the capacity to see things not simply as they were given, yielded to the desire for predictability, repetition, and stability. The world portrayed as objective reality, unchallenged by critical reason, was no more than an illusion maintained by the artificial exclusion of contingency. In modernity, the Enlightenment, once the grand critical enterprise and a destroyer of myths, had itself become a closed myth: a witness to the experience that "demythologization devours itself." When done, it left behind nothing but the affirmation of what existed as "demythologization recoils into the mythus."[28] Worst of all, the controlling human being was itself reduced to the level of an object.

Ironically, reason itself was bringing about its own destruction. The new world of intertwined instrumental reason and power had cut reason off from its sustaining root: reason's original alienation from nature that triggered an ongoing challenge to the given without aspirations to or hope for a stable answer. To avoid closure, the existential gap between the given historical condition and human expectations (particularly the ethical one of the avoidance of suffering) had to remain open at all times. The reform of the irrational society by critical theory remained the permanent goal.

On the broad definition of the specific problems to be remedied the Frankfurt scholars agreed. They were *Verdinglichung* and its connected *Verblendung*—the deception built into the structure of the liberal-capitalist mass society and its mass production that lured people (including the working classes) into accommodation to the wrong life because it promised security, wealth, and superficial meaning. The price of the *verwaltete Gesellschaft* (Horkheimer's term for the administratively ordered and controlled society that brought comfort via the promised secure existence) was a human life of vastly diminished dimensions. "Once the threads have been cut [tying life to the vital experience], joy and happiness may survive as images of the past, but their vitality has been extinguished, and the images cannot last for very long."[29] Here, Adorno and Horkheimer had resisted the affirmation structural postmodernists had given to such a society. But their call for constant change differed from that of the poststructuralist postmodernist's remedy: change for change's sake. Theirs was directed at substantial changes.

Changing the Vision for the Future

Eventually Horkheimer abandoned his early faith in radical changes in the existing society and accommodated himself to the continuance of human suffering. Adorno, however, still looked, in his last two works, *Negative Dialektik* (1966) and *Aesthetische Theorie* (1970), for a description of the desired society and the agent that could steer history toward it. The ideal of a nonhegemonical and nonexclusive mode of conceptual comprehension of the world (shared with poststructuralist postmodernists) could never be realized since the given always distorted it. Nevertheless, the good must remain visible in theory, although the praxis of life seemed beyond redemption. Rarely did Adorno see a possibility for the nonidentical to assert itself in the world dominated by the principle of exchange, although he insists that it never is completely absorbed by it. With critical reason rendered impotent by instrumental reason in modern culture, Adorno also had only qualified hopes for the critical capacity and role of art with its different cognition of the world. In it, he discerned the spur of the nonidentical that enabled art to envision a different human condition. Adorno never clarified how art could indeed be the agent of change. But, the purely technical fascinations and qualities of modern art disappointed him. Whatever was left of artistic creativity were mere products of the *Kulturindustrie* (aesthetic enterprises of routine productivity).

Herbert Marcuse staked his case on a revolution that no longer relied on the nationalization of production, the now powerless proletariat, activist expectations from the marginalized people of the globe, or the progressive elite leading the masses to a new enlightenment. The key to true change was a new role for the libido. The one-dimensional bourgeois-capitalist and communist societies that delayed all gratification and deprived libido of much of its energy in the interest of work and productivity must yield to a society marked by an unfettered eros and a lack of oppression. The end stage would be an age of endless continuity that had a remarkable similarity to Kojève's first vision of an age of sex and games.

On their parts, Adorno and Horkheimer had long left Marcuse's optimism behind. The future carried a close resemblance to the structural postmodernist postmodernity—a life frozen into routine. A life marked by the absence of concrete hope (Adorno) and the resignation to a world of continued suffering (Horkheimer). In their *Dialectic of Enlightenment* they had still held out the hope that the admonition would be heeded "that the Enlightenment *must consider itself,* if men are not to be wholly betrayed." The new mythology could be destroyed by an enlightenment that was "not paralyzed by the fear of truth" as the constant critique of the given. Otherwise the false clarity of facts "condemns the spirit to increasing darkness." True clarity would be based on the "*petitio principii*—that social freedom is inseparable from enlightened thought."[30] Progress was not progress if it merely produced material comfort and ease and left the many dominated by a few. Their admonition was not heeded. The age of relentless and continuous change guided by critical reason or eros would not arrive. Life had disappointed the Frankfurt scholars as it had the postmodernists whose hopes had been affined in their expectations from either endless change or continuity.

Habermas: From Instrumental to Communicative Reason

Jürgen Habermas did not share the resignation of the later Frankfurt school to reason's negative turn as an inescapable fate. With his belief in reason's centrality and beneficence intact, he also considered the postmodernist abandonment of reason and, with it, of the Enlightenment unjustified. Instead he urged his contemporaries to bring to its proper conclusion the "unfinished project of modernity." Habermas judged those who abandoned modernity to be conservatives (really reactionaries). That characterization became well known when he used it for the French postmodernists in the context of his debate with Lyotard. The postmodernists separated theory from praxis. On his part, Habermas continued to work in the reform spirit of the Frankfurt School or Critical Theory, which—in earlier times—had affirmed the feasibility of constructing a truly modern society.

From the late 1960s, Habermas has argued the case of thought that went beyond the discussion of means (methods) to that of aims and goals as the only way to avoid Max Weber's vision of a quasi-posthistoric "iron cage" society. He also objected to the poststructuralist postmodernists' deconstruction of all stable elements of truth as the path to avoid suffering, oppression, and domination. That goal needed the reaffirmation of the metanarrative of emancipation (progress). In the debate with Lyotard, he argued that without the proper metanarrative there would neither be an ideal society to aspire to nor an action program to reach it. In other words, the existential tension cannot be abolished but must be channeled properly. Habermas advocated consensus without coercion as the facilitating means for achieving the "ought to be" status. Lyotard argued that any "consensus is only a particular stage of the discussion [in the sciences], not its end. Its end is paralogy."[31] Habermas's affirmation of consensus as the goal and end of history was a metanarrative no less dangerous than any other. The contention that history was discontinuous and aimless appeared to Lyotard as the safer alternative.

Habermas's historical metanarrative knew a development from an undifferentiated state of unity and cohesion to one of ever greater social differentiations. In modernity such unity was difficult to achieve since the increasing rationality separated two once-unified components of society from each other—the guiding and explanatory system and the *Lebenswelt* (best but not entirely accurately rendered as the world human beings actually lived in).

The explanatory system relied on instrumental (*zweckrational*) action, one that had a clearly defined goal and followed a set of rules. This system, growing more and more intricate conceptually, produced a world that resembled the "iron cage" (Max Weber), the "administered world" of Adorno and Horkheimer, and the static postmodernity of the structural postmodernists. Organization increased, meaning decreased. An ironic result showed. The more instrumental rationality dominated, the weaker the once firm solidarity of society became, and the more restricted were the problems posed and the solutions found. The bureaucratic state triumphed. In a dangerous development, the rationalization process threatened the *Lebenswelt*. Habermas spoke even of a colonization of the life world. In a similarly defined situation, structural postmodernists had declared the ironic ending the inevitable one. Poststructuralists who negated all such metanarratives had affirmed the sole reality of ceaseless change. In contrast, Habermas developed an ideal (for postmodernists, privileged) path to social integration. It relied on a linguistic solution.

In the *Lebenswelt* integration occurred through communicative action. The latter always involved others and their willingness to understand. Its guidance and substance came from the experiential knowledge of life and its forum of action was the speech act. The goal of communicative action was not to affirm the postmodernists' plurality but to reach consensus. The result was to be a society from which power and coercion were absent in communicative action. In that society the system and the *Lebenswelt* were reintegrated and the conditions for finishing the project of modernity were given. History had followed its true telos.

Critics have raised questions about what could account for the stipulated desire in human beings to come to a consensus and whether power could be neutralized. Postmodernists have suspected the continuing presence of metaphysics in the ideal of consensus. Marxists have pointed to the distortions of power resident in all contexts and their influence on the noncoercive purity of the consensus. And, in general, there has been the question about the presumption of a natural, historically developed, or rationally evident preference for harmony without which Habermas's theory of history would lose its foundation. In his recent writings, Habermas has tried to modify his views on the basis of a less sanguine assessment of the human readiness for noncoercive communication. That modification put an even greater distance between his views and those of the postmodernists but left the preference for change guided by communicative reason intact. The completion of the project of modernity relied on the peaceful reconciliation of change and continuity and not postmodernist separation.

■ 20 POSTMODERNISM AND FEMINIST HISTORY

Women's History in the Progressive Mode

At the very core of progress resided the concept of emancipation that has energized the dynamics toward equality. Among the major obstacles in the way of emancipation has stood the male/female divide with its historical inequalities. For decades, the arguments used in favor of women's history were indeed couched in terms of emancipation and other progressive ideas and ideals. Full justice for the cause of women was seen as an integral part of history's goal of universal emancipation, which entailed the advance of women from the condition of enforced silence to that of equality of voice. That seemingly good fit between progress and women's causes had a persuasive influence on the thinking and writing of women's history. It also helped that women historians remained in general agreement with contemporary history's epistemology, which was considered to be neutral in the male/female controversies. Nevertheless, women's history was decidedly revisionist in spirit, determined to break through the barriers of the male-dominated historiography. The demand was for the long-withheld inclusion and equality for women's history in the accounts of history and for women historians in the historical professional. As an important part of feminist activism, women's historians strove to bring to public awareness the so far suppressed story of the role of women in the past. The result was expected to render major support to the struggle against patriarchal ideas and institutions—the theory upholding them and the practices buttressing them. In history, their detrimental effects showed in the diminution if not neglect of women and their roles. Much criticism was aimed at the division of life into private and public spheres, where private meant the essentially female and not proper part of historical accounts. The critique even encompassed the widely used periodization scheme for Western history with its underlying progressive assumption of a general amelioration of the human condition. That progress had left women behind (Joan Kelly, Judith M. Bennett). In the new view, the discriminatory binary definition of the gender relationship (weak/strong, able/unable, etc.) had to yield to a reality-based and morally justifiable one. Such a women's history knew the equality but not necessarily the sameness of women and men in all aspects of life, including the opportunity to write history. With such a program women's history remained well within the framework of progressive history and the epistemology of existing historiography.

The Shift to Gender History

Judged by the standards of contributions to historical knowledge and to the women's cause, women's history proved to be abundantly successful. Yet some women's historians experienced a distinct sense of unease in the midst of this success. By the late 1980s, with women's history widely accepted as an essential part of historiography, questions emerged concerning basic concepts and interpretations. They did so in an intellectual climate that had its origin in the social and cultural upheavals of the 1960s and 1970s and, in the 1980s, was powerfully reshaped by postmodernism. The climate was marked by a strong animus against the Enlightenment and its understanding of the role of reason and progress and affected many of progressive history's key elements, which had been tightly woven into women's history. Now, some feminists raised the question whether reliance on the theoretical propositions of the progress view of history offered a sufficient and proper argument for the cause of women. Was the integration of women's history into the mainstream of historiography, particularly academic history, under these conditions the proper ultimate goal? The search for an answer led to a broader theoretical base for the history of women. Rather than augmenting or adjusting the epistemology of women's history, some feminist scholars called for a radical revision of history's theoretical structure. A major element in the ensuing debate concerned doubts about the continuing ability of women's history to stimulate and support activism after the achievement of equity. And postmodernist theories, by the 1980s already a significant influence on the debate about history in general, offered themselves, to some feminist scholars persuasively, as guides in formulating questions and answers.

Gender history's prominent advocate, Joan Wallach Scott, described the situation in the 1980s as marked by a serious dilemma in thinking about women's history. Argued on the basis of equality of all human beings, women's history would eventually blend into social history as a fully recognized field in historical inquiry. Argued on the basis of a natural permanent difference between the sexes it would maintain a separate status and remain isolated or ghetto-bound (Denise Riley). In her resolution to the perceived dilemma of equality versus difference, Scott shifted the focus away from women's history to gender history. She considered gender (be it male or female) the most crucial shaping force in history. This change, a response to her own complaint about the lack of theoretical consciousness among historians, involved a decisive link to poststructuralist postmodernism.

Consequently, opponents of the stipulation of equality to men as the ultimate goal (with all the theoretical implications) rejected the Enlightenment frame of reference as too limited and improper for feminist history. That frame became outdated with the "Death of Man," (referring to the human being that could transcend subjectivity), "Death of History," (as an ordered and meaningful entity), and "Death of Metaphysics" (an affirmation of permanence and universality).[32] In that connection, the postmodernist view of the world and its phenomena as being in complete flux proved of great assistance. The idea of a world in flux, which seemed totally malleable, exerted a strong attraction. In it, an authoritative truth and striven-for objectivity were detrimental concepts made stable by means of referentiality and binary oppositions. Once they accepted the tenet of the absolute dominance of change over continuity, feminist historians would bring new arguments and counterarguments to bear on the debate in and about history. The effect on the history of women was twofold. On the one hand, feminists lost concepts that had been sources of stability, hope, and legitimation; on the other hand, the search for appropriate substitutes could get underway. Postmodernism offered concepts useful for a perpetual feminist critique of the existing social order: heterogeneity, pluralism, marginalization, exclusion, and the "other." With long-standing feminist positions at stake, the debate about the desirability of adjustments on terms of postmodernism became intense.

In between Women's and Gender History

A crucial issue in the debate turned out to be the very concept of "woman." So far, it had been the object of much theorizing, but discussions had been governed by the goal to establish a stable identity. Arguments for features characteristic for women, among them special female empathy, reluctance to be aggressive, or preference for consensus, were suggested as "natural" (universal) qualities. In line with postmodernist thought, some feminist historians rejected stipulations of such inherent or innate characteristics since they were considered products of thinking in terms of essentialism and universalism. One of its detrimental consequences had been the definition of "man" with firm characteristics that appeared to justify male superiority. To some degree, women historians also used such legitimation when they amassed proofs for the achievements of women in the past. But the concept of a firm and separate woman's identity had served and was serving as an effective bond of unity and a guide for feminist action. Hence the universalizing approach retained a strong following. Reason, truth, and objectivity were not necessarily seen as patriarchal tools. Some liberal, conservative, and Marxist women were convinced of the need for a measure of stability in female identity in order to retain strength for the argument on behalf of women's rights. The commonality was beneficial even on a global scale.[33] Yet women's historians with a postmodernist perspective saw much greater advantage in the condemnation of all that was stable with its freedom for constructing and acting.

Much like Joan Wallach Scott, Judith Butler opposed vigorously any entity "woman" with its binary tendencies. Biology was not the shaping force of human destiny. The ideal must be entities with fluid definitions and borders. They must be free floating. Toril Moi, writing primarily in literary theory, added her influence. Gender was no longer the result of given but of constructed characteristics. The history of women had made its poststructuralist postmodernist turn. Its impact on the history of women stretched well beyond the concept of gender. Gender history needed the postmodernist world of complete and ceaseless flux. That world was one of discontinuity and ruptures, constructed entities, heterogeneity, and a lack of uniformity and overall unity.

The quest for a many-faceted concept of "women" corresponded to that world and also reflected the reality of the women's movement in which the variety of women became a significant factor calling for recognition. Postmodernist theory offered the solution in the ideal of heterogeneity seen in the ethnic, social, sexual, and educational differences among women. The previous common denominator definition of "woman" had established a firm presence where a flexible one was needed. The latter was thought to be unable to suppress the "other" among women. In that spirit, Marxism was rebuked for using "the generalizing categories of production and class to delegitimate demands for women, black people, gays, lesbians, and others whose oppression could not be reduced to economics."[34] On that point, some feminist historians saw in the recognition of such "otherness" a mandate for gender construction. Constructed and changing gender identities seemed to be the perfect match for the pluralistic world with its agonistic gender relations. From it would be banished closures. In a recent study, Bonnie

Smith demonstrated how modern definitional closures were used to exclude women from being recognized and accepted as professional historians.[35]

Women's ultimate goal must be to control the power over the definition of their own gender and, on that basis, reconstruct history. In Scott's case, Foucault proved of special influence with his nexus between power and knowledge. It was male power that had impressed its concepts and interpretations of what exactly the term female meant on history and history writing. But the influence of poststructuralist postmodernism on the history of women was much wider, because corollaries of the acceptance of a world in complete and ceaseless flux were many. Four of them brought changes with multiple impact: a world marked by discontinuity and ruptures, unstable constructed entities, heterogeneity, and a lack of uniformity and overall unity. To historians fell the task of laying bare the power configurations responsible for the specific gender constructions in the contexts of the past. That meant the deconstruction of traditional history. Feminist history must not be "the recounting of great deeds performed by women but the exposure of the often silent and hidden operations of gender that are nonetheless present and defining forces in the organization of most societies."[36] To that undertaking, postmodernism rendered significant assistance through its calls for pluralism and heterogeneity and its avoidance of all universalizing tendencies. Quietly put aside was the presence of the still permanent bodily divide between male and female and the implication of limits to the freedom of construction therefrom.

For critics, there remained the question of how persuasive gender construction could be on behalf of the feminist cause. Feminists supportive of modernism argued that the patriarchal mind set, older than modernity, was most effectively eroded by women historians pointing out the inner contradiction between the logic of emancipation and that of actually existing institutions and practices. Opposing modernity harbored the danger that the element of hope and the instrumental use of emancipatory ideals would be lost. If all constructions were declared to be equal, could any one of them carry more weight than the other? Could they legitimize the feminist struggle since in the constructed world legitimizing rationale, aim, or guidance for it could not be found? The only prospect appeared to be an endless struggle between the established order (the dominant gender definition) and the "other" (the excluded ones) with equally endless changes in dominance. Thus, theoretically, any lasting resolution was excluded. A Foucauldian struggle for the power over constructing the male and female definitions would stretch endlessly into the future.

In the end, the concept of gender and any theory built on it inherited postmodernism's nonreferentiality problem. Two manifestations could be observed. First, and specific to this case, gender was linked to a material referent—the body, male or female. All definitions of gender must take account of it. There, the postmodernist assumption of unlimited possibilities did not quite apply. The second manifestation came in the absolute dominance of change. Any definition of gender was a closure, representing a specific ordering of the web of life, and hence itself needed deconstruction. If it claimed more, it tried to assume the quality of a universal essence in the stipulated purely contextual and fluid world. Women's history and the progress view of history had an ambiguous relationship and now postmodernism and gender history duplicated that: enhancements and hindrances alternated.

Has gender history finally replaced women's history? Not yet. So far, gender history opened another way to look at the issue of the male/female divide and, as has been usual in such cases, contributed new insights to history. Or as it looked from another and grander perspective, a full exploration of what history would look like if women's and gender history had "achieved its grandest ambition—the ambition to rewrite all of history from the standpoint of gender."[37] The settlement of that issue depended on proof of the feasibility of a world in total flux as the precondition of the world of pure construction. Until then, gender history will coexist with women's history and general history in some tension but also in a state of mutual stimulation. As for poststructuralist postmodernism, its views on history proved to have an uneasy fit with the goals and strategies of the history of women. One could add: as has been the case with other activist endeavors concerned with historiography. The need for developments and aims legitimated by life has not yet found persuasive support for the presupposition of an inherently meaningless world temporarily ordered by constructs chosen from a myriad of others of equal value.

PART 5

CONCLUDING OBSERVATIONS

A Proper Moment for Assessment

This exploration of the postmodernist challenge to history occurs at a moment when the exuberant hopes and the excessive zeal generated by modernity have diminished and postmodernism has been, for some time now, in the aftermath of its creative period. Even the debates on postmodernism have become somewhat predictable. At this point, it becomes feasible to answer some important questions concerning the degree and kind of impact postmodernism has had or might still have on not just the discipline of history but also the historical understanding of human life in general.

Postmodernism has proved to be neither a fad (although a measure of faddishness has marked it) nor a product of an overheated intellectual fashion industry. But neither has it turned out to be what postmodernists have expected it to be: the ultimate answer to life in general and historical understanding in particular. And far from being an isolated and rather inexplicable phenomenon, postmodernism has been part of a broad response to a disenchantment with and skepticism about modernity that, by 1945, had gathered formidable strength, first in Europe and then in America. In this context, postmodernists strove to supplant the progressive view of history with a more appropriate and final one. Looking back at this endeavor, the question can be asked: to what extent has postmodernism succeeded in doing so. Will, in the twenty-first century, historical thought and practice conform to postmodernist designs in a posthistoric postmodernity or is the postmodernist challenge destined to become another episode in the history of historiography?

The Complex Relationship between Postmodernity and Modernity

The postmodernism debate has been so intense because it reached well beyond the repertoire of methods and techniques presently used in historical practice. Postmodernism's ambition to purge from the future human condition the vicissitudes manifest in modernity—often explicitly widened to include all of history—pushed the discussion of the theoretical aspects of history to the level of basic propositions concerning the world and human life. Historians, as reluctant participants in the debate, were forced to defend the basic propositions used in "doing history."

The postmodernist challenge's significant impact cannot be properly understood unless one focused attention on the postmodernist stipulation of a sharp break between modernity and postmodernity and of the need for a radical change in the human condition connected with it. For bringing that about, postmodernists had recourse to the reinterpretation of the role of time. Giving such weight to time in historical thought was not in itself a challenge to history. History's very claim to be a special way of thinking about life has always been based on its insistence that every one of the myriad aspects of human life involved the temporal dimension. Time was not just a neutral space in which historical events occurred but was an essential and formative part of all of human experience. The awareness of the finiteness of life and of the intertwined but often contradictory desires for change and continuity in human thought and action, together with the existential tension produced by them, were integral elements of the historical nexus between past, present, and expectations for the future. Such nexus building engaged in daily life as well as in historical analysis witnessed to the historical quality of life.

Postmodernist theories became a serious challenge when they rejected the contention that the existentially important simultaneous presence of the two temporal experiences constituted an unalterable part of human life. These theories maintained that the exclusive dominance of either change or continuity was not only possible but was the necessary condition for a posthistoric postmodernity. As separate and dominant organizers of human life, each of the two temporal experiences would establish and maintain the proper human condition. At first glance, such a separation of the two time experiences seemed to be quite novel. Yet, as was seen before, early Greek philosophers already discussed such a possibility in their theories of the "natural" state. Heraclitus had stipulated the exclusive dominance of change and the illusory nature of duration and continuity. Other philosophers thought change to be a temporary phenomenon and permanence the true reality. Now, postmodernists wished for the dominance of either change or continuity so as to bar the vicissitudes of the past from future human life.

These considerations focused attention on two unexpected but important links between modernity and postmodernity. The progressive theory of history had already contained such a separation of the two aspects of time. The historical period had been seen as the age in which relentless and increasingly dominant change drove the human race toward the perfectly rational age. In that dynamic period, all attempts at closures were harmful because they were not based on a fully developed rationality. The Enlightenment promised the perfected rationality that would bring a proper and final closure. Then, continuity would prevail and change would be reduced to benign minor adjustments. Postmodernists, too, separated change and continuity but in a radically different way.

In a further striking similarity to modernity, each of the two visions of postmodernity also began with a new enlightenment. That of structural postmodernism revealed how wrong the common understanding of the nature and goals of progress had been. Progress had not failed but simply never had aimed at a state of affairs that people had hoped for—one of freedom, happiness, and virtue. Now, people finally understood that they longed above all for the security of utter continuity, and postmodernity simply brought about that desired state. As for historians, they were not called to alter their methods of work prompted by the new enlightenment. They only must be more accurate in observing the objective structural forces. Even for verifying their expectations for the future, historians needed only to wait for the actualization of the postmodernity dominated by continuity.

In contrast, poststructuralist postmodernism's enlightenment revealed progress to be an immoral script for history. Hence the historian's task in making postmodernity real was the rejection, directly, of the progressive view of history and, indirectly, of all traditional views of history. That rejection entailed a complete revision of how historians thought about their role, especially the search for one truth. Change must be championed unconditionally and immediately in life and historical theory so as to assure the dominance of such new postmodernist ethical and political ideals as plurality, diversity, and heterogeneity. Guided by this presupposition, postmodernist theory had an impact on traditional historiography that amounted to a complete revision.

These considerations have made visible the postmodernist retention of another key feature of modernity. One that most historians have rejected as detrimental to a proper history: the reductionist approach. Progressive views of history had reduced the complex web of life to a simplified hierarchy of forces and structures ultimately structured and dominated by reason. Now, postmodernists proposed a new reductionism when they reached for their dominating organizing principle into the human temporal experience. In one case continuity and in the other change became the key to the explanation of life and its history.

Furthermore, it has become clear that at the root of both postmodernist endeavors to describe or even bring about an ultimate and proper state of human existence was a moral and political quest. The choice between change and continuity was to be no less than that of the *summum bonum* (highest good) fit to determine the proper shape of postmodernity. In either case, the result would be the suppression of the vicissitudes that had marked life in the historical period. But as was seen, change or continuity came to be considered as purely formal categories for the shaping of life. The mere fact that one or the other would prevail sufficed to bring about the proper order without reliance on the perfection of a specific aspect of human life. Not having understood that fact had been the great failing of past historical interpretations. Now, affirmation of it would inspire hope for the future.

On their part, poststructuralist postmodernists could not simply assume a passive stance in the shaping of posthistoric postmodernity. They had to work out the appropriate theory as the blueprint for postmodernity. The task involved the purge of all objective, inherent, and thus continuous elements (now seen as metaphysical) from historical thought. Affected would be the concepts of metanarrative, truth, the use of history, and the historicity of life. That struggle was to be at the core of the postmodernist challenge to history. When the resultant theories yielded inconclusive results, they foreshadowed problems to come in their application to historical thought and practice.

The Stubborn Persistence of the Metanarrative

Lyotard's exhortation to be incredulous toward metanarratives was one thing, the avoidance of writing metanarratives was another. Indeed, the very stipulation of a postmodernity established a rudimentary but important metanarrative—the period of modernity was followed by that of postmodernity.

Structural postmodernists expanded that dual scheme to a tripartite sequence: era of natural stability—historical period of instability (modernity as its peak and end)—postmodern stability. However, their view of history entailed no objections to the metanarrative (or in their terminology, the philosophy of history) as long as it was the right one.

Poststructuralist postmodernists objected to metanarratives as products of "essentialist" or "foundationalist" thinking. Metanarratives stipulated one overall meaning and order of history and one force to bring it about. They blocked the unimpeded change necessary for the directionless fluid world with its multiple truths. Yet, in their own ways, even Foucault, Derrida, and Lyotard spoke about the past in terms of at least rudimentary narratives. Foucault relied on epistemes for configuring whole cultures and periods and an endless wavelike dynamics, which included periods and turning points. Derrida returned, however tentatively, to the concept of emancipation and talk of a new democracy, not yet defined. Lyotard sketched a world that developed from the harmony between the narrative and social bonds to the dominance of scientific discourse to the agonistic struggle between incommensurable language games (later a coexistence of phrase regimes). These responses hinted at the contradiction between rigid negation of any inherent overall order and its silent accommodation—a problem that was bequeathed to those who tried to write accounts in the spirit of the pioneers.

Yet the difficulties besetting attempts to free postmodernist theories from the grip of the metanarrative did not end there. The underlying ethical and political motive for postmodernism involved the expectation that postmodernity was the period when the existential tension would be resolved in a world dominated by one or the other temporal experience. Then, that which "ought to be" will be that which "is." That stipulation raised the question whether postmodernism did not by the logic of its overall argument reintroduce a progressive metanarrative when an imperfect age would be followed by a much better, if not perfect one.

In this context, the issue of postmodernity as a utopian period arose. In their defense, postmodernists could point to the absence of the utopian stipulation of general happiness from the characteristics of postmodernity. The postmodernity of the structural postmodernists resembled the traditional utopia in one respect: it was completely stable and uneventful. But it offered few "happy" versions. Most often, postmodern society was characterized as petrified, crystallized, or demonstrating an animal-like existence. Critics could point to these insights as proof that a one-dimensional temporal perspective produced a human condition that really was no longer truly human. Poststructuralist postmodernists also held out scant hope for happiness. They rejected that long-standing crucial feature of utopias, the passive and happy adjustment to endless stability. Instead, they demanded from everybody the ascetic denial of the longing for closure (continuity) and the engagement in a daily struggle to keep change unimpeded.

In an important unresolved ambiguity the range of validity claimed for postmodernist views on the course of history was left unclear. Structural postmodernists did not hesitate to assume universal validity for their findings. None of their theoretical tenets prevented such a claim, only life could disprove it. Poststructuralist postmodernists faced their own stern injunction against claims to universal validity for their projections for the future. But if their suggested postmodernity were only contextual—valid for Western culture only—critics could point to the cyclical philosophy of history as the plausible theoretical framework for both postmodernities. The static posthistory of structural postmodernists fit perfectly to a culture's ahistorical state after all creativity had been exhausted in the period of decadence. And the postmodernity of poststructuralist postmodernists with its multitude of equally nonbinding truths could be seen as marked by the extreme relativism typical for late stages of decadence.

The Issue of Truth without Stability

The inconclusive arguments against the metanarrative, while chronologically primary, were logically dependent on the even more crucial one against a correct and binding truth. They pointed to the decisive difference on the issue of referentiality between the poststructuralist postmodernists and most historians. And the debate of that point could not be postponed. These postmodernists urgently demanded thoroughgoing reforms in historical thought because there could be no wait for postmodernity to be established since there was no stable end stage to be ushered in. Postmodernity began when the conscious struggle on behalf postmodernist concepts began. They were to be tools for organizing and forever guiding the postmodern world of constant flux. Most important were actions directed against the to-be-expected recurring attempts to reshape the dangerous link between truth and authority. Such attempts aimed at giving legitimacy once more to closures in theory and in life's practice (usually on the basis of essences, foundations, or stable natures). They impeded, naively or intentionally but always dangerously, the ceaseless process of change. Without the key reform of truth finding and of the concept of truth itself and a constant struggle to preserve the results, the vicissitudes of history would return.

The role of the linguistic turn has been seen widely as the decisive inspiration for poststructuralist postmodernism when it actually was the instrument ready at hand to realize the world of dominant change. The turn promised to free postmodernist theory of direct cognitive links with anything once seen as objective or material (the extralinguistic). The objective or material reality, now considered inaccessible, was subject to the intertwining of change and continuity and, therefore, an obstacle to the world of pure change. Once the separation of words and world was achieved and the world of words accepted as the effective reality, such obstacles would disappear. A world of pure human construction became feasible.

The main problem with the poststructuralist postmodernist theory of truth derived from the difficulties encountered in banning all elements of continuity from such a world. Gadamer and Heidegger "solved" the problem by conceding a strictly circumscribed degree of stability in their works (prejudgments and tradition). Foucault and Derrida tried to shed such unwanted remainders of stability in the midst of a world of discursive and textual constructs. Yet Foucault did not succeed in giving the crucial concept of power a clearly discursive reality. Derrida conceded that stable elements were clinging to language. Neither could Derrida demonstrate that the differentiation process and the whole from which it "arose" were purely discursive phenomena.

The incomplete realization of nonreferentiality in postmodernist theory persisted in the application of that theory to history. There was, first, the difficulty in accounting for the conceded universal human need for order and meaning, itself not a linguistic construct. Poststructuralist narrativists encountered the problem in clarifying the status of the poetic choice and the literary forms, both formal universals that left basic questions open. The new cultural historians were troubled by the uneasy relationship between the ideal of a "pure" semiotic system and the need for social actions in concrete contexts as well as the inescapable ties between cultural narratives and the material world. The difficulties were also visible in the "identity" debates, particularly in the new cultural histories, where the nonreferentiality problem returned in the concept's implied continuity. Attempts to revise Marxist and feminist historical thought in the poststructuralist postmodernist vein faced related problems.

Finally, historians also could ask whether postmodernist fears of a controlling absolute truth were actually justified in the case of history. Perhaps excluding brief moments of exhilaration over discoveries, most practicing historians have never claimed to pronounce the absolute truth. Ideologues have. A product of conscientious use of proper and commonly accepted procedures, historical truth has been critically assessed and modified in increasingly sophisticated ways, which made it conditionally and partially "durable." Authoritative truth under strict critical control would be a fitting description. Poststructuralist postmodernist answers have not addressed such objections by historians, because for them these objections were still in the old mode of reasoning and, thus, needed no answer. The separation of words from the world must be accepted as given and historical inquiry redirected at clarifying the ways in which historical accounts were constructed linguistically. Truth and truth finding were exclusively formal matters—concerned only with that and how things change discursively and textually. The material content of a specific context need be part of the inquiry only to the extent that it fit that criterion. The world of dominant change could not accommodate another truth.

Problems with History's Usefulness

The so-called lessons of or from history have been properly never those that simply equated experiences of the past with those of the present. Instead, they derived from careful, methodical, and skillful assessments of the past and its contexts, the results of which were incorporated not mechanically but creatively into a new historical nexus. Life's past successes figured in them and so did, perhaps even more so, its failures. Moreover, since life necessitated constant historical nexus building, such "lessons" were not a matter of choice. After all, the past was the still active extended human existential experience, admittedly incompletely known.

Still, even postmodernists shaped their visions of postmodernity according to one "master lesson," the one that told what of the past from now on must be avoided. From it, postmodernists derived their insights for building the proper nexus toward postmodernity. Structural postmodernists considered all previous nexuses flawed by erroneous perceptions of the working of progress. The turbulence so characteristic of history was a result. But by virtue of a now full enlightenment the true aim of progress had become clear: the final static postmodernity. That last, the postmodernist nexus would be accurate. Afterwards, the historical inquiry had done its duty. In postmodernity, minuscule nexuses would record the pulsations of routine life only—yielding annals of the endlessly the same not like their ancient and medieval forerunners of the significant or extraordinary. The relative uselessness of history would signal the advent of the posthistoric postmodernity.

Poststructuralist postmodernists, too, saw in the transition from modernity to postmodernity the last historical nexus, which yielded the only acceptable lesson from history. Once more, a new enlightenment ended the long series of illusory nexuses with its reliance on continuity. The new linguistically constructed world knew none of the objective limits, recurrences, perimeters, and other "resistances" to change with which human beings had wrestled. These objective structures had disappeared as false sources of lessons. In a more technical language, such elements of an objective order were metaphysical elements that had become unnecessary detractions.

Future "lessons" would be simple and formal, derived from the guiding one: change was the key reality. As a guide for action in an inherently meaningless world, Foucault suggested the alternating valuation of power, as positive when it was used to oppose and negative when used to defend the established system of order. Derrida turned to the "presence—absence" duality for the guide in decision making and action, all of it driven by the concern for the "other." In neither case did past and present particulars of contexts matter: who established what, opposed whom, or why should that which was present be replaced by that which was absent in an endless and in itself meaningless chain. The ideals of heterogeneity and pluralism could serve as meanings, but like the ideal of pure change they remained formal guides only.

The problems in translating these postmodernist tenets into a new answer to the question of history's utility have so far proved insuperable. This problem of an unresolved legitimation for postmodernist theory's utility for action was a particularly serious one. For ethical and political reasons, poststructuralist postmodernists had asked for a radical rethinking of progress. Now, in the world of change with infinite possibilities of equal value for actions, guidance from the content of history—past existential experience—was absent.

The Missing Postmodernist Histories

In the end, the most telling indicator for the problems with an exclusive affirmation of either continuity or change has been the absence of persuasive successes in the translation of postmodernist theories into viable historical writings.

An assessment of the creative potential of postmodernism in terms of historical accounts produced in full conformity with postmodernist theory will have to differentiate between its two versions. All structural postmodernists could do was to demonstrate how human life foreshadowed the approaching static postmodernity. Such accounts remained within the perimeters of the traditional approaches to history. They would tend to show in the past the signs of the expected development. Historiography would change in postmodernity but not before.

The expectations from poststructuralist postmodernists were much higher. They had to be fervent activists on behalf of the desired postmodernity since the latter needed a conscious effort for its realization and, once established, for its maintenance. The world of flux had to be defended constantly against the centuries-old longings and habits of closure—the reliance on illusory elements of permanence. The new type of historicity and way of writing history had to be realized immediately. Proper historical accounts were needed as witnesses to the emerging or even already existing postmodernity.

What, then, have been the results of the decades long, ardent push toward radical change in historiographical practice? Have there been works that reflected postmodernist theory in its purity?

The situation has not been promising. In sharp contrast to the rich harvest of theoretical writings on what historiography should be, the harvest was poor of historical accounts that fully qualified as poststructuralist postmodernist. Even the ardent advocate of poststructuralist postmodernism, Keith Jenkins, admitted that truly "postmodernist histories are 'histories of the future,' are histories 'which have not yet been,' . . . they are clearly not yet in existence." He could only point to works that were "intimations of postmodern-type histories at least according to some 'trend-spotters.'"[1] Among the most prominent of them he listed works by Simon Schama, Natalie Zemon Davis, and Emmanuel Le Roy Ladurie. Yet neither Davis nor Ladurie qualified as examples. And Simon Schama in his *Dead Certainties: (Unwarranted Speculations)* (1991), had indeed mixed "purely imagined fiction" (invented witnesses and dialogues) into historical accounts without identifying them as such in the text. But Schama resumed here the habit of historians, practiced until well into the eighteenth century, to present what would today be put into abstract considerations as narrative sketches or invented speeches and dialogues. Modern historians have rejected that practice. Yet with its by and large conscientious use of sources, Schama's experiment represented more an echo of old narrative history than a postmodernist testimony.

Indeed, no historical account of note has conformed to such crucial tenets as the impossibility of a nonlinguistically mediated access to the past (nonreferentiality), the absence of closures, exceptionless multiperspectivity, or the dominance of power as energizing force. Elements have always surfaced that did not fit into the confines of a linguistically or discursively constructed fluid world. This should not have been a surprise since purity had even escaped the pioneering authors.

Perhaps one could argue that the postmodernist endeavor had not yet fully enlightened historians about the necessity of using the new opportunities open to them. Yet, while postmodernists could praise some works as harbingers of great things to come, critics among historians saw only the lacuna—for them a proof of the impossibility to write historical accounts that adhered strictly to the poststructuralist postmodernist precepts.

Does History Have a Future?

Postmodernists formulated answers to this question in the contexts of their theories on postmodernity. Structural postmodernists foresaw a severely limited role for historians in their postmodernity. Poststructuralist postmodernists expected a radical move away from traditional historical understanding in theirs. As it has been put, a history insisting on the reference to the actual past was the old world's "concept of last resort, a floating signifier, the alibi of an alignment with obligatory values. It pertains to no signified at all."[2] Epistemologically that was translated into the affirmation of a linguistically constructed world in which the past existential experience could no longer be the direct referent. Once history would respond completely to that and other theoretical tenets it would lose its legitimacy as a separate endeavor. Making these expectations actuality depended, first, on whether postmodernist theories were persuasive enough in their logic, coherence, and consistency to be reliable predictors for the envisioned postmodernity. And, secondly, on whether life would conform or could be made to conform to theoretical expectations.

In matters of theory, indications have not been positive. In poststructuralist postmodernism, which carried the heaviest theoretical burden, multiple unresolved theoretical problems have become visible. They have not remained problems of concepts, ideas, and techniques, as the theoretical problems have not been technical glitches but testimonies to life's resistance to attempts at totalizing and simplifying explanations. Life, the final arbiter on historical theories and nexuses, also has given few indications of an impending realization of the theoretical blueprints for the two postmodernities.

The prospects for the postmodernity of structural postmodernists have not looked promising. Life has not yet made all people immune to those aspirations that produced such routine-transcending phenomena as great literature, works of science and technology, commercial empires, architecture, and writings about the sacred. The forces of sameness have indeed received much support from standardization, commodification, and mass communications but also have evoked formidable negative reactions, among them profound existential boredom.

As for the realization of the poststructuralist postmodernist world of ceaseless change without stability, there has been much delight in the world of lessening restraints but no great enthusiasm for the asceticism that required abstaining from all certainties and stabilities in the interest of flux. The admonition against closures has not been heeded. People have still striven for change in order to achieve the "right" conditions, hoping that these would offer at least temporary continuity. Neither has it been shown how collective life could be sufficiently and successfully organized in a totally fluid world. While the world of linguistic constructs with its infinite possibilities for combinations does, theoretically, deprive continuity of chances for its realization, there have been no signs that life can be made to conform fully to that model. Only if one or the other postmodernity became the form of actual life could historians become either simple annalists or simply analysts of how the natural and human world was constructed linguistically.

Among those poststructuralist postmodernists with high hopes for a replacement of traditional history by its postmodern counterpart, some have expected a broad interdisciplinary endeavor to prevail. Yet apart from some interdisciplinary cooperation and a few institutes of "cultural studies," little has transpired to justify such expectations. Perhaps the suspicion was justified that institutional inertia was simply too strong. Yet experiments in interdisciplinary cooperation have been willingly engaged in and have proven most fruitful, while a unified discipline has remained a distant possibility, at best. Developments also have not favored the quite logical view that if only the present and the future were to be left as active temporal aspects in the nexus, history would become redundant. The past was not easily ignored. In short, there has been no evidence for the contention that "we can now 'forget history' for postmodern imaginaries *sans history*" and "that history *per se* is slipping out of conversations; that it does not seem urgent or much to the point any more."[3]

Even the advocate of poststructuralist postmodernism Patrick Joyce has asked: "Does this mean that postmodernism has had its day?" He added, "I think not" because he observed a partial and pragmatic acceptance of elements of postmodernist thought in historiographical practice. He still regretted that "large sectors of the History discipline are totally impervious, and in some instances extremely hostile, to postmodernism in whatever form."[4] While he suspected a lack of enlightenment or at least of fair play on the part of historians, the deep theoretical divide between traditional historiography and postmodernist thought was no phenomenon of scholarly inertia or thoughtless rejection. Postmodernists had been too ready to identify history with modernity's progress view of history, although the history of historiography showed such a limitation to be inappropriate. But historical knowledge and understanding have been shown to be by far more substantial. In Western culture, they have reflected, however imperfectly, the existential experience since ancient Greece. This self-limitation of postmodernist criticism made it not surprising that at the end of the creative phase of poststructuralist postmodernism stood not a radical historiographical revolution but, as Joyce conceded, some pragmatic acceptance of elements of postmodernist thinking about history.

Calls for Selective Listening to Postmodernism

Postmodernists have complained frequently and bitterly about the historian's lagging response to their challenge. In typical fashion, Patrick Joyce regretted the insignificant impact of the postmodernist challenge on the field of history: "Far from being beleaguered, the commanding heights of academy history seem secure against the skirmishing bands outside, though some notable walls have fallen, chiefly in the United States"[5] Others have pleaded for a mutual relenting: "A theoretical *hauteur* instructs a redoubt of methodological conservatism, and the latter shouts defiantly back. Between the two lies a silence, a barrier that in these tones cannot be crossed."[6]

After more than three decades of controversy, a diminution of postmodernist innovative energy, and problems besetting the quest for a totally new inquiry and age, on the one side, and the recognition that if not postmodernist theory in toto so at least a few postmodernist diagnoses and tenets had merit, on the other side, historians have with prudent caution begun to explore possible adjustments in thinking about their practices. Some postmodernists saw in this wish to find a *via media* between fervent advocacy and unremitting rejection of poststructuralist postmodernism a mere tactical move. However, many historians considered calls for a moderately adjusted historical thought a valid and time-proven reaction. John Toews suggested guidelines for an accommodation when he defined experience as not directly available to the historian but being mediated by meaning, which was itself "constituted by and through language." However, that was no one-way process since human experience, in turn, shaped or at the least delimited the construction of meanings. Neither language nor experience could be considered reality in isolation from each other. And, one must add, there also was neither need nor possibility to define the world as all change and no continuity.

Calls for mutual listening and calm discussion were raised. "For progress to be made in understanding the truth and objectivity of history, each side must attend more closely to what the other is saying."[7] C. Behan McCullagh tried to persuade historians to give up assumptions of a direct, linguistically unmediated, and hence objective correspondence between reality and accounts as naive. However, he demonstrated to postmodernists that their views, based on the radical separation of reality from accounts, were equally illusory. Historians affirm and postmodernists negate too much too soon.

A general, none-too-specific concession of some value to postmodernist thought became fairly common. The prominent representative of social history, Lawrence Stone, provided a good example. He never relented on the historian's *conditio sine qua non,* the ability of historians to have access to the nonlinguistically mediated reality. Pure textualism created a hall of mirrors in which texts, completely isolated from material contexts, reflected endlessly one another. However, historians could profit from a greater awareness of the complexity of texts and the insights of the new cultural anthropology. But, although Stone praised the work of Clifford Geertz, he remained rather skeptical of the latter's symbolic anthropology with its conflation of the real and the imagined. In what would turn out to be a typical response for historians, Stone's willingness to concede to postmodernism some beneficial impact on the discipline of history remained strictly controlled.

Other historians were willing to venture further in their appreciation of the "semiotic challenge." Medievalists, accustomed to complex textual problems, had to be especially concerned with the consequences of the postmodernist language-based concept of reality. Gabrielle Spiegel discerned in postmodernist innovations a spur to a fuller historical understanding. In her assessment of postmodernism she came to view language as neither the creator of reality (literature) nor as the transparent and neutral medium (scientific history). Historians could accept discursive practices as partners of their concern with and insistence on the materiality of the past (through evidence). If, however, texts formed their own independent world then "historical study can scarcely be distinguished from literary study, and the 'past' dissolves into literature."[8]

The marks of postmodernism will remain on historiography. As serious endeavors to remedy the actual and perceived flaws of modernity's approach to life and history, the two varieties of postmodernism have failed as grand theories of human life but have issued challenges that historians will not soon forget. The extremity of postmodernist views made them falter but in the process they became useful by what they have pointed out. One important contribution, in which both postmodernisms shared, was the salutary redirection of the historian's attention to the basic philosophical presuppositions of "doing history." On other issues they parted company.

Structural postmodernists will be credited with having rescued from intermittent forgetting the lesson that human life and its history have an ironic component. Decisions and actions taken in accordance with a well-worked-out historical nexus produced nevertheless unexpected consequences. Even a theory such as progress that seemed to allow for no contingent elements was granted no exception. Hence all actual consequences of historical developments, even those which worked against the logic of theoretical expectations, must engage the attention of scholars.

Poststructuralist postmodernist theories have enriched our knowledge of the process by which we relate to the world. In the actual existential experience and its analysis, language as discourse and text as well as the narrative will be granted a considerably enhanced role. When historians balance the objectively given and the interpretatively constructed, they will treat language as a much more active partner. And the web of meanings will overcome its status as poor cousin of materiality. And the ethical implications of epistemological theory, such as the exclusion of moral issues from attention by the choice of methods and presuppositions, will not be forgotten.

The postmodernist challenge will leave historians equipped with a richer repertory of questions and a new sense for the proper possibilities and limits of historical inquiry. But the attractions of grand simplifications through reductionism of any kind have been once more thoroughly explored and found unable to master properly and effectively the web of past life. Modernists and postmodernists alike have treated the complexity of life and the related inconclusiveness and indeterminacy of knowledge as a problem with an easily obtainable solution. A final enlightenment did tell about the true nature and aim of life. Modernity found the key to the solution in the perfection of rationality that would resolve the tension defined as that between rational knowledge and ignorance wedded to oppression. Structural postmodernists perceived reason as solving the problem by guiding life to a postmodernity of the endless continuity of a rigidly routine life. For poststructuralist postmodernists change yielded the key to the solution. Its world was a symbolic, linguistic, or rhetorical one that transmuted all existential issues (the great and little ones of life as lived) into internal difficulties of a world of pure construction. Yet these issues proved resistant to solutions by grand theoretical schemes concerning the temporal dimensions. What had looked like a soluble theoretical problem turned out to be a constant feature of the human condition: the endless task of finding a balance between the inescapable need for certainty (with its necessary element of continuity) and the equally inescapable fact of ceaseless change. The incompleteness and temporariness of historical accounts simply reflected those of life.

History in the Aftermath of the Postmodernist Challenge

Compared with postmodernist theories, with their clear-cut solutions to the tensions besetting the existential experience as well as inquiries into it, history's ways of inquiry and their results have looked messy and of small proportions. But they have endured, not the least because they have remained open to revisions, rectifications of balances in emphasis, and novel insights, thus recognizing the elements of newness and of sameness in every historical context. Despite its obvious imperfections, the historical nexus, trying to account for as many aspects of life as possible and respecting the full dimension of time, has proved a sturdy way to comprehend life. Not the least because historians have long known about the fallibility of their knowledge. In life, there have been the at least partial failures of all nexuses in their expectations for the future and in historical analysis there has been the awareness of the gap between that which happened in the past and the historical account of it. Historians have tried to narrow that gap as much as possible but no experienced historian has ever claimed to have closed it. Still, even in the face of the odds against them, historical accounts, built upon critical inquiry, have yielded a body of knowledge—sufficient rather than perfect—that has constituted the only available repository of the existential experience by actual people in actually existing past contexts. This hard-won foundation for life and for its historical accounts—while itself always open to revisions and argumentation—has proved indispensable.

All of that boded ill for history as a source of redemptive hopes. But in its own way, history has offered hope through affirming the possibility of gaining some lessons from the past—with great caution and moderation. The insights offered by the past were gleaned from stories of successes and failures, from understanding human possibilities and limits. They provided measured hopes for betterment (ethically and materially) but also warnings against simplistic expectations of perfection in the conduct and study of life. Thus, although the so-called Golden Age of history may well have faded away, history has retained its crucial and distinctive function in and value for human life. History—despite its flaws and intermittent misuse—has remained the only attempt to keep a record of the full existential experience of human beings who have actually lived at a given time and place. This assertion has not denied the value of those ways of thinking about the world and human life, which have at one time or the other contested the place of history such as philosophy, theology, the social sciences, and literature. But neither would or could history concede its place to them. Life, being historical in nature, has prescribed the general role of history and life's actual contexts have changed historiography's specific shape. That link has made history an existential necessity. Such history has been in the best sense empirical, that is, obligated to reflect the whole past human condition. Risky endeavors as they are, historical accounts, nevertheless, have informed us about glorious human achievements and the ash heaps of overreaching ambitions, the morally best and the abysmally evil, the needed balance between change and continuity, and hope on the human rather than the utopian scale. This record of the human experience over the millennia, always incompletely understood but cumulatively becoming clearer, has been the responsibility of historians to keep and make known and will be so in postmodernity and beyond.

NOTES

Part One. A Preliminary Exploration of the Postmodernist Challenge
  1. Carl Becker remained in the ranks of the New Historians for only a few years. By 1910, he began to doubt their trust in the truth-producing power of empirical research. See "Detachment and the Writing of History," *Atlantic Monthly* 106 (October 1910): 526–28.
  2. Gianni Vattimo, *The End of Modernity: Nihilism and Hermeneutics in Postmodern Culture*, trans. Jon R. Snyder (Oxford: Polity Press, 1988), vi.
  3. Ihab H. Hassan, "The Culture of Postmodernism," *Theory, Culture and Society* 2, no. 3 (1989): 119.
  4. Wolfgang Welsch, *Unsere postmoderne Moderne*, 2nd ed. (Weinheim: VCH, Acta humaniora, 1988).
  5. Stefano Rosso and Umberto Eco, "A Correspondence on Postmodernism," in *Zeitgeist in Babel: The Postmodernist Controversy*, ed. Ingeborg Hoesterey (Bloomington: Indiana University Press, 1991), 242.
  6. Ernest Gellner, *Postmodernism, Reason and Religion* (London: Routledge, 1992), 22.
  7. Hassan, "Culture of Postmodernism," 121.
  8. Susan Sontag, *Against Interpretation: And Other Essays* (New York: Farrar, Straus & Giroux, 1966), 298.
  9. Vattimo, *End of Modernity*, vi.
  10. Hans Bertens, *The Idea of the Postmodern: A History* (London: Routledge, 1995), 10–11.
  11. Dick Hebdige, *Hiding in the Light: On Images and Things* (London: Routledge, 1988), 195.
  12. Heinrich Klotz, *Die Moderne und Postmoderne: Architektur der Gegenwart, 1960–1980* (Braunschweig: Vieweg, 1984), 15 (author's translation).
  13. Patrick Joyce, "The Imaginary Discontents of Social History: A Note of Response to Mayfield and Thorne, and Lawrence and Taylor," *Social History* 18, no. 1 (1993): 83, and Allan Megill, "Recounting the Past: 'Description,' Explanation, and Narrative in Historiography," *American Historical Review* 94, no. 3 (June 1989): 631.
  14. Nancy Partner, "Historicity in an Age of Reality-Fictions," in *A New Philosophy of History*, ed. Frank Ankersmit and Hans Kellner (Chicago: University of Chicago Press, 1998), 22.
  15. Lucien Febvre, *A New Kind of History and Other Essays*, ed. Peter Burke, trans. K. Folca (New York: Harper & Row, 1973), 29.
  16. In the United States, history's longed-for emancipation from literature manifested itself symbolically when, in 1904, the historical conference connected with

the St. Louis World's Fair carried the designation Historical Science, while the earlier auxiliary historical conference at the World's Columbian Exhibition at Chicago still had been conducted under the label Historical Literature.

17. Rosso and Eco, "Correspondence on Postmodernism," 242–43.

18. Jean-François Lyotard, *The Postmodern Condition: A Report on Knowledge,* trans. Geoffrey Bennington and Brian Massumi, (Minneapolis: University of Minnesota Press, 1984), xxiii.

19. Jean-François Lyotard, *The Inhuman: Reflections on Time,* trans. Geoffrey Bennington and Rachel Bowlby (Stanford, Calif.: Stanford University Press, 1991), 34.

20. The title of Wolfgang Welsch's already cited book.

21. Keith Jenkins, ed., *The Postmodern History Reader* (London: Routledge, 1997), 3.

22. See John McGowan, *Postmodernism and Its Critics* (Ithaca, N.Y.: Cornell University Press, 1991), ix.

23. Zygmunt Bauman, *Intimations of Postmodernity* (London: Routledge, 1992), vii–viii.

24. The term's first known use came as *post-historique* in Célestin Bouglé, *Qu'est-ce que la sociologie?* (1905; Paris: F. Alcan, 1921), 86. Further use followed in works by Bertrand de Jouvenel, Hendrik de Man, and Arnold Gehlen in the late 1940s and 1950s. For a more recent discussion of the term, see Ilie Paunescu, "L'entrée dans la posthistoire: critères de définition," *History and Theory* 35, no. 1 (1996): 56–79.

25. Andreas Huyssen, "The Search for Tradition: Avant-garde and Postmodernism in the 1970s," *New German Critique* 22 (1981): 30.

26. Jenkins, *Postmodern History Reader,* 8.

27. Foucault established a periodization: Renaissance (?–1660), classical (1660–1800), and modern (1800–1950) implicitly followed by the contemporary period. Baudrillard produced his periodization without clear chronological division.

28. Typical representatives of the two sides in the controversy were Hans Blumenberg, *The Legitimacy of the Modern Age,* trans. Robert M. Wallace (Cambridge: MIT Press, 1983) and Carl L. Becker, *The Heavenly City of the Eighteenth-Century Philosophers* (New Haven, Conn.: Yale University Press, 1932).

29. The most useful reference here is to Condorcet, "Sketch for a Historical Picture of the Progress of the Human Mind," in Keith Michael Baker, ed., *Condorcet: Selected Writings* (Indianapolis: Bobbs-Merrill, 1976).

30. See Michael Koehler, "'Postmodernismus': ein begriffsgeschichtlicher Überblick," *Amerikastudien* 22, no. 1 (1977): 8–18. Also, Margaret A. Rose, *The Postmodern and the Post-industrial: A Critical Analysis* (Cambridge: Cambridge University Press, 1991), 3–20 and Welsch, *Unsere postmoderne Moderne,* 12–17.

31. See Dick Higgins, *A Dialectic of Centuries: Notes Towards a Theory of the New Arts* (New York: Printed Editions, 1978), 7.

32. Rudolf Pannwitz, *Werke,* vol. 2, *Die Krise der europäischen Kultur* (Nuremberg: H. Carl, 1917), 64 (Author's translation).

33. Federico de Onis Sanchez, *Antología de la Poesia Española e Hispanoamericana* (Madrid: [Imp. de la Lib. y casa edit. Hernando (s. a.)], 1934), xviii. As these essentially literary categories were later on used in various anthologies, the term postmodernism survived in this limited connotation.

34. Joseph Hudnut, "The Post-modern House," *Architectural Record* 97 (May 1945): 70–75.

35. Arnold Toynbee, *A Study of History* (London, 1939), 5:43 (there postmodern was written as Post-Modern). Also in the abridgment of *A Study of History* by D. C. Somervell (New York: Oxford University Press, 1946), 39.

36. At this point, the controversy whether Enlightenment-born modernity and modernism could actually be held responsible for fascism must be mentioned although it cannot be explored in this context. For a guide to the controversy, see the debates in connection with the German *Historikerstreit*. For example, Rudolf Augstein, ed., *Historikerstreit: Die Dokumentation der Kontroversen um die Einmaligkeit der national-sozialistischen Judenvernichtung* (München: R. Piper, 1987).

37. Lucien Febvre, *A New Kind of History and Other Essays*, ed. Peter Burke, trans. K. Folca (New York: Harper & Row, 1973), 29.

38. Some of his work of that period appeared in Charles Olson, *Human Universe, and Other Essays*, ed. Donald Allen (New York: Grove Press, 1967).

39. Elizabeth Deeds Ermarth, *Sequel to History. Postmodernism and the Crisis of Representational Time* (Princeton, N.J.: Princeton University Press, 1992), xi.

Part Two. Postmodernity as the Triumph of Continuity

1. Cournot's work was first dealt with in Célestin Bouglé, *Qu'est-ce que la sociologie?* (Paris, 1921), earlier published in *Revue de metaphysique et morale* (1905). Much later, in the 1950s, the German anthropologist Arnold Gehlen discovered Cournot in the context of the German "Posthistoire" debate.

2. The natural order produced a harmonious undifferentiated society. One must note here that even Condorcet, speaking of his vision of the end stage, hinted at a return to natural harmony. He described the human race as "emancipated from its shackles, released from the empire of fate . . . with man restored to his natural rights and dignities." Keith Michael Baker, ed., *Condorcet: Selected Writings* (Indianapolis: Bobbs-Merrill, 1976), 281.

3. Antoine Augustin Cournot, *Oeuvres Completes*, vol. 3, *Traité de l'enchaînement des idées fondamentales dans les sciences et dans l'histoire*, ed. Nelly Bruyère (Paris: Librairie Philosophique J. Vrin, 1982), 484. (All translations of Cournot's text are by the author.)

4. Cournot, *Traité*, 480.

5. Ibid., 485, 487.

6. Ibid., 484.

7. Ibid., 485.

8. Henry Adams, *Mont-Saint-Michel and Chartres* (Garden City, N.Y.: Doubleday, 1959), 337.

9. The German term is left standing since the English "rationalization process" has too strong a post-Freudian connotation.

10. Max Weber, *Gesammelte Politische Schriften*, 3rd rev. ed., ed. Johannes Winckelmann (Tübingen: Mohr, 1971), 332. (Author's translation.)

11. Weber, *Gesammelte Politische Schriften*, 63.

12. Max Weber, *The Protestant Ethic and the Spirit of Capitalism*, trans. Talcott Parsons (New York: Scribner, 1958), 182.

13. William M. Sloane, "History and Democracy," *American Historical Review* 1, no. 1 (October 1895): 1–23.

14. For an excellent contemporary statement of the situation see Woodrow Wilson's Chairman's Address, "The Variety and Unity of History," in *Congress of*

Arts and Science: Universal Exhibition, St. Louis, 1904, ed. Howard J. Rogers (Boston, 1906), 2: 3–20.

15. They were edited and published by one of the participants, Raymond Queneau. English edition: Alexandre Kojève, *Introduction to the Reading of Hegel,* assembled by Raymond Queneau, ed. Allan Bloom, trans. James H. Nichols, Jr. (New York, Basic Books, 1969). Specifically, the lectures were on Hegel's *Phenomenology of Spirit.*

16. They included Queneau himself, Georges Bataille, Jacques Lacan, André Breton, and Maurice Merleau-Ponty. Some would add Jean-Paul Sartre to that list.

17. Allan Bloom's pronouncement that the *Introduction* "constitutes the most authoritative interpretation of Hegel" can only be affirmed in the sense of "imaginative." Kojève, *Introduction,* ix. Bloom did study for a period with Kojève.

18. The focus on the master-slave relationship was not at all idiosyncratic to Kojève. It formed the nucleus of many a Hegel interpretation from Marx to Kojève's contemporary, Jean Hyppolite.

19. In her book *Alexandre Kojève: The Roots of Postmodern Politics* (New York: St. Martin's Press, 1994), Shadia B. Drury makes the interesting attempt to see the master/state and slave/family juxtaposition as one of masculinity and femininity. The perspective is insightful, but, as she herself states, not Kojève's.

20. Kojève, *Introduction,* 35.

21. Ibid., 159 n. 6. Note to the second edition.

22. Ibid., 158 n. 6.

23. Ibid.

24. Ibid., 160 n. 6. Note to the second edition.

25. Ibid., 160 n. 5.

26. Actually, one cannot be sure how seriously he ever entertained the contention. While he stipulated, still in 1968, that history would end not so much with Napoleon but with Stalin, friends of Kojève stated that he, even during the 1930s, was not really enamored by Stalin.

27. Kojève, *Introduction,* 161 n. 6. Note to second edition.

28. Both, the Belgian de Man and the Frenchman Jouvenel, came from affluent families, worked, in the 1930s, on behalf of socialism, were disappointed with the result, collaborated, in the 1940s for a brief period, with Germany, and ended up, in the mid-1940s, as disillusioned exiles in Switzerland.

29. That view separated de Man from the large literature that held the masses responsible for the active undermining of Western culture, as in José Ortega y Gasset's *The Revolt of the Masses* (New York: W. W. Norton, 1957).

30. Bertrand de Jouvenel, *On Power: Its Nature and the History of Its Growth,* trans. J. F. Huntington (New York: Viking, 1949), 356–57, 362. Ironically, Jouvenel became a well-known expert in forecasting in the modernist manner. See his *The Art of Conjecture,* trans. Nikita Lang (New York: Basic Books, 1967).

31. See the works by Max Scheler and Helmuth Plessner.

32. Arnold Gehlen, *Studien zur Anthropologie und Soziologie,* ed. Heinz Maus and Friedrich Fürstenberg (Berlin: Luchterhand, 1963), 18. (This and the following quotes from Gehlen's works are translations by the author.)

33. Gehlen, *Studien zur Anthropologie und Soziologie,* 316.

34. Characteristically, Gehlen spoke of an *Entscheidungszumutung* (the unwelcome demand to make decisions), clearly implying that to make decisions was a

burden for human beings that they were tempted to shed. The concept was developed in his *Urmensch und Spätkultur: Philosophische Ergebnisse und Aussagen* (Frankfurt am Main: Athenäum, 1964).

35. For his views on posthistory see Gehlen, "Über die kulturelle Kristallisation," in *Studien zur Anthropologie und Soziologie*, 323.

36. Roderick Seidenberg, *Posthistoric Man: An Inquiry* (Chapel Hill: University of North Carolina Press, 1950) and *Anatomy of the Future* (Chapel Hill: University of North Carolina Press, 1961).

37. Seidenberg, *Posthistoric Man*, 91.

38. Seidenberg, *Anatomy of the Future*, 160.

39. Carl L. Becker, *Progress and Power* (New York: A. A. Knopf, 1949), 112 as cited in Seidenberg, *Posthistoric Man*, 56.

40. Seidenberg, *Posthistoric Man*, 91.

41. Ibid., 91. Although these laws were strictly speaking not laws but conventions and statistical averages, "they approximate even if they do not with final exactitude, an underlying invariance in the processes of nature" [use for human area], p. 71.

42. Ibid., 72.

43. Seidenberg, *Anatomy of the Future*, 126.

44. Seidenberg, *Posthistoric Man*, 25.

45. Ibid., 194.

46. Ibid.

47. See Walter W. Rostow's influential book *The Stages of Economic Growth: A Non-Communist Manifesto* (Cambridge: Cambridge University Press, 1960).

48. Francis Fukuyama, *The End of History and the Last Man* (New York: Free Press, 1992), xii.

49. Fukuyama, *End of History*, 162–63.

50. Ibid., xi.

51. Ibid., xii.

52. Ibid., 328 and 329.

53. For a special treatment of this issue see among others Alex Callinicos, *Theories and Narratives. Reflections on the Philosophy of History* (Durham, N.C.: Duke University Press, 1995), 16–20 and Christopher Bertram and Andrew Chitty, eds. *Has History Ended? Fukuyama, Marx, Modernity* (Aldershot, England: Avebury, 1994), 1–10.

Part Three. Postmodernity as the Age of Dominant Change

1. Hans Kellner, "Narrativity in History: Poststructuralism and since," *History and Theory* Beiheft 26 (1987), 2.

2. For an early use of the term, see Richard Rorty, ed., *The Linguistic Turn: Recent Essays in Philosophical Method* (Chicago: University of Chicago Press, 1967), 3.

3. The Anglo-American philosophical turn to language (G. E. Moore, L. Wittgenstein, J. L. Austin, G. Ryle, P. F. Strawson) had no important links to poststructuralist postmodernism.

4. The new linguistic theories were proposed by Saussure (1857–1913) in a series of lectures at the University of Geneva (published posthumously in 1916) and by Jakobson between 1915 and 1920 in Moscow (later in Prague and New York by Jakobson and his followers).

5. On that point see scholars who argue in the mode of Gottlob Frege that language had a double nature: a meaning system (*Sinngebung*) and a link to the real world (*Bedeutung*). The sentence, not words, provided the moments of unity.

6. Among the vast literature on the natural language idea see Umberto Eco, *The Search for the Perfect Language* (Oxford, England: Blackwell, 1995).

7. In the early 1940s, Jakobson exerted some influence on Claude Lévi-Strauss to take linguistics as a model for his structuralism.

8. Friedrich Nietzsche, *Untimely Meditations,* trans. R. J. Hollingdale (Cambridge: Cambridge University Press, 1983), 57–123. Another plausible translation rendered the German title as *History in the Service and Disservice of Life* (Gary Brown).

9. See Lévi-Strauss's preference for the "cold" (traditional, slowly changing if not stable) cultures over the "hot" (modern, technologically advanced) ones because of their perceived lesser ability to do harm.

10. Thomas Haskell, *Objectivity Is Not Neutrality: Explanatory Schemes in History* (Baltimore: Johns Hopkins University Press, 1998), 14.

11. Roland Barthes, "Historical Discourse," trans. Peter Wexler, in Michael Lane, ed., *Introduction to Structuralism* (New York: Basic Books, 1970), 145.

12. Barthes, "Historical Discourse," 154.

13. For a further elaboration on the reality effect see Frank R. Ankersmit, *The Reality Effect in the Writing of History: The Dynamics of Historiographical Topology* (Amsterdam: Koninklijke Nederlandse Akademie van Wetenschappen: Noord-Hollandsche, 1989).

14. Barthes, "Historical Discourse," 155.

15. David Harlan, "Intellectual History and the Return of Literature," *American Historical Review* 94, no. 3 (June 1989): 581.

16. Hayden White, *Metahistory: The Historical Imagination in Nineteenth-Century Europe* (Baltimore: Johns Hopkins University Press, 1973), 2.

17. Besides Barthes, Northrop Frye and Michel Foucault were important influences.

18. White, *Metahistory,* 46.

19. See Frank R. Ankersmit, *Narrative Logic: A Semantic Analysis of the Historian's Language* (The Hague: Martinus Nijhoff, 1983), 96–104.

20. Frank R. Ankersmit, "Reply to Professor Zagorin," *History and Theory* 29, no. 3 (1990): 281.

21. Carl L. Becker, "Detachment and the Writing of History," *Atlantic Monthly* 106 (October 1910): 526–28.

22. Frank R. Ankersmit, "The Dilemma of Contemporary Anglo-Saxon Philosophy of History," in *Knowing and Telling History: The Anglo-Saxon Debate, History and Theory* Beiheft 25 (1986), 19.

23. Hans Kellner, *Language and Historical Representation: Getting the Story Crooked* (Madison: University of Wisconsin Press, 1989), 24.

24. Frank R. Ankersmit, "Historiography and Postmodernism," *History and Theory,* 28, no. 2 (1989): 144.

25. White, *Metahistory,* 31.

26. Barthes, "Historical Discourse," 148 and 149.

27. Hayden White, *The Content of the Form: Narrative Discourse and Historical Representation* (Baltimore: Johns Hopkins University Press, 1987), 209.

28. Frank R. Ankersmit, *History and Tropology: The Rise and Fall of Metaphor* (Berkeley: University of California Press, 1994), 33–34.

29. Ankersmit, "Historiography and Postmodernism," 149.

30. See Hayden White's "The Burden of History," in *Tropics of Discourse: Essays in Cultural Criticism* (Baltimore: Johns Hopkins University Press, 1978), 27–50.

31. In the context of White's work, the term "existential" is best understood in the Sartrean sense of living authentically in an as such senseless world.

32. Ankersmit, "History and Postmodernism," 152.

33. Ankersmit, "Reply to Professor Zagorin," 294.

34. White, "Burden of History," 27.

35. Frank R. Ankersmit and Hans Kellner, eds., *A New Philosophy of History* (Chicago: University of Chicago Press, 1995).

36. For the following, see Nancy Partner, "Historicity in an Age of Reality-Fiction," in Ankersmit and Kellner, eds., *New Philosophy of History,* 21–39.

37. Paul Ricoeur, *Time and Narrative,* trans. Kathleen McLaughlin and David Pellauer (Chicago: University of Chicago Press, 1984), 3.

38. David Carr, "Narrative and the Real World: An Argument for Continuity," *History and Theory* 25, no. 2 (1986): 117.

39. Roger Chartier, *On the Edge of the Cliff: History, Language, and Practices,* trans. Lydia Cochrane (Baltimore: Johns Hopkins University Press, 1997), 4.

40. Chartier, *On the Edge of the Cliff,* 1.

41. Cited by Chartier, *On the Edge of the Cliff,* 1 and n. 1.

42. Ibid., 8 and 26.

43. Dominick LaCapra, *Rethinking Intellectual History: Texts, Contexts, Language* (Ithaca, N.Y.: Cornell University Press, 1983), 72.

44. Leopold von Ranke, "On the Character of the Historical Science" (manuscript of the 1830s), in *Leopold von Ranke: The Theory and Practice of History,* ed. Georg G. Iggers and Konrad von Moltke, trans. Wilma A. Iggers and Konrad von Moltke (Indianapolis: Bobbs-Merrill, 1973), 33.

45. The specific German meaning of *Geisteswissenschaft* cannot be rendered properly into English by one term. *Wissenschaft* refers here not simply to science but to an inquiry with a rigorous set of rules and *Geist* (in Dilthey's case) to the dynamic and creative force in the human realm.

46. Martin Heidegger's *Being and Time,* trans. Joan Stambaugh (Albany: State University of New York Press, 1996). Original German edition as *Sein und Zeit* in 1927.

47. However, in recent works Derrida came close to such authenticity with his concept of indecidability in moral decisions that could be resolved through action outside a limiting framework.

48. See Sartre's related views, as discussed in chapter 14.

49. Michel Foucault, *The Order of Things: An Archaeology of the Human Sciences* (New York: Pantheon Books, 1970), xi.

50. Michel Foucault, *The Archaeology of Knowledge,* trans. A. M. Sheridan Smith (New York: Pantheon Books, 1972), 191.

51. Saussure would diverge here also from the development of linguistic philosophy, where Ludwig Wittgenstein abandoned the concept of a well-defined language whole in favor of language games.

52. Jacques Derrida, *Margins of Philosophy,* trans. Alan Bass (Chicago: University of Chicago Press, 1982), 9.

53. The term is derived from the Latin *differre* that in English led to two verbs differ and defer (the one with a spatial reference and the other a temporal one). Derrida created the noun *différance* to gain access to the two meanings in one word.

54. Derrida, *Margins of Philosophy,* 7.

55. When he rejected any final stability, Derrida broke with Heidegger, who, as it seemed to him, was searching for a Being (*Sein*) behind the beings (*Seiendes*). Although Heidegger's *Sein* was here not understood as an ultimate foundation for beings, but as a transcending of the principle of differentiation, Derrida could not agree to that.

56. The religious aspect of Derrida's thought has been dealt with extensively by John Caputo. Other scholars have pointed to Jewish mysticism as one of Derrida's inspiration. As for negative theology as an influential pattern, see Harold Coward and Toby Foshay, eds., *Derrida and Negative Theology* (Albany: State University of New York Press, 1992).

57. Derrida, *Margins of Philosophy,* 21.

58. Peggy Kamuf, ed., *A Derrida Reader: Between the Blinds* (New York: Columbia University Press, 1991), ix.

59. See Lyotard's key work of that period, *Économie libidinale,* trans. Iain Hamilton Grant (Bloomington: Indiana University Press, 1993).

60. The observer is reminded of the many neo-platonist schemes where from an unnameable whole (the "One") emanates the differentiated world. However, there the results of the emanation had strong fixed identities rather than being traces of the process itself.

61. John Caputo, *Radical Hermeneutics: Repetition, Deconstruction, and the Hermeneutics Project* (Bloomington: Indiana University Press, 1987) and Roy Martinez, ed., *The Very Idea of Radical Hermeneutics* (Atlantic Highlands, N.J.: Humanities Press, 1997).

62. Gianni Vattimo, *The End of Modernity: Nihilism and Hermeneutics in Postmodern Culture,* trans. Jon R. Snyder (Baltimore: Johns Hopkins University Press, 1988), 159. The cultures referred to were archaic cultures.

63. David D. Roberts, *Nothing but History: Reconstruction and Extremity after Metaphysics* (Berkeley: University of California Press, 1995), 252 and the theme of the book.

64. Roberts, *Nothing but History,* 292.

65. "Weak" in the sense of Gianni Vattimo's *pensiero debole.*

66. Sande Cohen, *Historical Culture: On the Recoding of an Academic Discipline* (Berkeley: University of California Press, 1986), 329.

67. Patrick Joyce, "History and Postmodernism," *Past and Present* 133 (November 1991): 208.

68. Keith Jenkins, *Why History? Ethics and Postmodernity* (London: Routledge, 1999), 95.

69. Alun Munslow, *Deconstructing History* (London: Routledge, 1997), 1.

70. Munslow, *Deconstructing History,* 5.

71. Jenkins, *Why History?,* 3.

72. Hans Kellner, "Introduction: Describing Reinscriptions," in Frank R. Ankersmit and Hans Kellner, eds., *A New Philosophy of History* (Chicago: University of Chicago Press, 1995), 10.

73. Richard Evans, *In Defence of History* (London: Granta Books, 1999), 8. (English edition only.)

74. Arthur Marwick, "The Approaches to the Study of History: The Metaphysical (including 'Postmodernism') and the Historical," *Journal of Contemporary History* 30 (1995): 5 and Gabrielle Spiegel, "History and Postmodernism," *Past and Present* 135 (May 1992): 195.

75. Gertrude Himmelfarb, "Some Reflections on the New History," *American Historical Review* 94, no. 3 (June 1989): 668.

76. See Donna Haraway, "Situated Knowledge: The Science Question in Feminism and the Privilege of Partial Perspective," *Feminist Studies* 14, no. 3 (Fall 1988): 577–78.

77. Munslow, *Deconstructing History,* 164.

78. Keith Jenkins, ed. *The Postmodern History Reader* (London: Routledge, 1997), 17.

79. Jenkins, ed., *Postmodern History Reader,* 6.

80. Peter Novick, *That Noble Dream: The "Objectivity Quest" and the American Historical Profession* (Cambridge: Cambridge University Press, 1988). Title of chapter 16.

81. Jenkins, *Why History?,* 3.

82. Geoffrey R. Elton, *Return to Essentials: Some Reflections on the Present State of Historical Study* (Cambridge: Cambridge University Press, 1991), 11.

83. See Thomas Haskell, *Objectivity Is Not Neutrality: Explanatory Schemes in History* (Baltimore: Johns Hopkins University Press, 1998).

84. David Harlan, *The Degradation of American History* (Chicago: University of Chicago Press, 1997), xx.

85. Harlan, *Degradation of American History,* 94.

86. Jenkins, *Why History?,* 4 and 12.

87. Joyce Appleby, "One Good Turn Deserves Another: Moving beyond the Linguistic. A Response to David Harlan," *American Historical Review* 94, no. 5 (December 1989): 1332.

88. Jean-François Lyotard et al., *Immaterialität und Postmoderne,* trans. Marianne Karbe (Berlin: Merve, 1985), 33. (Author's translation.) A volume connected with a presentation at the Centre Georges Pompidou in 1985.

89. Jean-François Lyotard, *The Postmodern Condition: A Report on Knowledge,* trans. Geoffrey Bennington and Brian Massumi (Minneapolis: University of Minnesota Press, 1984), xxiv.

90. Exceptions have been few. For two of them, see Thomas Jung, *Vom Ende der Geschichte: Rekonstruktion zum Posthistoire in kritischer Absicht* (Münster: Waxmann, 1989) and Roderick Seidenberg, *Posthistoric Man* (Chapel Hill: University of North Carolina Press, 1950), see part ii.

91. Karl Popper, *The Open Society and Its Enemies* (Princeton, N.J.: Princeton University Press, 1950; Preface 1944) and Karl Popper, *The Poverty of Historicism* (Boston: Beacon Press, 1957).

92. See Allan Megill's attempt to systematize categories of narratives beyond the "narrative proper": master narratives (segment of history), grand narratives (universal history without inherent principle of order), and metanarratives (universal history with such a principle). " 'Grand Narrative' and the Discipline of History," in Ankersmit and Kellner, eds., *A New Philosophy of History* (Chicago: University of Chicago Press, 1995), 152–53.

93. Lyotard, *Postmodern Condition,* xxiv.

94. Lyotard, *Immaterialität,* 65. Remarks in response to Lyotard's question by Bernard Blistene. (Author's translation.)

95. See his engagement (to 1964) with the *Socialism or Barbarism* movement that tried to strip the limiting forms of orthodoxy from Marxism, including the strictly determinist scheme for overall history.

96. Lyotard, *Immaterialität,* 35. Remark by Giairo Daghini addressed to Lyotard. (Author's translation.)

97. Lyotard, *Postmodern Condition,* 46 and xxiii.

98. See Lyotard, *Immaterialität,* which signaled such a turn in his thoughts about immaterial phenomena.

99. Michel Foucault, *The Order of Things: An Archeology of the Human Sciences* (New York: Pantheon Books, 1973), 168.

100. Jacques Derrida, *Of Grammatology,* trans. Gayatari Chakravorty Spivak (Baltimore: Johns Hopkins University Press, 1976), 158. A controversial statement that Derrida had to explain a few times, in the process modifying its bluntness. He would point out that while we had no access to a not linguistically mediated reality, he did not deny its existence.

101. Derrida, *Of Grammatology,* 49.

102. Ibid., 14.

103. Jacques Derrida, "Deconstruction and the 'other,' " in Richard Kearney, *States of Mind: Dialogues with Contemporary Thinkers* (New York: New York University Press, 1995), 166.

104. Derrida, "Deconstruction," 166.

105. Jean Baudrillard, *Forget Foucault,* trans. Sylvère Lotringer (New York: Semiotext(e), 1987), 63.

106. "Nietzsche, Genealogy, History," in Michel Foucault, *Language, Counter-Memory, Practice,* ed. Donald F. Bouchard, trans. Donald F. Bouchard and Sherry Simon (Ithaca, N.Y.: Cornell University Press, 1977), 151.

107. John Toews, "Intellectual History after the Linguistic Turn: The Autonomy of Meaning and the Irreducibility of Experience," *American Historical Review* 92 (1987): 906.

108. David Harlan, "Intellectual History and the Return of Literature," *American Historical Review* 94 (1989): 585.

109. Toews, "Intellectual History," 882.

110. Robert F. Berkhofer, Jr., *Beyond the Great Story: History as Text and Discourse* (Cambridge: Harvard University Press, 1995), 38.

111. For a more general view of the links between Western culture and colonialism see Edward Said, *Culture and Imperialism* (New York: Knopf, 1993).

112. Robert Young, *White Mythologies: Writing History and the West* (London: Routledge, 1990).

113. Elizabeth Deeds Ermarth, *Sequel to History: Postmodernism and the Crisis of Representational Time* (Princeton, N.J.: Princeton University Press, 1992), 10.

114. Ermarth, *Sequel to History,* 14.

115. Ibid., 25.

116. William Sewell, Jr., "The Concept(s) of Culture," in *Beyond the Cultural Turn: New Directions in the Study of Society and Culture,* ed. Victoria Bonnell and Lynn Hunt (Berkeley: University of California Press, 1999), 36.

117. Clifford Geertz, *The Interpretation of Cultures* (New York: Basic Books, 1973), 452 and 5.

118. Geertz, *Interpretation of Cultures*, 20 and 27.

119. Ibid., 28.

120. For a statement on anthropological developments from a perspective that sharply separates content from form, see the introductory chapter in James Clifford and George E. Marcus, eds., *Writing Culture: The Poetics and Politics of Ethnography* (Berkeley: University of California Press, 1986), 1–26.

121. Anne Kane, "Reconstructing Culture in Historical Explanation: Narration as Cultural, Structure and Practice," *History and Theory* 39, no. 3 (October 2000): 315.

122. See Richard Biernacki, "The Shift from Signs to Practices in Historical Inquiry," *History and Theory* 39, no. 3 (October 2000): 294.

123. Lucien Febvre, *A New Kind of History and Other Essays*, trans. K. Folca, ed. Peter Burke (New York: Harper & Row, 1973), 2.

124. Prominent representatives: Alf Lüdtke, Hans Medick, and Lutz Niethammer.

125. See here the conflicts with the German *Historische Sozialwissenschaft*, particularly Hans Wehler and Jürgen Kocka.

126. Among the early representatives were Carlo Ginzburg and Carlo Poni.

127. Carlo Ginzburg, *Clues, Myths, and the Historical Method*, trans. John Tedeschi and Ann C. Tedeschi (Baltimore: Johns Hopkins University Press, 1989), 164.

128. Carlo Ginzburg, *The Cheese and the Worms: The Cosmos of a Sixteenth-Century Miller*, trans. John Tedeschi and Ann C. Tedeschi (Baltimore: Johns Hopkins University Press, 1980), xxiii.

129. Edward Muir, "Introduction: Observing Trifles," in *Microhistory and the Lost Peoples of Europe: Selections from Quaderni Storici*, eds. E. Muir and G. Ruggiero (Baltimore: Johns Hopkins University Press, 1991), xiv.

130. H. Aram Veeser, "Introduction," in *The New Historicism*, ed. H. Aram Veeser (New York: Routledge, 1989), xi.

131. Stephen Greenblatt, *Shakespearean Negotiations: The Circulation of Social Energy in Renaissance England* (Berkeley: University of California Press, 1988), 86.

132. For a review of such narratives, see Sarah Maza, "Stories in History: Cultural Narratives in Recent Works in European History," *American Historical Review* 101, no. 5 (December 1996): 1493–1515.

133. Emmanuel Le Roy Ladurie, *Montaillou: The Promised Land of Error*, trans. Barbara Bray (New York: Vintage Books, 1979).

134. Emmanuel Le Roy Ladurie, *Carnival in Romans*, trans. Mary Feeney (New York: George Braziller, 1979), xvi.

135. Natalie Zemon Davis, *Fiction in the Archives: Pardon Tales and Their Tellers in Sixteenth-Century France* (Stanford, Calif.: Stanford University Press, 1987).

136. Robert Darnton, *The Great Cat Massacre and Other Episodes in French Cultural History* (New York: Basic Books, 1984), 3.

137. Darnton, *Great Cat Massacre*, 3.

138. Judith R. Walkowitz, *City of Dreadful Delight: Narratives of Sexual Danger in Late-Victorian London* (Chicago: University of Chicago Press, 1992).

139. Susan Pedersen, "The Future of Feminist History," *Perspectives: American Historical Association Newsletter* 38, no. 7 (October 2000): 22.

140. See Ihab Hassan's critical remark, himself in earlier years an advocate of a poststructuralist postmodernism, in his recent *The Postmodern Turn: Essays in Postmodern Theory and Culture* (Columbus: Ohio State University Press, 1987), 5.

141. Claude Lévi-Strauss, *A World on the Wane,* trans. John Russell (London: Criterion, 1961), 397. But this "death of man" was one in entropy caused by the relentless abolition of differences, much in the manner of structural postmodernism.

142. Madeleine Chapsal, "La plus grande revolution depuis l'existentialisme," *L'Express* 779 (23–29 May 1966), 121 as cited in James Miller, *The Passion of Michel Foucault* (New York: Simon & Schuster, 1993), 149.

143. Michel Foucault, *The Order of Things: An Archeology of the Human Sciences* (New York: Pantheon Books, 1970), 386.

144. Richard Kearney, *States of Mind: Dialogues with Contemporary Thinkers* (New York: New York University Press, 1995), 174–75.

145. See Jacques Derrida, *Margins of Philosophy,* trans. Alan Bass (Chicago: University of Chicago Press, 1982), section "The Near End of Man," 119–23.

146. Jean-François Lyotard, *The Postmodern Condition: A Report on Knowledge,* trans. Geoffrey Bennington and Brian Massumi (Minneapolis: University of Minnesota Press, 1984), 15.

147. Kearney, *States of Mind,* 168.

148. Jacques Derrida, *Limited Inc,* ed. Gerald Graff, trans. Samuel Weber and Jeffrey Mehlman (Evanston, Ill.: Northwestern University Press, 1988), 260.

149. Derrida, "Afterword: Toward an Ethic of Discussion," in *Limited Inc,* 112.

150. Keith Jenkins, *Why History?: Ethics and Postmodernity* (London: Routledge, 1999), 2.

151. David Harlan, *The Degradation of American History* (Chicago: University of Chicago Press, 1997), 213.

152. Harlan, *Degradation,* xxxiii.

153. Joyce Appleby, Lynn Hunt, and Margaret Jacob, *Telling the Truth about History* (New York: W. W. Norton, 1994), 3.

154. Appleby et al., *Telling the Truth,* 4.

155. Ibid., 6.

Part Four. Poststructuralist Postmodernism and the Reshaping of Society

1. Martin Jay, *Fin-de-Siècle: Socialism and Other Essays* (London: Routledge, 1988), 2.

2. Norman Geras, *Discourses of Extremity: Radical Ethics and Post-Marxist Extravagances* (London: Verso, 1990), 64.

3. See Antonio Callari and David F. Ruccio, *Postmodernism, Materialism, and the Future of Marxist Theory: Essays in the Althusserian Tradition* (Hanover, N.H.: Wesleyan University Press, 1996), 9–10.

4. Stuart Hall, "The Toad in the Garden: Thatcherism among the Theorists," in *Marxism and the Interpretation of Culture,* ed. Cary Nelson and Lawrence Grossberg (Urbana: University of Illinois Press, 1988), 73.

5. Among the group were E. P. Thompson, Eric Hobsbawm, Rodney Hilton, and Christopher Hill.

6. Ernesto Laclau, "Metaphor and Social Antagonisms," in *Marxism and the Interpretation of Culture,* ed. Nelson and Grossberg, 250.

7. Edward P. Thompson, *The Making of the English Working Class* (New York: Vintage Books, 1968).

8. Fredric Jameson, "Cognitive Mapping," in *Marxism and the Interpretation of Culture,* ed. Cary Nelson and Lawrence Grossberg (Urbana: University of Illinois Press, 1988), 347.

9. Ernest Mandel, *Late Capitalism*, trans. Joris De Bres (London: Verso, 1975).

10. See the theme and title of an article by Fredric Jameson, "Postmodernism and Cultural Logic of Late Capitalism," *New Left Review* 146 (April 1989): 31–45.

11. Alex Callinicos, *Against Postmodernism: A Marxist Critique* (New York: St. Martin's Press, 1990), 7.

12. David Harvey, *The Condition of Postmodernity: An Inquiry into the Origins of Cultural Change* (Oxford, England: Blackwell, 1989), 38.

13. Harvey, *Condition of Postmodernity*, 156, 121, and 328.

14. Edward W. Soja, *Postmodern Geographies: The Reassertion of Space in Critical Social Theory* (London: Verso, 1989), 59.

15. For the concept of cognitive mapping see Jameson, "Cognitive Mapping," in *Marxism and the Interpretation of Culture*, 347–60. Earlier, he had called cognitive mapping a code word for class consciousness, *New Left Review* 146 (April 1989): 44.

16. Soja, *Postmodern Geographies*, 62.

17. Terms used by Ferenc Feher in "Redemptive and Democratic Paradigms in Radical Politics," *Telos* 63 (Spring 1985): 147–67.

18. Dick Hebdige, *Hiding in the Light: On Images and Things* (London: Routledge, 1988), 195.

19. See Geras, *Discourses of Extremity*, 102–3

20. Raymond Williams, *Marxism and Literature* (Oxford, England: Oxford University Press, 1977), 83.

21. In mid-1980, a conference was held at Cerisy, France, with the theme "Les fins de l'homme: A partir du travail de Jacques Derrida" (The Ends of Man: Spinoffs of the Work of Jacques Derrida). It spawned a Center for Philosophical Research on the Political led by Jean-Luc Nancy and Philippe Lacoue-Labarthe who also edited the conference proceedings (Paris: Galilee, 1981). The center closed in 1984. For an informative summary assessment of the debate see Nancy Frazer, "The French Derrideans: Politicizing Deconstruction or Deconstructing the Political?" in Gary B. Madison, *Working through Derrida* (Evanston, Ill.: Northwestern University Press, 1993), 51–76.

22. Barry Smart, *Modern Conditions, Postmodern Controversies* (London: Routledge, 1992), 219.

23. The *Institute*, founded in 1924, was located in Frankfurt am Main (to 1933), Geneva (to 1934), New York and California (to 1949–50) and again Frankfurt a. M. It must be stated here that this account with its special objective of locating affinities emphasizes certain themes without always pointing out the differences that divide the Frankfurt scholars. No claim for a uniform message of the school is made, although many major themes dealt with were broadly held by most of them.

24. Max Horkheimer and Theodor W. Adorno, *Dialectic of Enlightenment*, trans. John Cumming (New York: Continuum, 1991), xi. German edition: *Dialektik der Aufklärung* (New York, 1944).

25. That and other works were written and published in German, in isolation from the American environment. The assessment prevailed that the Marxist roots and the German intellectual aura and terminology were hardly promising for publishing success or even friendly acceptance there.

26. Horkheimer and Adorno, *Dialectic of Enlightenment*, 12.

27. Ibid., xvi.

28. Theodor W. Adorno, *Negative Dialectics*, trans. E. B. Ashton (New York: Seabury Press, 1973), 402.

29. Max Horkheimer, *Sozialphilosophische Studien: Aufsätze, Reden, und Vorträge (1930–1972)*, 2nd ed. (Frankfurt a. M.: Fischer Athenäum, 1981), 54. (Author's translation.)

30. Horkheimer and Adorno, *Dialectic of Enlightenment*, xv, xiv, and xiii.

31. Jean-François Lyotard, *The Postmodern Condition: A Report on Knowledge*, trans. Geoffrey Bennington and Brian Massumi (Minneapolis: University of Minnesota Press, 1984), 65–66.

32. For this argument see Jane Flax, *Thinking Fragments: Psychoanalysis, Feminism, and Postmodernism in the Contemporary West* (Berkeley: University of California Press, 1990), 32–34.

33. See, for example, Martha C. Nussbaum's attempt to systematize the elements of the common humanity as a "universal framework to assess the quality of life for women" in India and the West in a list of ten "central human functional capabilities." Martha C. Nussbaum, "Defense of Universal Values," in James P. Sterba, ed., *Controversies in Feminism* (Lanham, Md.: Rowman and Littlefield, 2001), 7 and 14–15.

34. Linda Nicholson, *Conflicts in Feminism* (New York, 1990), 11 as cited by Carol A. Stabile, "Postmodernism, Feminism, and Marx," in Ellen Meiksins Wood and John B. Foster, eds., *In Defense of History: Marxism and the Postmodern Agenda* (New York: Monthly Review Press, 1997), 136.

35. Bonnie Smith, *The Gender of History: Men, Women, and Historical Practice* (Cambridge: Harvard University Press, 1998).

36. Joan Wallach Scott, *Gender and the Politics of History* (New York: Columbia University Press, 1988), 27.

37. Susan Pedersen, "The Future of Feminist History," *Perspectives, American Historical Association Newsletter* 38, no. 7 (October 2000): 21.

Part Five. Concluding Observations

1. Keith Jenkins, ed., *The Postmodern History Reader* (London: Routledge, 1997), 28.

2. Sande Cohen, *Historical Culture: On the Recoding of an Academic Discipline* (Berkeley: University of California Press, 1986), 329.

3. Keith Jenkins, *Why History? Ethics and Postmodernity* (London: Routledge, 1999), 9.

4. Patrick Joyce, "A Quiet Victory: The Growing Influence of Postmodernism in History," *Times Literary Supplement,* 26 October 2001, 15.

5. Patrick Joyce, "History and Postmodernism," *Past and Present* 133 (November 1991): 204.

6. Geoff Eley and Keith Nield, "Starting Over: The Present, the Post-Modern and the Moment of Social History," *Social History* 20 (1995): 364.

7. C. Behan McCullagh, *The Truth in History* (London: Routledge, 1998), 4.

8. Gabrielle Spiegel, "History and Post-Modernism," *Past and Present* 135 (May 1992): 197.

SELECT BIBLIOGRAPHY

In the age of vast electronic databases and access to online catalogs of numerous libraries, the ideal of comprehensiveness can yield its place to other objectives in the compilation of bibliographies. This bibliography supports the purpose of this book: to be a guide in the assessment of the postmodernist challenge to long-standing ways of the historical understanding of life. Besides documenting the resources used by the author, the selected works will facilitate the readers' own explorations.

GENERAL WORKS

Anderson, Perry. *The Origins of Postmodernity.* London: Verso, 1998.

Attridge, Derek, Geoff Bennington, and Robert Young, eds. *Post-Structuralism and the Question of History.* Cambridge: Cambridge University Press, 1987.

Baker, Keith Michael. *Condorcet: Selected Writings.* Indianapolis: Bobbs-Merrill, 1976.

Bauman, Zygmunt. *Legislators and Interpreters: On Modernity, Post-Modernity and Intellectuals.* Cambridge, England: Polity Press, 1987.

————. *Intimations of Postmodernity.* London: Routledge, 1992.

————. *Postmodernity and Its Discontents.* New York: New York University Press, 1997.

Bernstein, Richard J. *The New Constellation: The Ethical-Political Horizons of Modernity/Postmodernity.* Cambridge: MIT Press, 1992.

Hans Blumenberg. *The Legitimacy of the Modern Age.* Trans. Robert M. Wallace, Cambridge: MIT Press, 1983.

Bürger, Peter. *Theory of the Avant-Garde.* Trans. Michael Shaw. Minneapolis: University of Minnesota Press, 1984.

Burke, Peter, ed. *New Perspectives on Historical Writing.* 2nd ed. University Park: Pennsylvania State University Press, 2001.

Callinicos, Alex. *Theories and Narratives: Reflections on the Philosophy of History.* Durham, N.C.: Duke University Press, 1995.

Connor, Steven. *Postmodern Culture: An Introduction to Theories of the Contemporary.* New York: Basil Blackwell, 1989.

Docherty, Thomas, ed. *Postmodernism: A Reader.* New York: Columbia University Press, 1993.

Febvre, Lucien. *A New Kind of History and Other Essays.* Ed. Peter Burke. Trans. K. Folca. New York: Harper & Row, 1973.

Gross, Mirjana. *Von der Antike bis zur Postmoderne: Die zeitgenössische Geschichtsschreibung und ihre Wurzeln.* Vienna: Böhlau, 1998.

Hassan, Ihab. *The Postmodern Turn: Essays in Postmodern Theory and Culture.* Columbus: Ohio State University Press, 1987.

Hebdige, Dick. *Hiding in the Light: On Images and Things.* London: Routledge, 1988.

Hoeveler, J. David, Jr. *The Postmodernist Turn: American Thought and Culture in the 1970s.* New York: Twayne Publishers, 1996.

Hoesterey, Ingeborg, ed. *Zeitgeist in Babel: The Postmodernist Controversy.* Bloomington: Indiana University Press, 1991.

Hutcheon, Linda. *The Politics of Postmodernism.* London: Routledge, 1989.

Iggers, Georg. *Historiography in the Twentieth Century: From Scientific Objectivity to the Postmodern Challenge.* Hanover, N.H.: Wesleyan University Press, 1997.

Jung, Thomas. *Vom Ende der Geschichte: Rekonstruktionen zum Posthistoire in kritischer Absicht.* Münster: Waxmann, 1989.

Kaplan, E. Ann, ed. *Postmodernism and Its Discontents: Theories, Practices.* New York: Harvester Wheatsheaf, 1991.

Kaye, Harvey J. *The Powers of the Past: Reflections on the Crisis of History and the Promise of History.* Minneapolis: University of Minnesota Press, 1991.

Klotz, Heinrich. *Die Moderne und Postmoderne: Architektur der Gegenwart, 1960–1980.* Braunschweig: Vieweg, 1984.

Lessing, Theodor. *Geschichte als Sinngebung des Sinnlosen oder die Geburt der Geschichte aus dem Mythos.* 1921. Reprint, Hamburg: Rütten and Löning, 1962.

Marsden, Gordon, ed. *After the End of History.* London: Collins and Brown, 1992.

McCullagh, C. Behan. *The Truth of History.* London, Routledge, 1998.

McDonald, Terrence, ed. *The Historic Turn in the Human Sciences.* Ann Arbor: The University of Michigan Press, 1996.

McGowan, John. *Postmodernism and its Critics.* Ithaca, N.Y.: Cornell University Press, 1991.

Meyer, Martin. *Ende der Geschichte?* Munich: C. Hanser, 1993.

Nicholson, Linda J. *The Play of Reason: From the Modern to the Postmodern.* Ithaca, N.Y.: Cornell University Press, 1999.

Norris, Christopher. *What's Wrong with Postmodernism: Critical Theory and the Ends of Philosophy.* Baltimore: Johns Hopkins University Press, 1990.

Pangle, Thomas. *The Ennobling of Democracy: The Challenge of the Postmodern Era.* Baltimore: Johns Hopkins University Press, 1992.

Renner, Rolf Günter. *Die postmoderne Konstellation: Theorie, Text, und Kunst im Ausgang der Moderne.* Freiburg im Breisgau: Rombach, 1988.

Sarup, Madan. *An Introductory Guide to Post-Structuralism and Postmodernism.* New York: Harvester Wheatsheaf, 1988.

Seidman, Steven, ed. *The Postmodern Turn: New Perspectives on Social Theory.* Cambridge: Cambridge University Press, 1994.

Sontag, Susan. *Against Interpretation: And Other Essay.* New York: Farrar, Straus & Giroux, 1966.

Southgate, Beverly. *Why Bother with History? Ancient, Modern, and Postmodern Motivations.* Harlow, England: Pearson Education, 2000.

Vattimo, Gianni. *The End of Modernity: Nihilism and Hermeneutics in Postmodern Culture.* Trans. Jon R. Snyder. Oxford, England: Polity Press, 1988.

Wakefield, Neville. *Postmodernism: The Twilight of the Real.* London: Pluto Press, 1990.

Waugh, Patricia, ed. *Postmodernism: A Reader.* London: E. Arnold, 1992.

Welsch, Wolfgang. *Unsere postmoderne Moderne.* 2nd ed. Weinheim: VCH, Acta Humaniora, 1988.

Wilson, Norman J. *History in Crisis? Recent Directions in Historiography.* Upper Saddle River, N.J.: Prentice Hall, 1999.

PUBLICATIONS FOCUSING ON STRUCTURAL POSTMODERNISM

Abramowski, Günter. *Das Geschichtsbild Max Webers: Universalgeschichte am Leitfaden des okzidentalen Rationalisiserungsprozesses.* Stuttgart: Klett, 1966.

Bell, Daniel. *The End of Ideology: On the Exhaustion of Political Ideas in the Fifties.* 2nd rev. ed. New York: Collier Books, 1962.

———. *The Coming of the Post-Industrial Society: A Venture in Social Forecasting.* New York: Basic Books, 1973.

———. *The Cultural Contradictions of Capitalism.* New York: Basic Books, 1976.

———. *The Winding Passage: Essays and Sociological Journeys, 1960–80.* Cambridge, Mass.: Abt Books, 1980.

Bertram, Christopher, and Andrew Chitty, eds. *Has History Ended? Fukuyama, Marx, Modernity.* Aldershot, England: Avebury, 1994.

Cournot, Antoine Augustin. *Oeuvres Completes.* Ed. Nelly Bruyère. Vol. 3. *Traité de l'enchaînement des idées fondamentales dans les sciences et dans l'histoire.* Paris: Librairie Philosophique J. Vrin, 1982.

de Jouvenel, Bertrand. *On Power: Its Nature and the History of Its Growth.* Trans. J. F. Huntington. Indianapolis: Liberty Fund, 1948.

———. *The Art of Conjecture.* Trans. Nikita Lang. New York: Basic Books, 1967.

de Man, Hendrik. *Vermassung und Kulturverfall. Eine Diagnose unserer Zeit.* Bern: A. Franke, 1951.

Drury, Shadia B. *Alexandre Kojève: The Roots of Postmodern Politics.* New York: St. Martin's Press, 1994.

Etzioni, Amitai. *The Active Society: A Theory of Societal and Political Processes.* New York: Free Press, 1968.

Featherstone, Mike. *Consumer Culture and Postmodernism.* London: Sage, 1991.

Fukuyama, Francis. *The End of History and the Last Man.* New York: Free Press, 1992.

Gehlen, Arnold. *Studien zur Anthropologie und Soziologie.* Ed. Heinz Maus and Friedrich Fürstenberg. Berlin: Luchterhand, 1963.

———. *Urmensch und Spätkultur: Philosophische Ergebnisse und Aussagen.* Frankfurt am Main: Athenäum, 1964.

Kojève, Alexandre. *Introduction to the Reading of Hegel: Lectures on the Phenomenology of Spirit.* Assembled by Raymond Queneau. Ed. Allan Bloom. Trans. James H. Nichols, Jr. New York: Basic Books, 1969.

Lentricchia, Frank. *After the New Criticism.* Chicago: University of Chicago Press, 1980.

Niethammer, Lutz. *Posthistoire: Has History Come to an End?* Trans. Patrick Camiller. London: Verso, 1992.

Ortega y Gasset, José. *The Revolt of the Masses (Rebelión de las masas).* New York: W. W. Norton, 1957.

Rose, Margaret A. *The Post-Modern and the Post-Industrial: A Critical Analysis.* Cambridge: Cambridge University Press, 1991.

Rostow, Walt W. *The Stages of Economic Growth.* Cambridge: Cambridge University Press, 1960.

Seidenberg, Roderick. *Posthistoric Man: An Inquiry.* Chapel Hill: University of North Carolina Press, 1950.

———. *Anatomy of the Future.* Chapel Hill: University of North Carolina Press, 1961.

Touraine, Alain. *The Post-Industrial Society; Tomorrow's Social History: Classes,*

Conflicts and Culture in the Programmed Society. Trans. Leonard F. X. Mayhew. New York: Random House, 1971.

Weber, Max. *Gesammelte Politische Schriften.* 3rd rev. ed. Tübingen: Mohr, 1971.

———. *The Protestant Ethic and the Spirit of Capitalism.* Trans. Talcott Parsons. Los Angeles: Roxbury Publishing Co., 1996.

Williams, Howard, David Sullivan, and E. Gwynn Matthews. *Francis Fukuyama and the End of History.* Cardiff: University of Wales Press, 1997.

PUBLICATIONS CONCERNING POSTSTRUCTURALIST POSTMODERNISM

On Developments Related to the Rise of Poststructuralist Postmodernism

Aarsleff, Hans. *From Locke to Saussure: Essays on the Study of Language and Intellectual History.* Minneapolis: University of Minnesota Press, 1982.

Berman, Art. *From the New Criticism to Deconstruction: The Reception of Structuralism and Post-Structuralism.* Urbana: University of Illinois Press, 1988.

Carr, David. "Narrative and the Real World: An Argument for Continuity." *History and Theory* 25, no. 2 (1986): 117–31.

Culler, Jonathan D. *Ferdinand de Saussure.* 2nd rev. ed. Ithaca N.Y.: Cornell University Press, 1986.

Descombes, Vincent. *Modern French Philosophy.* Trans. L. Scott-Fox and J. M. Harding. Cambridge: Cambridge University Press, 1980.

Dews, Peter. *The Limits of Disenchantment: Essays on Contemporary European Philosophy.* London: Verso, 1995.

Easthope, Antony. *British Post-Structuralism.* London: Routledge, 1988.

Eribon, Didier, and Claude Lévi-Strauss. *Conversations with Claude Lévi-Strauss.* Chicago: University of Chicago, Press, 1991.

Ferraris, Maurizio. *History of Hermeneutics.* Trans. Luca Somigli. Atlantic Highlands, N.J.: Humanities Press, 1996.

Heidegger, Martin. *Being and Time.* Trans. Joan Stambaugh. Albany: State University of New York Press, 1996.

Koelb, Clayton, ed. *Nietzsche as Postmodernist: Essays Pro and Contra.* Albany: State University of New York Press, 1990.

Lane Michael, ed. *Introduction to Structuralism.* New York: Basic Books, 1970.

Leach, Edmund. *Claude Lévi-Strauss.* Rev. ed. New York: Viking Press, 1974.

Megill, Allan. *Prophets of Extremity: Nietzsche, Heidegger, Foucault, Derrida.* Berkeley: University of California Press, 1985.

Nietzsche, Friedrich. *Untimely Meditations.* Trans. R. J. Hollingdale. Cambridge: Cambridge University Press, 1983.

Pace, David. *Claude Lévi-Strauss: The Bearer of Ashes.* London and Boston: Routledge and Kegan Paul, 1983.

Rorty, Richard, ed. *The Linguistic Turn: Recent Essays in Philosophical Method.* Chicago: University of Chicago Press, 1967.

On the New Narrativism

Ankersmit, Frank R. *Narrative Logic: A Semantic Analysis of the Historian's Language.* The Hague: Martinus Nijhoff, 1983.

———. *The Reality Effect in the Writing of History: The Dynamics of Historiographical Topology.* Amsterdam: Koninklijke Nederlandse Akademie van Wetenschappen: Noord-Hollandsche, 1989.

———. *History and Tropology: The Rise and Fall of Metaphor.* Berkeley: University of California Press, 1994.

Ankersmit, Frank R., and Hans Kellner, eds. *A New Philosophy of History.* Chicago: University of Chicago Press, 1995.

Arac, Jonathan, ed. *After Foucault: Humanistic Knowledge, Postmodern Challenges.* New Brunswick, N.J.: Rutgers University Press, 1988.

Bann, Stephen. *The Clothing of Clio: A Study of the Representation of History in Nineteenth-Century Britain and France.* Cambridge: Cambridge University Press, 1984.

Barthes, Roland. "Historical Discourse." Trans. Peter Wexler. In *Introduction to Structuralism,* edited by Michael Lane. New York: Basic Books, 1970.

Berkhofer, Robert F., Jr.. *Beyond the Great Story: History as Text and Discourse.* Cambridge: Harvard University Press, 1995.

Bouwsma, William. "From History of Ideas to History of Meaning." In *The New History: The 1980s and beyond: Studies in Interdisciplinary History,* edited by Theodore Rabb and Robert Rotberg. Princeton, N.J.: Princeton University Press, 1981.

Canary, Robert H., and Henry Kozicki. eds. *The Writing of History: Literary Form and Historical Understanding.* Madison: University of Wisconsin Press, 1978.

Carrard, Philippe. *Poetics of the New History: French Historical Discourse from Braudel to Chartier.* Baltimore: Johns Hopkins University Press, 1992.

Chartier, Roger. *On the Edge of the Cliff: History, Language, and Practices.* Trans. Lydia Cochrane. Baltimore: Johns Hopkins University Press, 1997.

de Certeau, Michel. *The Writing of History.* Trans. Tom Conley. New York: Columbia University Press, 1988.

Friedlander, Saul, ed. *Probing the Limits of Representation: Nazism and the "Final Solution".* Cambridge: Harvard University Press, 1992.

Harlan, David. "Intellectual History and the Return of Literature." *American Historical Review* 94, no. 3 (June 1989): 581–609.

Hollinger, David. "The Return of the Prodigal: The Persistence of Historical Knowledge." *American Historical Review* 94, no. 3 (June 1989): 610–21.

Jacoby, Russell. "A New Intellectual History." *American Historical Review* 97, no. 2 (April 1992): 405–24.

Kellner, Hans. *Language and Historical Representation: Getting the Story Crooked.* Madison: University of Wisconsin Press, 1989.

———. "Narrativity in History: Poststructuralism and since." *History and Theory* 26, no. 4, Beiheft 26 (1987): 1–29.

LaCapra, Dominick. *History and Criticism.* Ithaca, N.Y.: Cornell University Press, 1985.

———. "Intellectual History and Its Ways." *American Historical Review* 97, no. 2 (April 1992): 425–39.

LaCapra, Dominick, and Steven L. Kaplan. *Modern European Intellectual History: Reappraisals and New Perspectives.* Ithaca, N.Y.: Cornell University Press, 1982.

Nelson, John S., Allan Megill, and Donald N. McCloskey, eds. *The Rhetoric of the Human Sciences: Language and Argument in Scholarship and Public Affairs.* Madison: University of Wisconsin Press, 1982.

Orr, Linda. *Headless History: Nineteenth-Century French Historiography of the Revolution.* Ithaca: Cornell University Press, 1990.

Ricoeur, Paul. *Time and Narrative.* 3 vols. Chicago: University of Chicago Press, 1984–88.

Rigney, Ann. *The Rhetoric of Historical Representation: Three Narrative Histories of the French Revolution.* Cambridge: Cambridge University Press, 1990.

Schama, Simon. *Dead Certainties: (Unwarranted Speculations).* New York: Alfred A. Knopf, 1991.

Simons, Herbert W. *Rhetoric in the Human Sciences.* London: Sage, 1989.

Tompkins, Jane P., ed. *Reader-Response Criticism: From Formalism to Post-Structuralism.* Baltimore: Johns Hopkins University Press, 1980.

Veyne, Paul. *Writing History: Essay on Epistemology.* Middleton, Conn.: Wesleyan University Press, 1984.

White, Hayden. *Metahistory: The Historical Imagination in Nineteenth-Century Europe.* Baltimore: Johns Hopkins University Press, 1973.

———. *Tropics of Discourse: Essays in Cultural Criticism.* Baltimore: Johns Hopkins University Press, 1978.

———. *The Content of the Form: Narrative Discourse and Historical Representation.* Baltimore: Johns Hopkins University Press, 1987.

———. "The Burden of History." In *Tropics of Discourse: Essays in Cultural Criticism.* Baltimore: Johns Hopkins University Press, 1978.

On the New Type of Knowledge (Truth, Metanarrative, and the Utility of History)

Works with a General Scope

Arac, Jonathan, ed. *After Foucault: Humanistic Knowledge, Postmodern Challenges.* New Brunswick N.J.: Rutgers University Press, 1988.

Baker, Peter. *Deconstruction and the Ethical Turn.* Gainesville: University Press of Florida, 1995.

Barrett, Michèle. *The Politics of Truth: From Marx to Foucault.* Cambridge, England: Polity Press, 1991.

Berkhofer, Jr., Robert. *Beyond the Great Story: History as Text and Discourse.* Cambridge: Harvard University Press, 1995.

Best, Steven, and Douglas Kellner. *Postmodern Theory: Critical Interrogations.* New York: The Guilford Press, 1991.

Caputo, John D. *Radical Hermeneutics: Repetition, Deconstruction, and the Hermeneutic Project.* Bloomington: Indiana University Press, 1987.

Culler, Jonathan D. *On Deconstruction: Theory and Criticism after Structuralism.* Ithaca, N.Y.: Cornell University Press, 1982.

Dussen, W. J. van der, and Lionel Rubinoff. *Objectivity, Method, and Point of View: Essays in the Philosophy of History.* Leiden: E. J. Brill, 1991.

Grumley, John. *History and Totality: Radical Historicism from Hegel to Foucault.* London: Routledge, 1989.

Kearney, Richard. *States of Mind: Dialogues with Contemporary Thinkers.* New York: New York University Press, 1995.

Krieger, Murray. *The Aims of Representation: Subject, Text, History.* New York: Columbia University Press, 1987.

Lawson, Hilary. *Reflexitivy: The Postmodern Dilemma.* London: Hutchinson, 1985.

Macdonnell, Diane. *Theories of Discourse: An Introduction.* Oxford, England: Basil Blackwell, 1986.

Martinez, Roy, ed. *The Very Idea of Radical Hermeneutics.* Atlantic Highlands, N.J.: Humanities Press, 1997.

Megill, Allan, ed. *Rethinking Objectivity.* Durham, N.C.: Duke University Press, 1991.

Novick, Peter. *That Noble Dream: The "Objectivity Quest" and the American Historical Profession.* Cambridge: Cambridge University Press, 1988.

Roetzer, Florian. *Conversations with French Philosophers.* Trans. Gary E. Aylesworth. Atlantic Highlands, N.J.: Humanities Press, 1995.

Works Focusing on Poststructuralist Postmodernist Authors, Works, and Themes

Arac, Jonathan, Wlad Godzich, and Wallace Martin, eds. *The Yale Critics: Deconstruction in America.* Minneapolis: University of Minnesota Press, 1983.

Baudrillard, Jean. *Forget Foucault.* Trans. Sylvère Lotringer. New York: Semiotext(e), 1987.

————. *Jean Baudrillard: Selected Writings.* Ed. Mark Poster. Stanford, Calif.: Stanford University Press, 1988.

————. *Symbolic Exchange and Death.* Trans. Iain Hamilton Grant. London: Sage, 1993.

Bernstein, Geoffrey, and Jacques Derrida. *Jacques Derrida.* Trans. G. Bernstein. Chicago: University of Chicago Press, 1993.

Benjamin, Andrew E., ed. *A Lyotard Reader.* Oxford, England: Blackwell, 1989.

Bennington, Geoffrey. *Lyotard: Writing the Event.* New York: Columbia University Press, 1988.

Bennington, Geoffrey, and Jacques Derrida. *Jacques Derrida.* Trans. Geoffrey Bennington. Chicago: University of Chicago Press, 1991.

Caputo, John. *Foucault and the Critique of Institutions.* University Park: Pennsylvania State University Press, 1993.

————. *Deconstruction in a Nutshell: A Conversation with Jacques Derrida.* New York: Fordham University Press, 1997.

————. *The Prayers and Tears of Jacques Derrida: Religion without Religion.* Bloomington: Indiana University Press, 1997.

Cohen, Tom. *Jacques Derrida and the Humanities: A Critical Reader.* Cambridge: Cambridge University Press, 2001.

Coward, Harold, and Toby Foshay, eds. *Derrida and Negative Theology.* Albany: State University of New York Press, 1992.

Critchley, Simon. *The Ethics of Deconstruction: Derrida and Levinas.* West Lafayette, Ind.: Purdue University Press, 1999.

Critchley, Simon, et al. *Deconstruction and Pragmatism.* Ed. Chantal Mouffe. London: Routledge, 1996.

Derrida, Jacques. *Speech and Phenomena, and Other Essays on Husserl's Theory of Signs.* Evanston, Ill.: Northwestern University Press, 1973.

————. *Of Grammatology.* Trans. Gayatari Chakravorty Spivak. Baltimore: Johns Hopkins University Press, 1976.

————. *Margins of Philosophy.* Trans. Alan Bass. Chicago: University of Chicago Press, 1982.

————. *Limited Inc.* Ed. Gerald Graff. Trans. Samuel Weber and Jeffrey Mehlman. Evanston, Ill.: Northwestern University Press, 1988.

Dreyfus, Hubert L., and Paul Rabinow. *Michel Foucault: Beyond Structuralism and Hermeneutics.* 2nd ed. Chicago: University of Chicago Press, 1983.

Ellis, John M. *Against Deconstruction.* Princeton N.J.: Princeton University Press, 1989.

Eribon, Didier. *Michel Foucault.* Trans. Betsy Wing. Cambridge: Harvard University Press, 1991.

Foucault, Michel. *The Order of Things: An Archaeology of the Human Sciences.* New York: Pantheon Books, 1970.

———. *The Archaeology of Knowledge.* Trans. A. M. Sheridan Smith. New York: Pantheon Books, 1972.

———. *Language, Counter-Memory, Practice: Selected Essays and Interviews.* Ed. Donald F. Bouchard. Trans. Donald F. Bouchard and Sherry Simon. Ithaca, N.Y.: Cornell University Press, 1977.

———. *Madness and Civilization. A History of Insanity in the Age of Reason.* New York: Vintage Books, 1988.

Goodchild, Philip. *Deleuze and Guattari: An Introduction to the Politics of Desire.* London: Sage, 1996.

Harlan, David. *The Degradation of American History.* Chicago: University of Chicago Press, 1997.

Haskell, Thomas. *Objectivity Is Not Neutrality: Explanatory Schemes in History.* Baltimore: Johns Hopkins University Press, 1998.

Kamuf, Peggy, ed. *A Derrida Reader: Between the Blinds.* New York: Columbia University Press, 1991.

Lyotard, Jean-François. *The Postmodern Condition: A Report on Knowledge.* Trans. Geoffrey Bennington and Brian Massumi. Minneapolis: University of Minnesota Press, 1984.

———. *The Differend: Phrases in Dispute.* Minneapolis: University of Minnesota Press, 1988.

———. *The Inhuman: Reflections on Time.* Trans. Geoffrey Bennington and Rachel Bowlby. Stanford, Calif.: Stanford University Press, 1991.

Madison, Gary B., ed. *Working through Derrida.* Evanston, Ill: Northwestern University Press, 1993.

Megill, Allan. "The Reception of Foucault by Historians." *Journal of the History of Ideas* 48, no. 1 (January–March 1987): 115–41.

Pefanis, Julian. *Heterology and the Postmodern: Bataille, Baudrillard, Lyotard.* Durham, N.C.: Duke University Press, 1991.

Racevskis, Karlis. *Michel Foucault and the Subversion of the Intellect.* Ithaca, N.Y.: Cornell University Press, 1983.

Rojek, Chris, and Bryan S. Turner, eds. *Forget Baudrillard?* London: Routledge, 1993.

Royle, Nicholas. *After Derrida.* Manchester, England: Manchester University Press, 1995.

Schultz, William R. *Jacques Derrida: An Annotated Primary and Secondary Bibliography.* New York: Garland Publications, 1992.

von Ranke, Leopold. "On the Character of the Historical Science" (manuscript of the 1830s), in *Leopold von Ranke: The Theory and Practice of History.* Ed. Georg G. Iggers and Konrad von Moltke. Trans. Wilma A. Iggers and Konrad von Moltke. Indianapolis: Bobbs-Merrill, 1973.

Williams, James. *Lyotard: Towards a Postmodern Philosophy.* Oxford, England: Polity Press, 1998.

Works Concerning the Metanarrative

Ermarth, Elizabeth Deeds. *Sequel to History: Postmodernism and the Crisis of Representational Time.* Princeton, N.J.: Princeton University Press, 1992.

Lévi-Strauss, Claude. *A World on the Wane.* Trans. John Russell. London: Criterion, 1961.

Popper, Karl. *The Open Society and Its Enemies.* Princeton, N.J.: Princeton University Press, 1950.

———. *The Poverty of Historicism.* Boston: Beacon Press, 1957.

Said, Edward. *Orientalism.* New York: Vintage Books, 1979.

———. *Culture and Imperialism.* New York: Knopf, 1993.

Stannard David. *American Holocaust: Columbus and the Conquest of the New World.* New York: Oxford University Press, 1992.

Todorov, Tzvetan. *The Conquest of America: The Question of the Other.* New York: Harper Collins, 1985.

Windschuttle, Keith. *The Killing of History: How Literary Critics and Social Theorists are Murdering Our Past.* New York: The Free Press, 1997 (chapters 2, 3, 4, and 9).

Young, Robert. *White Mythologies: Writing History and the West.* London: Routledge, 1990.

Assessments

Advocacy

Ankersmit, Frank R. "Reply to Professor Zagorin." *History and Theory* 29, no. 3 (1990): 275–96.

———. "Historiography and Postmodernism." *History and Theory* 28, no. 2 (1989): 134–53.

Bertens, Hans. *The Idea of the Postmodern: A History.* London: Routledge, 1995.

Cohen, Sande. *Historical Culture: On the Recoding of an Academic Discipline.* Berkeley: University of California Press, 1986.

Jenkins, Keith. *On "What is History?": From Carr and Elton to Rorty and White.* London: Routledge, 1995.

———. *Why History? Ethics and Postmodernity.* London: Routledge, 1999.

———. "A Postmodern Replay to Perez Zagorin." *History and Theory* 39, no. 2 (May 2000): 181–200.

Jenkins, Keith, ed. *The Postmodern History Reader.* London, Routledge, 1997.

Joyce, Patrick. "History and Post-Modernism." *Past and Present* 133 (November 1991): 206–9.

———. "A Quiet Victory: The Growing Influence of Postmodernism in History." *Times Literary Supplement,* 26 October 2001, 15.

Lyon, David. *Postmodernity.* Minneapolis: University of Minnesota Press, 1994.

Munslow, Alun. *Deconstructing History.* London: Routledge, 1997.

Roberts, David D. *Nothing but History: Reconstruction and Extremity after Metaphysics.* Berkeley: University of California Press, 1995.

Critique

Appleby, Joyce, Lynn Hunt, and Margaret Jacob. *Telling the Truth about History.* New York: W. W. Norton, 1994.

Elton, Geoffrey R. *Return to Essentials: Some Reflections on the Present State of Historical Study.* Cambridge: Cambridge University Press, 1991.

Evans, Richard J. *In Defence of History.* London: Granta Books, 1997: New York: W. W. Norton, 1999.

Gellner, Ernest. *Postmodernism, Reason and Religion.* London: Routledge, 1992.

Himmelfarb, Gertrude. *The New History and the Old.* Cambridge: Harvard University Press, 1987.

————. *On Looking into the Abyss: Untimely Thoughts on Culture and Society.* New York: Knopf, 1994.

Palmer, Bryan. *Descent into Discourse: The Reification of Language and the Writing of Social History.* Philadelphia: Temple University Press, 1990.

Racevskis, Karlis. *Postmodernism and the Search for Enlightenment.* Charlottesville: University of Virginia Press, 1993.

Spiegel, Gabrielle. *The Past as Text: The Theory and Practice of Medieval Historiography.* Baltimore: Johns Hopkins University Press, 1997 (Introduction and chapters 1–3).

————. "History and Post-Modernism." *Past and Present* 135 (May 1992): 194–208.

Stone, Lawrence. "History and Post-Modernism." *Past and Present* 135 (May 1992): 189–94.

Toews, John. "Intellectual History after the Linguistic Turn: The Autonomy of Meaning and the Irreducibility of Experience." *American Historical Review* 92 (1987): 879–907.

Windschuttle, Keith. *The Killing of History: How Literary Critics and Social Theorists are Murdering Our Past.* New York: The Free Press, 1997.

Zagorin, Perez. "History and Postmodernism: Reconsiderations." *History and Theory* 29, no. 3 (1990): 263–74.

————. "Rejoinder to a Postmodernist." *History and Theory* 39, no. 3 (May 2000): 201–9.

Zammito, John. "Are We Theoretical Yet? The New Historicism, the New Philosophy of History, and Practicing Historians." *Journal of Modern History* 65 (December 1993): 783–814.

POSTSTRUCTURALIST POSTMODERNISM: SPUR TO THE NEW
AND CHALLENGE TO THE ESTABLISHED IN HISTORY

Toward a New Cultural History

Aronowitz, Stanley. *Roll over Beethoven: The Return of Cultural Strife.* Hanover, N.H.: Wesleyan University Press, 1993.

Biernacki, Richard. "The Shift from Signs to Practices in Historical Inquiry." *History and Theory* 39, no. 3 (2000): 289–310.

Bonnell, Victoria E., and Lynn Hunt, eds., *Beyond the Cultural Turn: New Directions in the Study of Society and Culture.* Berkeley: University of California Press, 1999.

Chartier, Roger. *Cultural History: Between Practices and Representations.* Trans. Lydia G. Cochrane. Cambridge, England: Polity and Blackwell, 1988; Ithaca, N.Y.: Cornell University Press, 1988.

Clifford, James, and George E. Marcus, eds. *Writing Culture: The Poetics and Politics of Ethnography.* Berkeley: University of California Press, 1986.

Collins, Jim. *Uncommon Cultures: Popular Culture and Post-Modernism.* New York: Routledge, 1989.

Darnton, Robert. *The Great Cat Massacre and Other Episodes in French Cultural History.* New York: Basic Books, 1984.

Davis, Natalie Zemon. *Fiction in the Archives: Pardon Tales and Their Tellers in Sixteenth-Century France.* Stanford, Calif.: Stanford University Press, 1987.

Dirks, Nicholas B., ed. *In Near Ruins: Cultural Theory at the End of the Century.* Minneapolis: University of Minnesota, 1998.

Gallagher, Catherine, and Stephen Greenblatt. *Practicing New Historicism.* Chicago: University of Chicago Press, 2000.

Geertz, Clifford. *The Interpretation of Cultures: Selected Essays.* New York: Basic Books, 1973.

Ginzburg, Carlo. *The Cheese and the Worms: The Cosmos of a Sixteenth-Century Miller.* Trans. John Tedeschi and Anne C. Tedeschi. Baltimore: Johns Hopkins University Press, 1980.

———. *Clues, Myths, and the Historical Method.* Trans. John Tedeschi and Anne C. Tedeschi. Baltimore: Johns Hopkins University Press, 1989.

Greenblatt, Stephen. *Shakespearean Negotiations: The Circulation of Social Energy in Renaissance England.* Berkeley: University of California Press, 1988.

Hoeveler, J. David, Jr. *The Postmodernist Turn: American Thought and Culture in the 1970s.* New York: Twayne Publishers, 1996.

Hunt, Lynn, ed. *The New Cultural History.* Berkeley: University of California Press, 1989.

Kane, Anne. "Reconstructing Culture in Historical Explanation: Narration as Cultural Structure and Practice." *History and Theory* 39, no. 3 (October 2000): 311–30.

Kuper, Adam. *Culture: The Anthropologists' Account.* Cambridge: Harvard University Press, 1999.

Le Roy Ladurie, Emmanuel. *Carnival in Romans.* Trans. Mary Feeney. New York: George Braziller, 1979.

———. *Montaillou: The Promised Land of Error.* Trans. Barbara Bray. New York: Vintage Books, 1979.

Levi, Giovanni. "On Microhistory." In *New Perspectives on Historical Writing,* 2nd ed., edited by Peter Burke. University Park: Pennsylvania State University Press, 2001.

Lüdtke, Alf. *Alltagsgeschichte: Zur Rekonstruktion historischer Erfahrungen.und Lebensweisen.* Frankfurt am Main: Campus, 1989.

Maza, Sarah. "Stories in History: Cultural Narratives in Recent Writings in European History." *American Historical Review* 101, no. 5 (December 1996): 1493–1515.

McDonald, Terrence, ed. *The Historic Turn in the Human Sciences.* Ann Arbor: University of Michigan Press, 1996.

McGrane, Bernard. *Beyond Anthropology: Society and the Other.* New York: Columbia University Press, 1989.

Muir, Edward, and G. Ruggiero, eds. *Microhistory and the Lost Peoples of Europe: Selections from Quaderni Storici.* Baltimore: Johns Hopkins University Press, 1991.

Ortner, Sherry B., ed. *The Fate of "Culture": Geertz and beyond.* Berkeley: University of California Press, 1999.

Pfeil, Fred. *Another Tale to Tell: Politics and Narrative in Postmodern Culture.* London: Verso, 1990.

Poster, Mark. *Cultural History and Postmodernity: Disciplinary Readings and Challenges.* New York: Columbia University Press, 1997.

Rabb, Theodore, and Robert Rotberg, eds. *The New History, the 1980s and beyond: Studies in Interdisciplinary History.* Princeton, N.J.: Princeton University Press, 1981.

Sahlins, Marshall D. *Culture and Practical Reason.* Chicago: University of Chicago Press, 1976.

Sarup, Madan. *Identity, Culture, and the Postmodern World.* Ed. Tasneem Raja. Athens: University of Georgia Press, 1996.

Thomas, Brook. *The New Historicism: And Other Old-Fashioned Topics.* Princeton, N.J.: Princeton University Press, 1991.

Turner, Graeme. *British Cultural Studies: An Introduction.* Boston: Unwin Hyman, 1990.

Veeser, H. Aram, ed. *The New Historicism.* New York: Routledge, 1989.

Walkowitz, Judith R. *City of Dreadful Delight: Narratives of Sexual Danger in Late-Victorian London.* Chicago: University of Chicago Press, 1992.

The Postmodernist Challenge to Marxist Views of History

The Debate on How Much Marxism Should Yield to Postmodernism

Anderson, Perry. *Considerations on Western Marxism.* London: NLB, 1976.

Best, Steven. *The Politics of Historical Vision: Marx, Foucault, Habermas.* New York: Guilford Press, 1995.

Callinicos, Alex. *Against Postmodernism: A Marxist Critique.* Cambridge, England: Polity Press, 1989; New York: St. Martin's Press, 1990.

Callari, Antonio, and David F. Ruccio. *Postmodernism, Materialism, and the Future of Marxist Theory: Essays in the Althusserian Tradition.* Hanover, N.H.: Wesleyan University Press. 1996.

Docherty, Thomas. *After Theory: Postmodernism/Postmarxism.* New York: Routledge, 1990.

Eagleton, Terry. *The Illusions of Postmodernism.* Oxford, England: Blackwell, 1989.

Geras, Norman. *Discourses of Extremity: Radical Ethics and Post-Marxist Extravagances.* London: Verso, 1990.

Harvey, David. *The Condition of Postmodernity: An Inquiry into the Origins of Cultural Change.* Oxford, England: Blackwell, 1989.

Jameson, Fredric. *Postmodernism, or, the Cultural Logic of Late Capitalism.* Durham, N.C.: Duke University Press, 1991.

Kaye, Harvey J. *The British Marxist Historians: An Introductory Analysis.* 2nd ed. New York: St. Martin's Press, 1995.

Laclau, Ernesto, and Chantal Mouffe. *Hegemony and Socialist Strategy: Towards a Democratic Politics.* 2nd ed. London: Verso, 2001.

Makdisi, Saree, Cesare Casarino, and Rebecca E. Karl, eds. *Marxism beyond Marxism.* New York: Routledge, 1992.

Mandel, Ernest. *Late Capitalism.* Trans. Joris De Bres. London: Verso, 1975.

Milner, Andrew, Philip Thomson, and Chris Worth, eds. *Postmodern Conditions.* New York: Berg Publishers, 1990.

Mouffe, Chantal, ed. *Deconstruction and Pragmatism.* London, Routledge, 1996.

Nelson, Cary, and Lawrence Grossberg, eds. *Marxism and the Interpretation of Culture.* Urbana: University of Illinois Press, 1988.

Ryan, Michael. *Marxism and Deconstruction.* Baltimore: Johns Hopkins University Press, 1982.

Smart, Barry. *Modern Conditions: Postmodern Controversies.* London: Routledge, 1992.

Soja, Edward W. *Postmodern Geographies: The Reassertion of Space in Critical Social Theory.* London: Verso, 1989.

Thompson, Edward P. *The Making of the English Working Class.* New York: Vintage Books, 1968.

Wood, Ellen Meiksins, and John B. Foster, eds. *In Defense of History: Marxism and the Postmodern Agenda.* New York: Monthly Review Press, 1997.

The Frankfurt School and J. Habermas: Junctures with Postmodernist Thought

Adorno, Theodor W. *Negative Dialectics.* Trans. E. B. Ashton. New York: Seabury Press, 1973.

Bannet, Eve Tavor. *Postcultural Theory: Critical Theory after the Marxist Paradigm.* New York: Paragon House, 1993.

Bernstein, Richard J., ed. *Habermas and Modernity.* Cambridge: MIT Press, 1985.

Dews, Peter. *Logics of Disintegration: Post-Structuralist Thought and the Claims of Critical Theory.* London: Verso, 1987.

Gripp, Helga. *Jürgen Habermas.* Paderborn: Schöningh, 1984.

Horkheimer, Max, and Theodor W. Adorno. *Dialectic of Enlightenment.* Trans. John Cumming. New York: Herder and Herder, 1972; New York: Continuum, 1991.

Jay, Martin. *The Dialectical Imagination: A History of the Frankfurt School and the Institute for Social Research, 1923–1950.* Boston: Little, Brown, 1973.

———. *Adorno.* Cambridge: Harvard University Press, 1984.

———. *Marxism and Totality: The Adventures of a Concept from Lukács to Habermas.* Berkeley: University of California Press, 1984.

———. *Fin-de-Siècle: Socialism and Other Essays.* London: Routledge, 1988.

Pensky, Max, ed. *The Actuality of Adorno: Critical Essays on Adorno and the Postmodern.* Albany: State University of New York Press, 1997.

Poster, Mark. *Critical Theory and Poststructuralism: In Search of a Context.* Ithaca, N.Y.: Cornell University Press, 1989.

Tallack, Douglas, ed. *Critical Theory: A Reader.* London: Harvester Wheatsheaf, 1995.

Wolin, Richard. *The Terms of Cultural Criticism: The Frankfurt School, Existentialism, Poststructuralism.* New York: Columbia University Press, 1992.

Postmodernism and Feminism

Alcoff, Linda, and Elizabeth Potter, eds. *Feminist Epistemologies.* NewYork: Routledge, 1993.

Assiter, Alison. *Enlightened Women: Modernist Feminism in a Postmodern Age.* London: Routledge, 1996.

Barrett, Michèle, and Anne Phillips. *Destabilizing Theory: Contemporary Feminist Debates.* Stanford, Calif.: Stanford University Press, 1992.

Beer, Ursula. *Klasse und Geschlecht: Feministische Gesellschaftsanlayse und Wissenschaftskritik.* Bielefeld: AJZ Verlag, 1989.

Butler, Judith P. *Gender Trouble, Feminism, and the Subversion of Identity.* New York: Routledge, 1990.

Carroll, Berenice. *Liberating Women's History: Theoretical and Critical Essays.* Urbana: University of Illinois Press, 1970.

Chodorow, Nancy. *The Reproduction of Mothering: Psychoanalysis and the Sociology of Gender.* Berkeley: University of California Press, 1978.

Code, Lorraine. *What Can She Know? Feminist Theory and the Construction of Knowledge.* Ithaca, N.Y.: Cornell University Press, 1991.

Duby, Georges, and Michelle Perrot, eds. *A History of Women in the West.* 5 vols. Cambridge: Harvard University Press, 1994–96.

Elam, Diane. *Feminism and Deconstruction.* London: Routledge, 1994.

Feder, Ellen K., Mary Rawlinson, and Emily Zakin, eds. *Derrida and Feminism: Recasting the Question of Women.* London: Routledge, 1997.

Flax, Jane. *Thinking Fragments: Psychoanalysis, Feminism, and Postmodernism in the Contemporary West.* Berkeley: University of California Press, 1990.

Fraser, Nancy. *Unruly Practices: Power, Discourse, and Gender in Contemporary Social Theory.* Minneapolis: University of Minnesota Press, 1989.

Fraser, Nancy, and Sandra Lee Bartky, eds. *Revaluing French Feminism: Critical Essays on Difference, Agency, and Culture.* Bloomington: Indiana University Press, 1992.

History and Feminist Theory. Ed. Ann-Louise Shapiro. *History and Theory* Beiheft 31 (1992).

Irigaray, Luce. *This Sex Which Is Not One.* Ithaca, N.Y.: Cornell University Press, 1985.

Lennon, Kathleen, and Margaret Whitford. *Knowing the Difference: Feminist Perspectives in Epistemology.* London: Routledge, 1994.

Mohanty, Chandra Talpade, Ann Russo, and Lourdes Torres. *Third World Women and the Politics of Feminism.* Bloomington: Indiana University Press, 1991.

Moi, Toril. *French Feminist Thought: A Reader.* Oxford, England: Blackwell, 1987.

Nicholson, Linda J. *Gender and History: The Limits of Social Theory in the Age of the Family.* New York: Columbia University Press, 1986.

———. *Feminism/Postmodernism.* London: Routledge, 1990.

Offen, Karen. *European Feminisms, 1700–1950: A Political History.* Stanford, Calif.: Stanford University Press, 2000.

Offen, Karen, Ruth Roach Pierson, and Jane Rendall, eds. *Writing Women's History: International Perspectives.* Bloomington: Indiana University Press, 1991.

Perrot, Michelle, ed. *Une Histoire des femmes est-elle possible?* Paris: Rivages, 1984.

Riley, Denise. *"Am I That Name?": Feminism and the Category of "Women" in History.* Minneapolis: University of Minnesota Press, 1988.

Scott, Joan Wallach. *Gender and the Politics of History.* New York: Columbia University Press, 1988.

———. "Deconstructive Equality–versus–Difference: Or, The Uses of Poststructuralist Theory for Feminism." *Feminist Studies* 14, no. 1 (Spring 1989): 33–50.

Shapiro, Ann-Louise, ed. *Feminists Revision History.* New Brunswick, N.J.: Rutgers University Press, 1994.

Smith, Bonnie. *The Gender of History: Men, Women, and Historical Practice.* Cambridge: Harvard University Press, 1998.

Sterba, James, ed. *Controversies in Feminism.* Lanham, Md.: Rowman and Littlefield, 2001.

Whitford, Margaret. *Luce Irigaray: Philosophy in the Feminine.* London: Routledge, 1991.

INDEX